Foraging in the Tennessee River Valley, 12,500 to 8,000 Years Ago

A Dan Josselyn Memorial Publication

Foraging in the Tennessee River Valley, 12,500 to 8,000 Years Ago

Kandace D. Hollenbach

THE UNIVERSITY OF ALABAMA PRESS
Tuscaloosa

Manufactured in the United States of America

Typeface: Caslon

∞

The paper on which this book is printed meets the minimum requirements of American National Standard for Information Sciences-Permanence of Paper for Printed Library Materials, ANSI Z39.48-1984.

Library of Congress Cataloging-in-Publication Data

Hollenbach, Kandace D.

Foraging in the Tennessee River Valley, 12,500 to 8,000 years ago / Kandace D. Hollenbach.

p. cm.

Includes bibliographical references and index.

ISBN 978-0-8173-1643-3 (cloth : alk. paper) — ISBN 978-0-8173-5522-7 (pbk. : alk. paper) — ISBN 978-0-8173-8126-4 (electronic : alk. paper) 1. Paleo-Indians—Tennessee River Valley. 2. Indians of North America—Tennessee River Valley—Antiquities. 3. Plant remains (Archaeology)—Tennessee River Valley. 4. Hunting and gathering societies—Tennessee River Valley. 5. Excavations (Archaeology)—Tennessee River Valley. 6. Tennessee River Valley—Antiquities. I. Title.

E78.T33H65 2009

976.8′01—dc22

2008035775

For Michael

Contents

Illustrations

FIGURES

TABLES

Acknowledgments

The research presented here is based on work supported by the National Science Foundation under Grant No. 0332275, which enabled me to acquire nine AMS and two conventional radiocarbon dates, purchase a subscription to the Alabama Online Cultural Resource Database, and hire four undergraduate students to help sort samples.

This study builds on the work of my colleagues at Dust Cave. Boyce Driskell has organized an impressive group of researchers to work at the site, and our discussions over many seasons together in the field and beyond have greatly shaped my understanding of the prehistory of the region. Sarah Sherwood, Renee Walker, Scott Meeks, Lara Homsey, Nick Richardson, Sharon Freeman, and particularly Asa Randall have been wonderful sounding boards and have provided much food for thought. In addition, I thank the many field school students, supervisors, and volunteers, particularly Joe and Nancy Copeland and Bobby Stanfield, who worked at Dust Cave, Stanfield-Worley, LaGrange, and Rollins shelters. Their efforts produced the numerous botanical samples and archaeological context upon which I base my research.

This book has benefited greatly from the input of a number of people, including Margie Scarry, Boyce Driskell, Dick Yarnell, Steve Davis, Vin Steponaitis, Bruce Winterhalder, Kristen Gremillion, Leslie Bush, Amanda Tickner, Kim Schaefer, Jennifer Hora, Christine Kelleher, Bram Tucker, Amber VanDerwarker, Greg Wilson, Tony Boudreaux, and Mintcy Maxham, who all provided invaluable suggestions and encouraged me to think more broadly. I also thank the staff of the University of Alabama Press, whose suggestions have greatly improved this work.

Many thanks also go to my family for their support, particularly my brother Tom Detwiler, who helped me think around a number of technical jams. I also thank Peter Lauren, and Lucy for their boundless enthusiasm, but most of all I thank Michael. He has been more than patient and always encouraging in this process, for which I am grateful.

1
Introduction

Plants are inarguably a significant component of the diets of foraging peoples in nonarctic environments (Keeley 1999; Kelly 1983; R. Lee 1968; Walthall 1998b). As such, the decisions and activities associated with the gathering and use of plants are important to foragers' subsistence pursuits. It follows, then, that if we are interested in the lifeways of early foraging groups, such as the Late Paleoindian and Early Archaic peoples living in the southeastern United States, we must consider the role of plant resources, and the gatherers who procured them, in their subsistence strategies and mobility patterns.

Although our current models of southeastern Late Paleoindian and Early Archaic peoples have become increasingly sophisticated over time, they remain grounded on limited evidence. Stone tool data and environmental reconstructions, rather than food remains, are used to suggest subsistence strategies as well as settlement and mobility patterns. This is largely due to the nature of the archaeological record: organic remains are poorly preserved in the acidic soils of the Southeast. Faunal and botanical materials are often limited or absent from open-air sites. Regional data comparable to those available for stone tools are difficult to compile for organic remains.

Archaeological deposits protected within rockshelters provide a clear exception. Organic remains are consistently well preserved in their rain-protected deposits. Furthermore, rockshelters are distinct locations on landscapes that groups repeatedly visited. Because of this repeated use and remarkable preservation, significant quantities of well-preserved faunal and botanical remains can be recovered from rockshelter deposits. While rockshelter sites are unique in terms of their preservation, the activities conducted at rockshelters are comparable to those performed at open-air sites. Early rockshelter sites in the eastern United States can be separated into residential sites and hunting camps, based on artifact assemblages that reflect maintenance and manufacture of bone, wood, and stone tools; preparation of hides; and the use of hearths (Walthall 1998a). Because the artifact assemblages of rockshelter and open-air sites are similar, it is reasonable to assume that faunal and botanical assemblages would be similar, if open-air sites had comparable preservation of organic remains. The rich organic data recovered from rockshelters therefore may be considered representative of general subsistence and settlement strategies, and thus can significantly inform our views of lifeways of Late Paleoindian and Early Archaic peoples.

Animal remains from early deposits in rockshelters have been analyzed (e.g., Fowler 1959; Griffin 1974; Logan 1952; Parmalee 1962; Parmalee et al. 1976; Snyder and Parmalee 1992; Walker 1998), and the resulting data have been consulted in the construction of models of Late Paleoindian and Early Archaic lifeways in the Southeast (e.g., Meltzer and Smith 1986). However, similar research on plant remains has been performed less often (an exception is Parmalee et al. 1976). This is unfortunate, as plant remains are particularly important for understanding gathering activities, especially because tools used specifically for plant processing either do not preserve well or are not easily recognized (Anderson and Sassaman 1996). Inasmuch as plant foods comprised a significant portion of early foragers' diets, and the gathering and processing of these plant resources occupied a significant proportion of the population, namely women, children, and the elderly, an understanding of gathering activities and how they relate to peoples' use of the landscape is key.

To this end, I examine plant remains from four rockshelter sites in the Middle Tennessee River Valley with deposits dating to the Late Paleoindian/Dalton and Early Archaic periods. The data produced from this analysis provide a valuable baseline of plant food use by early foragers in the region, a baseline that is currently lacking for the Southeast as a whole. I then use this baseline data to construct a model of subsistence strategies and mobility patterns in the region, exploring how the practices associated with the use of plant resources articulate with the exploitation of other resources, such as animals and stone. In this way, I hope to expand our understanding of the lifeways of men, women, and children living in the Southeast approximately 10,000 years ago.

Below I describe archaeologists' current understanding of Late Paleoindian and Early Archaic foragers, as well as my own assumptions about the groups that occupied and moved across the northwest Alabama landscape. I then briefly sketch the development of models of Late Paleoindian and Early Archaic lifeways, noting in particular the evidence on which they were constructed. Finally, I discuss the tack that I will take in developing a model of subsistence strategies and mobility patterns in the Middle Tennessee River Valley through the course of this book.

DEFINING THE LATE PALEOINDIAN AND EARLY ARCHAIC PERIODS

Archaeologists differentiate between the Late Paleoindian and Early Archaic periods using a series of diagnostic hafted bifaces, or points. Radiocarbon dates from charcoal associated with points provide a chronological framework for these periods. The decision about which points belong to which period is somewhat arbitrary; as new sites are excavated and new dates procured, the lines between the periods are redrawn. Here I follow the scheme suggested by Sherwood and colleagues (2004) and Anderson and colleagues (1996), which is summarized in Figure 1.1.

The Late Paleoindian period in the Southeast is associated with relatively standardized lanceolate points found at sites throughout the region, while the subsequent Early Archaic period is defined by a succession of side-notched, corner-notched, and bifurcate points that are more regionally distinctive in style (Anderson et al. 1996). I should note that in my analysis I include deposits associated with Quad and Beaver Lake points, which are considered by some to be representative of the Middle Paleoindian period (e.g., Sherwood et al. 2004:544) and by others to be transitional between the Middle and Late Paleoindian periods (e.g., Anderson et al. 1996:12). Because peoples using Quad/Beaver Lake points and Dalton points exhibit broad similarities in toolkits and in land use (Sherwood et al. 2004:544; see Chapter 3), and because the Quad/Beaver Lake and Dalton occupations are difficult to parse at Dust Cave, I discuss them as a unit, but keep in mind that they are not coeval.

I also include samples associated with Kirk Stemmed points, which are commonly placed at the start of the Middle Archaic period (Anderson 1995; Goldman-Finn 1995b). However, at Dust Cave, dates from Kirk Stemmed deposits range between 10,200 and 7800 cal B.P. (Sherwood et al. 2004:548). As such, I consider them to represent the transition between the Early and Middle Archaic periods.

Based on these diagnostic point sequences and differences between the technologies associated with them, archaeologists have traditionally considered the lifeways of Late Paleoindian and Early Archaic peoples to be distinctly different from each other. They interpreted the relative uniformity

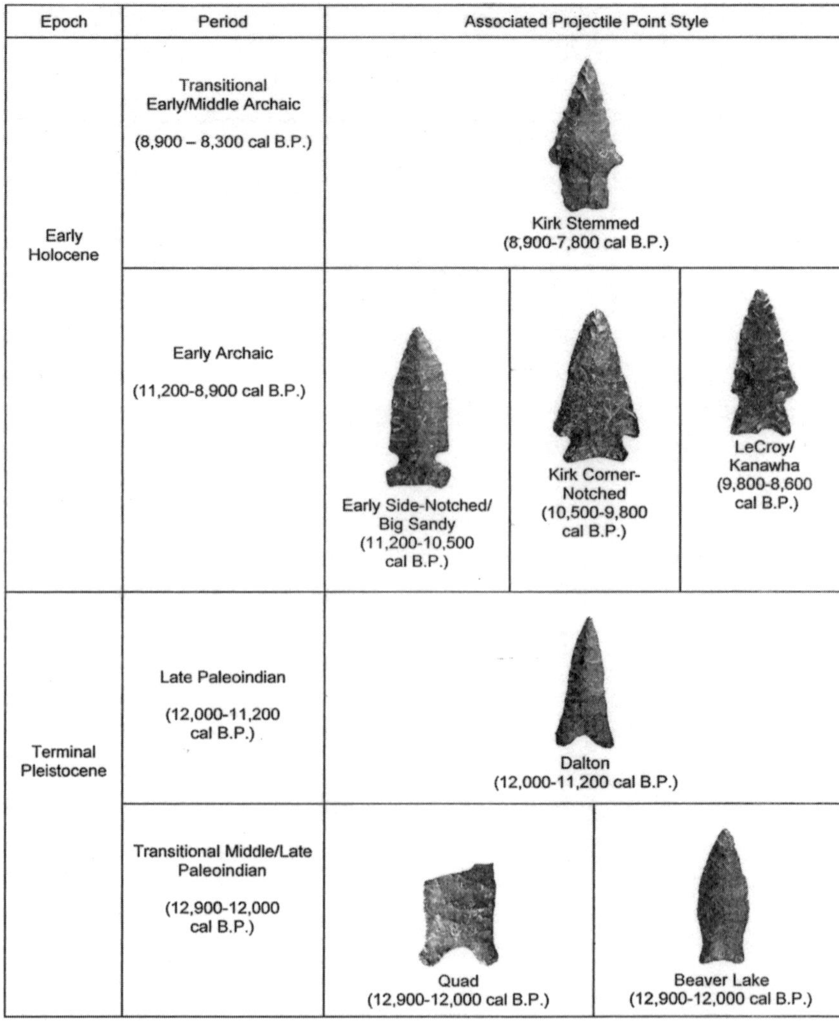

Figure 1.1. Point styles associated with the Late Paleoindian and Early Archaic periods in northwest Alabama.

of specialized Late Paleoindian toolkits across the Southeast as indicative of greater mobility: highly mobile hunters require a flexible technology that can be adapted to the task at hand (Cleland 1976:69; Goodyear 1982:384, 1989:2–4). In addition, Late Paleoindian points tend to be made from high-quality, sometimes nonlocal stone. The use of nonlocal stone suggests broad movements and/or trading relationships with neighboring groups (Goodyear 1989; Walthall 1980:35). Researchers have argued that this highly mobile lifestyle was organized around the focal hunting of larger game, such as deer (Caldwell 1958; Cleland 1976; Dragoo 1976). These lanceolate points require a significant investment of time and skill to make. The reasoning follows that the prey felled by these labor-intensive points must have been worth the effort it took to make them, and therefore the prey were probably larger in size and significant to Late Paleoindian peoples' subsistence.

In contrast, Early Archaic peoples were thought to have practiced a more generalized subsistence strategy, having adapted to locally available resources over the course of the preceding Paleoindian period (Caldwell 1958). This interpretation of local adaptations is based on the appearance of regional point styles, suggesting contact with a more limited group of neighbors. The more frequent use of local stone for the manufacture of tools is also interpreted as indicating local adaptations (Anderson and Schuldenrein 1983; Futato 1983). This reorganization from widespread to regionally defined mobility and subsistence strategies often has been attributed to the shift from Pleistocene to Holocene climatic and environmental conditions. Significant changes in plant communities presumably led to changes in the game available to hunter-gatherers on a regional level. Local variation in hunting strategies therefore gave rise to regional varieties of stone tools (Cleland 1976; Dragoo 1976).

Indeed, the division between the Late Paleoindian and Early Archaic periods has traditionally been defined as coincident with the Pleistocene/Holocene climatic transition (Anderson et al. 1996:14). This transition is marked by the close of the Younger Dryas event (ca. 12,900–11,650 cal B.P.), the last period of significant global cooling (Sherwood et al. 2004:544). More recent radiocarbon dates, as well as calibrations of these dates, indicate that the division between the two cultural periods is not as distinct as once supposed. Dalton materials, dating between 12,000 and 11,200 years ago, span this transition (Sherwood et al. 2004). Furthermore, differences between Late Paleoindian and Early Archaic subsistence strategies do not appear to be as significant as once thought (e.g., Detwiler 2001; Elston and Zeanah 2002; Walker et al. 2001).

CONSTRUCTING MODELS OF THE LATE PALEOINDIAN AND EARLY ARCHAIC PERIODS

While early work focused on the description of formal attributes of stone tools, particularly diagnostic points, and the construction of cultural trait lists (e.g., Lewis and Kneburg 1959), research on the Late Paleoindian and

Early Archaic periods in the 1950s through 1970s focused on developing the chronological sequence of diagnostic artifacts in the Southeast (Anderson and Sassaman 1996; Mason 1962). Archaeologists targeted sites with multiple cultural components, where the stratigraphic context of various points could reveal their relative chronological placement. Much of the early work was conducted at open-air sites, such as the Hardaway site in North Carolina (Coe 1964). Deeply buried components were also excavated at sites in river bottomlands, including the Doerschuk site in North Carolina (Coe 1964), the St. Albans site in West Virginia (Broyles 1971), and the Little Tennessee River sites—namely Icehouse Bottom, Rose Island, Calloway Island, and Bacon Farm—in eastern Tennessee (Chapman 1973, 1975, 1976, 1977, 1978). Excavators also targeted the extensive deposits of rockshelter sites. Among these are Stanfield-Worley Bluff Shelter (DeJarnette et al. 1962) and Russell Cave in Alabama (Griffin 1974), Modoc Shelter in Illinois (Fowler 1959), and Graham Cave (Logan 1952) and Rodgers Shelter (Wood and McMillan 1976) in Missouri (Figure 1.2).

The excavation of deep sites provided not only a sequence of points but also yielded faunal and plant remains largely absent from shallow open-air sites. Among the deep open-air sites at which organic materials were preserved and recovered are the Koster site in Illinois (Asch et al. 1972; Neusius 1982) and several of the Little Tennessee River sites (Chapman and Shea 1981). Rockshelter sites are particularly known for their remarkable preservation of organic remains. In-depth faunal analyses were conducted at Stanfield-Worley Bluff Shelter (Parmalee 1962) and Russell Cave (Griffin 1974), Modoc Shelter (Fowler 1959), Graham Cave (Logan 1952), and Rodgers Shelter (Parmalee et al. 1976). The plant assemblage from Rodgers Shelter was also reported in some detail (Parmalee et al. 1976).

Once the chronology of individual point styles had been refined, archaeologists focused their efforts on understanding the nature of toolkits and their relationship to site function. While archaeologists had interpreted the activities occurring on sites from the recovered artifacts for some time, they did not tie these activities into larger subsistence strategies and settlement systems until the 1970s. This trend was spurred by the development of middle-range theories, which used ethnographic and ethnoarchaeological observations to link toolkits and site patterns with settlement and subsistence modes. These theories organized settlement and subsistence strategies along logistical-residential, collecting-foraging, and focal-generalized continua (Binford 1979, 1980; Cleland 1976). Following middle-range theory, Binford (1979, 1980) characterized hunter-gatherer societies as *foragers* or *collec-*

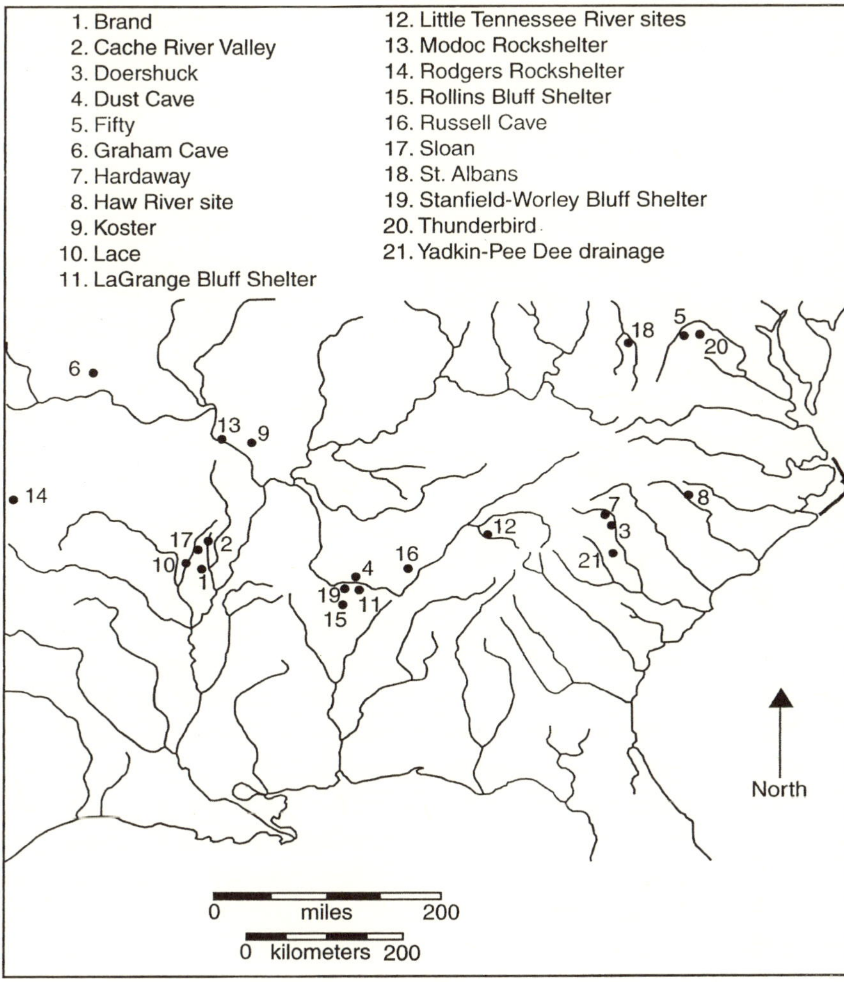

Figure 1.2. Map of Late Paleoindian and Early Archaic sites discussed in text.

tors, which use distinctly different toolkits. *Foraging* groups frequently move their residences to new patches of food as current patches are depleted, while *collecting* groups establish a single home base and launch logistical forays to gather resources from distant patches. *Foragers* with high residential mobility should use and discard more generalized, expedient tools, made on the spot as needs arise. *Collectors* with logistical mobility should have more specialized tools, designed for particular tasks, that are highly curated. In addition, markedly different toolkits should be found at the home bases and logistical camps of *collectors,* due to the different range of activities undertaken at each site. It should be stressed that a single group could display both *foraging* and *collecting* behaviors, depending on the season, the resource in question, and the like.

Using these middle-range theories, archaeologists ideally could interpret whether a site was used logistically or residentially, by *collectors* or *foragers,* based upon the nature and function of the artifact assemblage. An example of such a site-level approach is the study of the Brand site in Arkansas, where Goodyear (1974) used the diversity and spatial arrangement of the stone toolkit to argue that the site served as a hunting-and-butchering camp for a group of hunters.

A distinct advantage of these middle-range theories was that they simultaneously determined the probable functions of individual sites and placed them within the context of larger settlement systems, thus encouraging a regional perspective. Attempts to develop regional models of settlement and subsistence were further bolstered by large-scale survey and excavation projects, including those prompted by cultural resource management legislation. These projects facilitated the identification and exploration of multiple sites on a regional level. Examples include surveys and excavation of sites on Crowley's Ridge (Morse 1973, 1975a, 1975b) and in the Cache River Valley (Price and Krakker 1975) in northeastern Arkansas, the Little Tennessee River Valley in eastern Tennessee (Chapman 1973, 1975, 1976, 1977, 1978), and the Flint Run complex in Virginia (Gardner 1974, 1977).

Dan Morse developed one of the earliest settlement models, detailing the Dalton occupation of Crowley's Ridge in northeastern Arkansas. Based upon a broad survey combined with excavation of several key sites, including Lace (Redfield and Moselage 1970), Brand (Goodyear 1974; Morse 1973, 1975b), and Sloan (Morse 1975b, 1997b), Morse linked interpretations of stone tool clusters and densities, stone tool function, and environmental richness to understandings of hunter-gatherer lifeways. He suggested that bands organized their subsistence activities within the confines of watersheds, which provided an abundance of resources. Groups established base camps, like the Lace site, from which they set out on logistical forays to hunt, gather, and visit quarries and cemetery sites (Morse 1975a, 1975b, 1997a, 1997b; Morse and Morse 1983).

Using similar artifact data from Crowley's Ridge and the Cache River basin, Michael Schiffer (1975) developed a contrasting model for the region, suggesting instead that band territories crosscut river basins. He further contended that group mobility varied seasonally. Summer campsites were moved frequently, while during winter and early spring people established base camps near rivers, where resources were comparatively plentiful. Sites with high artifact densities such as Lace (Redfield and Moselage 1970) should therefore represent winter/spring camps, or summer campsites that were repeatedly revisited.

Rather than orient group movements to watersheds, William Gardner (1974, 1977, 1983) tethered settlement patterns in the Shenandoah Valley of Virginia to stone tool resources. He defined several site types in the Flint Run complex, including quarries, reduction stations, base camps, and hunting sites. These site types were based on the spatial relationship between local jasper outcrops and sites with extensive lithic assemblages, such as Thunderbird and Fifty, which Gardner included among base camps and quarries. He classed other sites with low artifact densities as reduction stations and hunting sites. Gardner (1974, 1977, 1983) hypothesized that movement between base camps, quarries, and hunting sites was directed by the need to periodically replenish toolkits.

As more detailed environmental reconstructions became available in the 1980s (e.g., Delcourt and Delcourt 1985; Delcourt and Delcourt 1981; Watts 1980; Watts and Stuiver 1980), researchers began to incorporate climatic shifts and local environmental conditions in their models of Paleoindian and Early Archaic lifeways. For example, Claggett and Cable's (1982) model of effective temperature and technological organization drew on paleoclimatic reconstructions as well as cross-cultural surveys linking hunter-gatherer subsistence strategies with environmental indicators. They postulated that residential mobility should have increased with the warming trend at the transition from the Late Pleistocene to the Early Holocene, in conjunction with a shift from boreal spruce to more productive oak-hickory forests. This accounted for the shift to a more expedient toolkit at the Haw River site in the Early Archaic than was used in the Late Paleoindian period.

Meltzer and Smith (1986) built their argument around environmental reconstructions, noting that although ecological communities in the Southeast were rapidly changing during the last several millennia of the Pleistocene, the habitats associated with this change were highly complex, diverse, and species-rich. They argued that such conditions favored generalized foraging rather than focal collecting strategies, not only in the Early Archaic but also during the Paleoindian period. They interpreted stone tool assemblages in the Southeast as relatively expedient in nature, particularly compared to highly curated assemblages from the Northeast, where Paleoindians appear to have focally exploited caribou herds.

In the late 1980s and 1990s, researchers joined considerations of environment and technological organization with explicit concern for biocultural needs and demographic structures. Group mobility and territorial organization were viewed not only in light of resource distribution but also with respect to the exchange of ideas, information, raw materials, and mates in regions with relatively low population densities (Anderson 1995).

A prime example is Anderson and Hanson's (1988) band-macroband model for the South Atlantic Coast. Addressing band-level subsistence strategies as well as social and biological needs for macroband aggregations, they postulated that territories coincided with river drainages, within which seasonal movements took place. During winter, bands established base camps in the more hospitable Coastal Plain, from which logistical forays were launched. These camps dispersed into the highly productive region above the Fall Line during spring and summer. Several bands from neighboring drainages aggregated in autumn at sites along the Fall Line, taking advantage of abundant nuts, seeds, and rutting deer. These meetings were opportunities to exchange raw materials, share information and technology, and find potential mates. In addition to minimum population estimates necessary to sustain bands and macrobands, Anderson and Hanson (1988) relied on reconstructions of regional environmental structures, as well as patterns of stone tool assemblages and raw material use along and across drainages, to support their model.

Recent models of Late Paleoindian and Early Archaic settlement and subsistence strategies largely constitute further refinements of existing models. Cable (1996) revisited the Haw River data (Claggett and Cable 1982) and reinterpreted the Late Paleoindian occupation as a field camp, rather than a base camp, within a logistical system that may be seasonally limited. He proposed that while groups likely behaved as collectors during the winter, targeting deer in particular, they might have adopted more generalized strategies during the warm season. These generalized strategies might then have been employed throughout the year as winters began to warm during the Early Holocene. Walthall (1998b) argued that winter base camps, posited in models such as Anderson and Hanson's (1988) and Schiffer's (1975), could not have been supported by the meager food resources available during the winter. Instead, Walthall (1998b) used several ethnographic examples to suggest that after aggregating with other bands during autumn, early prehistoric groups dispersed into the uplands to hunt deer and turkeys that were subsisting on the remaining mast resources. Daniel (1998, 2001) objected more broadly to the river-basin focus of seasonal rounds, particularly those hypothesized by Anderson and Hanson (1988). Examining patterns of raw material frequency across the Carolina piedmont and along Yadkin–Pee Dee drainage, Daniel argued that band territories were organized around the distribution of raw materials used to make stone tools, crosscutting—rather than being defined by—river drainages.

The overarching trends in the construction of models for Late Paleoindian and Early Archaic lifeways in the last 40 years demonstrate a broadening in both data and the theoretical arguments used to underpin these models. Archaeologists began to apply ethnographically and ethnoarchaeologically informed middle-range theory to the considerable data, particularly in the form of stone tools and debitage, derived from excavation and regional surveys in the 1960s and 1970s. A more explicit concern with ecological arguments developed as more detailed environmental reconstructions became available in the 1980s. Thereafter, researchers began to consider various resources, including biocultural, faunal, and tool-stone resources, in further detail. Thus, beginning with an assumption of seasonal rounds as noted among modern hunting and gathering groups, Southeastern archaeologists have used stone tool data, raw material distribution, animal behaviors, and demographic patterns to direct Late Paleoindian and Early Archaic peoples' seasonal movements.

The astute reader will note that discussion of use of plant resources is absent in these models. Gero (1995) suggests that the focus on stone tools and hunting is related to the bias of the researchers, who are primarily men. Because the gathering and processing of plant resources is largely women's work, male researchers have largely overlooked the use of plants. In fairness to these researchers, I suggest that gathering has been neglected because data associated with the use of plants are notably scarce for these early populations. The general paucity of plant data further underscores the importance of paleoethnobotanical studies of early sites in the Southeast, such as the one presented here.

THE PROJECT

I envision Late Paleoindian and Early Archaic foraging groups living in northwest Alabama as relatively mobile, spending perhaps several weeks at a particular campsite, but often shifting camp after only several days. I assume that much of the year they traveled in groups of approximately 10 to 15 people, defined by extended families—elder parents, their adult children, and their children's children. Smaller groups presumably aggregated several times a year to form bands of about 50 people, and perhaps yearly to form macrobands of about 400 people, in order to share information, resources, and camaraderie. As I argue throughout this book, there are relatively few differences between Late Paleoindian and Early Archaic peoples in the project area: both appear to have been generalists, relying on a range of wild plant and animal foodstuffs for subsistence.

I assume that the size of the groups was small enough, and their stays at particular campsites short enough, that they did not significantly alter local landscapes. However, it is quite likely that early foraging groups enhanced the productivity of local landscapes. In the immediate surroundings of campsites and along pathways and trails, they created, intentionally or not, small patches of disturbed habitats in which weedy (often edible) plants flourish. They may also have engaged in more obviously intentional activities, such as burning, pruning, and coppicing, to enhance the productivity of particular habitats (e.g., Fowler 1996). The scale of these landscape alterations, however, was presumably relatively small.

In order to address the settlement and subsistence strategies of early foragers, I rely on several concepts from the field of evolutionary ecology. These include discussions of the division of labor, as well as central place foraging theory. The former provides a basis for understanding the different goals and activities of women and men, gatherers and hunters. Central place foraging theory is used as a heuristic to clarify the variables that influence foragers' decisions about where to site base camps in relation to the distribution of various resources on the landscape.

I employ these theoretical constructs within the context—both physical and cultural—of northwest Alabama. The project area is defined by the boundaries of Lauderdale, Colbert, and Franklin counties (Figure 1.3), which encompass river valleys, rolling karstic plateaus, and deeply incised, sandstone-capped hills. In addition to a rich array of riverine and upland natural resources, this region claims one of the richest archaeological records of Paleoindian and Archaic sites in the Southeast.

Using a geographic information system, I apply central place foraging theory directly to this physical and cultural landscape. This allows me to compare various resources, both plant and animal, and determine whether foragers could profitably exploit them at any given distance from camp. The results suggest that the important variable is not whether the resources are plant or animal, but instead whether they require significant processing prior to consumption. Those with low costs are best procured close to camp. These low-cost resources also tend to be highly predictable yet highly seasonable and restricted on the landscape. Their predictability makes them particularly

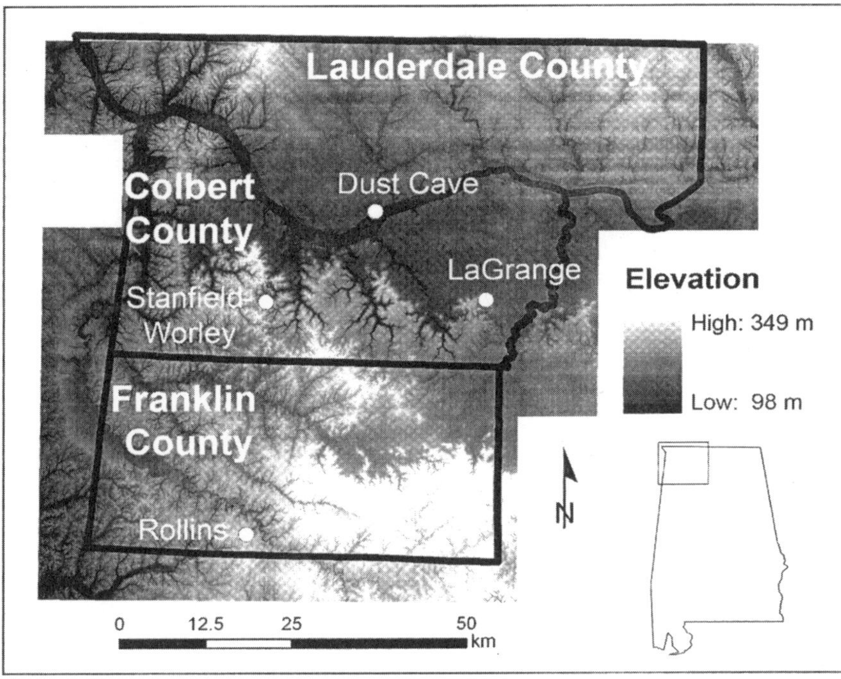

Figure 1.3. Map of the project area and the four rockshelter sites considered in this work.

suitable resources for women and children, who require stable nutrition; their limited availability in time and space requires seasonal movements across the landscape.

I then turn to plant data from four rockshelter sites in northwest Alabama (Figure 1.3). Among these sites is Dust Cave, dissolved from the limestone bluff that lines the northern edge of the Tennessee River floodplain in Lauderdale County. Two bluff shelters, both eroded from the sandstone caps of Little Mountain, are located in Colbert County. LaGrange Bluff Shelter is located on the escarpment between Little Mountain and the uplands of the Tennessee Valley, and Stanfield-Worley Bluff Shelter is nestled in a cove within the Little Mountain hills. The last bluff shelter site, Rollins, is located along the sandstone slopes of the Fall Line Hills in Franklin County.

Although the plant samples from the four sites were collected by various methods over the past 40 years, the excellent preservation of both plant and animal remains at the sites allows me to evaluate the use of plants by early foragers in relation to other subsistence pursuits. Using this subsistence data, the spatial distribution and seasonal availability of these resources, and the information about resource procurement derived from central place foraging theory, I construct a model of subsistence strategies and mobility patterns for early foragers living in the region. The outcome suggests that the decisions and activities of gatherers—women, children, and the elderly—do significantly shape settlement and subsistence strategies. Furthermore, women and children's need for reliable, predictable resources should influence settlement and subsistence strategies not only during the Late Paleoindian and Early Archaic periods in northwest Alabama but also for foraging peoples living in other times and places.

2
Modeling the Late Paleoindian and Early Archaic Periods in the Southeast

Foraging peoples can be described as relatively mobile groups who obtain more than 95 percent of their diet by hunting wild animals, gathering wild plant foods, collecting shellfish, and fishing (Lee and DeVore 1968:4; Panter-Brick et al. 2001). Lee and DeVore (1968:11–12) further add that foragers retain little in the way of personal property, live in groups that are relatively small (usually under 50), claim no exclusive rights to resources, do not amass food surpluses, and do not develop strong attachments to any particular site because of the frequency with which they move. The greatest similarity among foraging groups around the world, however, is that each employs a diversity of strategies and displays marked flexibility (Kelly 1995; Lee and DeVore 1968; Panter-Brick et al. 2001).

In this chapter, I present the theoretical framework that I use to address the diverse strategies employed by these early foragers. I approach the modeling of settlement and subsistence strategies from the perspective of evolutionary ecology. Use of this theoretical perspective is not new to southeastern archaeology; indeed, strands of evolutionary ecology appear in the models constructed by Meltzer and Smith (1986) and Cable (1996). However, I apply two approaches within evolutionary ecology—the division of labor and central place foraging theory—that have yet to be fully considered for southeastern Paleoindian and Early Archaic peoples. Below I discuss the basic assumptions of evolutionary ecology, its value to archaeological research, and the manner in which I will employ theories regarding the division of labor and central place foraging in my study. Please note that in the following discussion, as well as the remainder of this study, I use *foraging* in the broadest sense of the term, rather than Binford's (1979, 1980) more narrow definition (i.e., *foragers* versus *collectors*).

EVOLUTIONARY ECOLOGY

Evolutionary ecology approaches the study of behaviors from the standpoint of neo-Darwinian theory, asserting that natural selection affects the occurrence of particular behaviors. Of the available behaviors from which individuals can choose, those that provide individuals with an advantage in survival and sexual reproduction are "selected," or passed on to subsequent generations at higher rates than other behaviors (Kelly 1995:52; Smith and Winterhalder 1992; Winterhalder 1981:16). While these behaviors must be passed from parent to offspring for natural selection to operate, the mode of transmission need not be genetic: children may learn these behaviors through enculturation (Bettinger 1991:154; Kelly 1995:52), whether consciously or subconsciously (Winterhalder 1981:16).

Stated succinctly, evolutionary ecologists assume (1) that individuals make decisions (2) that maximize their ability to survive and raise offspring (3) within particular contexts (Bettinger 1991; Kelly 1995; Smith and Winterhalder 1992; Winterhalder and Smith 1992). I discuss each of these points in further detail below.

First, individuals make decisions to exhibit particular behaviors. This reflects not only that an individual must decide between a number of possible behaviors, but also the fact that variation among behaviors is necessary for natural selection to take place. It also highlights the individual as the basic unit of analysis in evolutionary ecology. This is important in part because fitness, or survival and sexual reproduction, is measured at the level of the individual. Furthermore, the actions and goals of individuals are held to be key to understanding social and ecological processes, an assumption termed *methodological individualism* (Smith 1988:225). Because "properties of groups . . . are a result of the actions of its individual members" (Smith and Winterhalder 1992:39), the individual should be prominent in analyses of these groups.

Second, individuals act as if they exercise rational choice in deciding which behavior(s) to adopt, such that they optimize their fitness, or ability to survive and produce viable offspring (Smith and Winterhalder 1992:45). Individuals must therefore evaluate various behaviors and choose the one with the highest payoffs (Kelly 1995:52). Of course, fitness is difficult for researchers to measure, much less for individuals to evaluate as they make decisions. Various proxy currencies are therefore used, which may either be maximized or minimized by individuals. For example, individuals may aim to maximize net energy returns from their food-getting pursuits, or maximize social capital from sharing foods. Conversely, they may strive to minimize the risk of being without food during lean times by storing or sharing foods, or minimize time spent foraging in order to have more time for other activities (Kelly 1995; Smith 1988; Smith and Winterhalder 1992:51). Individuals need not perform lengthy calculations to decide which behavior, among those available, provides the highest payoff. Instead, individuals probably learn rules of thumb that assist in such decision making (Kaplan and Hill 1992; Mithen 1989).

Third, the context within which these decisions are made is key. Natural selection is context specific: particular behaviors are adaptive only in particular contexts (Kelly 1995; Smith and Winterhalder 1992; Winterhalder and Smith 1992). Stockpiling meat for future use is adaptive in arctic climates but not in tropical ones where the meat would spoil quickly. Context includes more than local climate and physical environment, however. The social environment also plays a prominent role, and may include interactions with neighbors, the perceived value of resources, and cultural prescriptions (Smith and Winterhalder 1992). Evolutionary ecologists also recognize that individuals impact and influence their physical surroundings, for example by affecting prey populations (Belovsky 1988; FitzGibbon 1998), encouraging growth of particular plant species (Winterhalder and Goland 1993, 1997), and adopting new technologies (Winterhalder 1981). These actions change the payoffs of various behaviors, particularly interactions with animals, plants, and the landscape.

In order to understand how individuals make these decisions, evolutionary ecologists employ models as heuristic devices, simplifying complex processes in order to better define the problem, understand the data, test that understanding, and make further predictions (Winterhalder 2002; Winterhalder and Smith 1992:13). Models of adaptive strategies typically take the form of cost-benefit analyses using microeconomic models and detailed studies of available resources (Hames and Vickers 1982; Hawkes et al. 1982). These are often presented as mathematical algorithms. Models may also employ game theory analysis to understand the dynamics of interactions between individuals and groups (Smith 1988; Smith and Winterhalder 1992). It should be stressed that models are considered heuristic: they are not presumed to include all possible behaviors or incorporate all possible social and physical variables and constraints. Instead, they highlight a subset of these and suggest whether they are salient to the question at hand.

Among the behaviors, choices, and interactions modeled within evolutionary ecology, those associated with some economic choice or outcome are most commonly used within archaeology. These unquestionably have a social aspect as well, as economic choices are made within and shape social contexts. Some of the common topics addressed by these models include foraging strategies, such as the choice of food items as well as of resource patches (e.g., Belovsky 1988; Stiner et al. 2000); the placement of camp sites and decisions about the transport of goods to those sites (e.g., Gremillion 2006; Jones and Madsen 1989; Zeanah 2000), as well as decisions to move camp sites (e.g., Kelly 1997; Kelly and Todd 1988; Surovell 2000); the sharing of resources to reduce the risk of being without such resources at a later date (Winterhalder 1990); the division of labor by gender and age (e.g., Elston and Zeanah 2002); and the decision to tend gardens or animals rather than, or in addition to, hunting and gathering wild resources (e.g., Winterhalder and Goland 1993, 1997). This list is by no means exhaustive but suggests the range of subjects tackled by evolutionary ecology that have proven useful to archaeologists.

Models from evolutionary ecology are not always easily adapted to archaeological problems, however. Many of the algorithmic equations require detailed information, typically regarding the nature of resources, that is simply not available in most archaeological situations. This is particularly true of the Paleoindian and Early Archaic periods. Fine-grained reconstructions of local environments are not available for most regions. Even if organic remains are preserved, recovery biases are such that the full range of plant and animal resources used by a group cannot be known with certainty. Strict hypothesis testing thus is often not feasible.

While detailed modeling is not always possible, evolutionary ecology still provides valuable insights for archaeologists. Although the models may not be useful for directly evaluating and testing some types of archaeological data against expectations, they aid in interpretation of the data or recommend ways in which the data might be organized (Winterhalder 2002). They can provide an interpretive framework from which the data may be viewed. Perhaps the most significant manner in which these models facilitate interpretation is by encouraging researchers to perceive the archaeological record as the result of the decisions of individuals, who are situated, gendered, and have identities, histories, and agency. Further, this focus on the decisions of individuals widens the application of ethnographic analogy within archaeology (O'Connell 1995). The salient points of comparison between ethnographic and archaeological peoples become the decisions they face rather than similar technologies, subsistence strategies, and environments.

Here I use models developed within evolutionary ecology both to test my data and to provide an interpretive framework. I directly apply a model of central place foraging to explore why people occupied the four rockshelter sites, how they may have organized their movements between these and other open-air sites through the seasons of a year, and how gathering may have influenced these movements and occupations. I also use models of the division of labor to shape my discussion of gathering, although I do not employ specific models for this purpose. I discuss the two in turn below, beginning with the division of labor.

THE DIVISION OF LABOR

Ethnographic and historic accounts of hunter-gatherer groups consistently note a gendered division of labor, which in its simplest form equates gathering with women and hunting with men. More nuanced discussions broaden these categories, observing that women primarily target resources that may have higher processing costs and lower energy return rates but are relatively stable and reliable. Examples of such resources include plant foods, shellfish, and smaller animals. Men generally pursue larger prey with lower processing costs that yield higher energy return rates, but whose capture is much more unpredictable (Bird 1999; Hawkes 1996; Panter-Brick 2002).

Just as important as the consistency with which it is observed is the considerable flexibility in the division of labor, within as well as among various foraging societies (Kelly 1995; Panter-Brick 2002). Among some groups, women join men on hunting forays or hunt large animals themselves, although with different tools (Panter-Brick 2002). Men may also hunt smaller animals, fish, collect honey, and gather plant foods (Hawkes 1993, 1996; Walker et al. 2002). However, the general pattern of a sexual division of labor describes the majority of men's and women's activities both within and across groups.

The larger question is why this general pattern is so consistent across foraging societies. Evolutionary ecologists primarily address this question from two different perspectives: a conflict model, which stresses the differences in reproductive success of women and men; and a complementarity model, which highlights the interdependence of men and women due to their different life histories (Bird 1999). While they provide distinctly different explanations, both position the development of the division of labor in the evolutionary history of human primates.

Conflict Model

The conflict model relates the division of labor to differences in the reproductive strategies of men and women. A woman's reproductive success is limited by the number of children she can bear and raise to reproductive age. In contrast, a man's reproductive success is limited by his mating opportunities:

he can father many more children over his reproductive span than a woman can bear and raise. Men and women thus face different incentives. It is in a woman's best interest to invest in the well-being of her children, and her children's offspring, while a man's best strategy is to foster relationships that improve his opportunities to mate (Hawkes 1993:350, 1996).

Women can promote the well-being of their children through attentive care-giving to reduce children's exposure to danger, as well as by ensuring that they have adequate nutrition. Neither children nor pregnant or lactating mothers can go without food for long without incurring significant negative health effects. As such, we should expect mothers to target resources that are stable and predictable, such as plant foods and shellfish. Returns from hunting larger game are generally much less reliable; even skilled hunters can go days or weeks without success (Bird 1999; Hawkes 1996).

Women face a tradeoff between childcare and foraging to feed children and must weigh the benefits and costs of the two (Hawkes 1996). During seasons when foraging is more productive and/or danger to children from pests is lower (so that mothers need not be overly attentive), women spend more time foraging (Bird 1999:69; Hawkes 1996). Mothers may also decide to take children with them to pick berries, leave them at home to process foods like nuts, or allow them to forage for their own food during play, depending on which option yields the highest return rate and whether the immediate surroundings are safe for children (Hawkes 1996:291; Tucker and Young 2005). Importantly, women do not seem to choose between childcare and hunting. Not only do women in some societies hunt with nursing infants strapped to their backs (Kelly 1995:268), but also post-reproductive women do not hunt more frequently than younger women (Bird 1999:70). In addition, women who can leave their children at camp with older siblings, relatives, or other caretakers do not necessarily hunt more often (Bird 1999:70; cf. Kelly 1995:268). Instead, hunting by women seems to be related to local resource structures: women are more likely to hunt in areas where hunting provides a relatively predictable food supply (Bird 1999; Panter-Brick 2002). Indeed, women primarily hunt opportunistically, when they encounter small game while out gathering (Kelly 1995:267). Agta women, who are renowned for the frequency at which they hunt, use additional strategies, such as training and employing hunting dogs, that significantly improve their success rates compared to men (31 percent versus 17 percent) (Kelly 1995:268). The factor that best explains women's hunting appears to be whether they can reliably feed their children by engaging in it.

Men do not appear to be as concerned with predictable resources. Although they could feed their children more reliably by gathering and collecting food resources (Hawkes 1993:344), men instead generally choose to hunt larger animals. As noted above, returns from hunting larger game are highly variable. Even when hunters do return to camp with a successful kill, the carcass is often divided up among numerous families within the camp, so that the hunter's family does not gain any greater benefit from the meat itself. This communitywide sharing, which is observed in a number of modern hunter-gatherer groups (Kelly 1995), does not seem to reflect a direct investment by the hunter in the success of his children. Instead, hunters apparently gain social standing by felling and sharing larger prey (Bird 1999; Hawkes 1996). While increased social standing may garner better treatment for hunters' children from the community, this benefit may be incidental. Rather than provisioning their children, hunters appear to be strengthening social alliances through sharing meat; these social ties may lead to greater mating opportunities (Bird 1999; Hawkes 1993:349, 1996:297). This strategy promotes men's reproductive success, which is limited by mating opportunities.

Complementarity Model

The complementarity model approaches the division of labor from a different perspective, comparing the life histories of men and women rather than reproductive strategies. The main premise of the model is that hunting, particularly of larger animals, requires a significant learning investment in order for a hunter to be proficient. Observations of modern hunters support this: while adult humans reach their peak strength in their early twenties, hunters do not achieve their peak hunting returns until around the age of 35. This lag suggests that skill, gained only through frequent—if not daily—practice, is a significant component of hunting success (Kaplan et al. 2000; Kaplan et al. 2001).

Women simply may not have the time to invest in such practice. Assuming that women who are more than six months pregnant or nursing cannot go on hunting forays, a woman can only devote one-fourth of her reproductive life to hunting (Kaplan et al. 2001:306). Without the extended skill investment, hunting of larger game is not profitable for women, especially when compared to gathering. Men, unencumbered by pregnancy and lactation, are able to invest this time and eventually profitably hunt larger game at a high return rate. Presumably the decision to make such an investment is largely subconscious and highly enculturated. The nutritionally valuable meat they provide thus complements the plant foods that women gather. Furthermore, with these large packages of food provided by men, women in turn can spend more time caring for children. This cooperation between fathers and mothers leads to better outcomes for their children, and should therefore be favored by natural selection (Kaplan et al. 2001).

Comparing the Models

There are several important differences between the two models beyond life histories and reproductive strategies. Perhaps most importantly, they differ as to which parent provides the bulk of food for children. The conflict model asserts that women provide the majority of food opportunities for their children, whether through their own efforts or by bringing children with them on gathering forays so that children can gather food for themselves as well (Hawkes 1996; cf. Tucker and Young 2005). Men provide meat less frequently, but their own children do not appear to consume any more meat than other families with whom the kill is shared (Hawkes 1993, 1996). This is in stark contrast to the complementarity model in which fathers purportedly supply children with 97 percent of their caloric intake. Kaplan and colleagues (2001:308) arrive at this number by averaging the productivity of men and women in ten ethnographically observed foraging societies (Kaplan et al. 2000:Table 2). The authors note that men provide an average of 68 percent of calories while women provide 32 percent. Assuming that women consume 31 percent of all calories, men 39 percent, and children 31 percent, they conclude that women only produce 1 percent more than they consume. Men provide 29 percent more calories than they consume; these leftovers apparently comprise children's diets.

These calculations are problematic on several levels. First, they assume that children do not obtain any food for themselves. While it may be true that on average children forage at significantly lower rates than adults (Kaplan et al. 2000:160), they do acquire some food for themselves, of which Kaplan and colleagues (2000:168–169) provide several examples. Accordingly, a mother may choose gathering tasks that do not maximize her efforts alone, but those of her "team," which includes her children. For example, she may take her children with her to pick berries or dig young tubers because they can do so at a relatively efficient rate, even though the berry patch may be at some distance (Hawkes 1996; Tucker and Young 2005).

Perhaps more importantly, however, the calculations do not take into account the periodicity in returns of men's and women's food-getting efforts. While men may indeed on average provide more calories than women, these calories come in large packages (carcasses) that may be obtained only once a week or even once a month, and may not necessarily be storable. Of course periodicity may also be avoided by sharing, which Kaplan and colleagues (2000; 2001) assert does not significantly detract from the amount of meat available to a hunter's family. Instead, they suggest that hunters retain some control over the distribution of meat from their kills, and that they share only with those who will reciprocate. Reciprocal sharing would alleviate the periodicity of hunting and provide a more regular supply of meat to a group of families. Such a scenario is tenable as long as free-riding could be prevented, which is debatable (Bird 1999; Hawkes 1993).

Two additional points of difference follow from the first. Fathers are thought to invest significantly more energy in parenting, as suggested by the amount of food they provision to children, in the complementarity model (Kaplan et al. 2000; Kaplan et al. 2001). In contrast, men invest in parenting in the conflict model only if it coincides with strategies that increase their mating success (Bird 1999; Hawkes 1996). The roles of relatives other than fathers and mothers also differ between the two, beyond just the active foraging of children mentioned above. The availability of alternative caretakers, such as older siblings, other mothers, and grandmothers, significantly affects the foraging decisions of mothers in the conflict model. Grandmothers may also provision their grandchildren, thus furthering their own reproductive success (Hawkes 1996:292–293). In the complementarity model, however, it appears that only the families with whom hunters reciprocate play a significant role in food provisioning other than the father and mother (Kaplan et al. 2000:178–179).

Finally, the two models differ in their approach to hunting by women. The complementarity model persuasively argues that women do not hunt large game because they cannot invest the time to become efficient at it. But it does not address the fact that women do hunt with some regularity, sometimes alongside men (Bird 1999; Panter-Brick 2002:631). According the complementarity model, women such as the Agta apparently should not be hunting with infants strapped to their backs, but instead should be home nursing. The conflict model does allow for hunting by women, particularly when the risk of being unsuccessful is relatively low (Kelly 1995; Panter-Brick 2002).

Despite the differences between the two models, both place the biological differences between women and men at the base of the division of labor. The conflict model ties the division of labor to differences in reproductive success of men and women, and the complementarity model to differences in their reproductive lives. As such, both models incorporate the division of labor in the evolutionary history of humans.[1] This explains why a sexual division of labor is widely observed among modern foraging societies: not only do they presumably share a common ancestor but also the same reproductive strategies, as do all modern humans.

If this is the case, then it should be reasonable to assume that Paleoindian and Archaic foraging groups also practiced a sexual division of labor. However, we must also assume that this division of labor was highly flexible in the past, as it is today. Women likely targeted stable, predictable resources, including shellfish, fish, and smaller game in addition to plant foods. These resources may vary significantly in different ecological settings and different seasons (Panter-Brick 2002:633, 638). Men also probably gathered plant foods, not only for their own consumption while on forays but also for their families. In general, however, women probably performed the majority of gathering activities, as well as activities associated with processing and preparing both plant and animal foods, while men likely performed the majority of hunting activities, as well as specialized tool production.

Because the archaeological record is an accumulation of patterned behavior (Yarnell 1982), and because the general pattern among human foraging societies is that women gather and men hunt, it is reasonable to assume that women are responsible for the majority of gathered resources recovered from the occupation sites of foraging groups. In particular, women likely performed the majority of tasks associated with gathered plant foods, including monitoring, harvesting, and processing them.

I do not directly apply either the conflict or complementarity model to the data I analyze in this project. Instead, I draw from the models' similarities, which pose different foraging decisions for women and men based on their reproductive differences. As fully modern humans, Paleoindian and Archaic men and women faced similar decisions. I use this assumption to shape my interpretation of the plant remains from the four rockshelter sites examined in this project, arguing that they derive primarily from the efforts of women, children, and the elderly.

CENTRAL PLACE FORAGING THEORY

Of the numerous working theories in evolutionary ecology, central place foraging (hereafter CPF) is the most applicable to concerns of mobility and settlement patterns. This theory assumes that foragers return to a central place with the food they capture or collect, and that they attempt to maximize the rate of delivery of energy to that central place (Orians and Pearson 1979). In other words, individuals attempt to bring back to camp as large a quantity of energy (food) as possible while expending as little energy as possible in travel and transport. From these assumptions, CPF theory attempts to derive and test predictions regarding how far foragers will travel from their base camps in order to pursue food items (Gremillion 2006; Jones and Madsen 1989), or where foragers should locate their camps relative to the distribution of available resources (Orians and Pearson 1979; Zeanah 2000).

The theoretical answer to the latter is that central places should be situated such that travel time *to* and transport costs *from* foraging patches are minimized, with the result that central places are located at the "center of gravity" of food distribution (Orians and Pearson 1979; Zeanah 2000). How far foragers travel from these central places depends on the resource being targeted, and whether the benefits gained from the resource are greater than the costs of obtaining it. As such, foragers will travel much farther distances to pursue resources with high return rates, such as large mammals. The benefits, whether measured in terms of calories or in the prestige associated with sharing the meat with one's neighbors, outweigh the costs of travel from camp in search of prey and back to camp carrying the prey. Accordingly, the distance traveled to obtain items with lower return rates, such as plant foods, should be considerably less (Jones and Madsen 1989; Kelly 1995:141; Orians and Pearson 1979).

The net foraging return rate, or benefits minus the costs, of obtaining various resources and bringing them back to a central place can be calculated with the following equation (after Gremillion 2006):

$$r = \frac{e_{obt} - e_{exp}}{t}$$

where

r is return rate (kcal per hr)
e_{obt} is energy obtained per load (kcal)
e_{exp} is energy expended in procuring one load of the resource (kcal)
and t is time spent procuring one load (hr).

While the energy obtained per load can be readily determined from the caloric content of various foodstuffs, the energy expended in obtaining one load has several components. These include the energy used to walk to the patch where the resource can be found; energy used to harvest the resource (commonly referred to as handling costs); and energy used to carry the load back to camp. Similarly, time includes that spent traveling to and from camp, as well as spent harvesting (or handling) the resource. Including these components, the equation becomes (after Zeanah 2000:Table 1.4):

$$r = \frac{e_{obt} - [H_t * H_c + (\sum_{s=1}^{n} D_s * W_s) + (\sum_{f=1}^{n} D_f * L * U_f)]}{H_t + \frac{\sum_{s=1}^{n} D_s}{V}}$$

where

- H_t is handling time per load (hr)
- H_c is handling costs per load (kcal/hr)
- D_s is distance of slope *s* traveled to and from the nearest patch of the resource (km)
- W_s is cost of walking across slope *s* (kcal/km)
- D_f is distance of slope *f* from the nearest patch of the resource to camp (km)
- L is weight of one load of the resource (kg)
- U_f is cost of carrying one load across slope *f* (kcal/kg/km)

and V is walking speed (km/hr).

The equation can then be used to compare the return rates that various resources afford foraging groups, given the distribution of resource patches relative to campsites. Gremillion (2006) uses such an equation to compare the return rates of both wild and domesticate sumpweed and chenopod in floodplain and hillside settings to explore the range of options available to occupants of rockshelters in Kentucky. Comparing the return rates of mountain sheep and tansy mustard seeds, Zeanah (2000) demonstrates that the seasonal availability of resources can significantly influence the placement of base camps in the Great Basin. When mountain sheep are readily available, base camps should be located in the uplands, but when these highly ranked resources are scarce, foragers should shift camps to the lowlands to be nearer to resources like tansy mustard with lower return rates. The equation can also be employed to determine the distance of travel at which the energy spent procuring a particular resource is greater than that provided by the resource (Jones and Madsen 1989). Additionally, the benefits of processing items in the field can be weighed. While the energy obtained per load increases with the removal of low-utility parts (such as nutshells), the handling time and costs increase as well. Metcalfe and Barlow (1992) discuss the value of such an application in understanding field processing and transport of tool stone and carcass elements, as well as nuts. Bettinger and colleagues (1997) examine the payoffs of processing acorns and mussels, in the field versus at camp.

In keeping with central place foraging theory, I contend that Late Paleoindian and Early Archaic foragers located their base camps near important resources. Because foragers are less likely to travel long distances to obtain items with lower return rates, I expect that camps should be located nearer to these resources, such as plants and mussels, as long as they are sufficiently abundant in the landscape and critical to foragers' diets.

Gathered resources need not necessarily supply the bulk of foragers' calories to be important to their diets. Plant foods certainly supply vitamins and minerals unavailable from meat. But more importantly, gathered resources are predictable, and can fill gaps in the diet when hunters are unsuccessful. The predictability of gathered foods makes them particularly attractive to women, who need reliable sources of food for themselves and their children.

Because gathered resources were a key component of the diet, and because of their relatively low return rates, I suggest that site locations and mobility patterns are organized around the seasonal and spatial availability of plant foods and other gathered resources. More specifically, I hypothesize that early foragers chose their base camps so that women, children, and the elderly could exploit gathered foods residentially, while these groups exploited other resources, both animal and raw materials, logistically.

To test this hypothesis, I use the equation defined above to explore the influence of various resources, particularly plant foods but also animal and tool stone resources, on the choice of campsites. Similar to Zeanah (2000), I evaluate how the distribution of resources in space and time affects the payoffs of using such resources. The caloric content of various foodstuffs can be obtained from U.S. Department of Agriculture compilations (e.g., Kuhnlein and Turner 1991; U.S. Department of Agriculture, Nutrient Data Laboratory [USDA NDL] 2004), and the handling time and costs of most resources can be estimated from a number of experimental studies (e.g., Metcalfe and Barlow 1992; Munson 1984). With the aid of a geographic information system, I develop a map of resource distribution on the landscape of northwest Alabama and model the costs of obtaining resources on this landscape. By comparing these costs, I explore how the various resources influence site choice in the region, and in turn, how the activities of hunters and gatherers—men, women, children, and the elderly—shape site location and movement across the landscape.

The landscape is the center of this model, supplying resources and presenting challenges to foraging groups, who in turn may influence the availability of resources and shape the landscape. I describe both the physical and cultural landscape of northwest Alabama during the Late Paleoindian and Early Archaic periods in the next chapter.

NOTE

1. The division of labor may be a (perhaps relatively modern) social construct, in which men appropriate hunting and the value associated with it in order to secure higher stature within the group. This explains why women do not hunt and refer to hunting as men's work, even though they can and do hunt themselves (Brightman 1996). But it does not explain why men choose hunting rather than gathering; it is possible that plant foods could have been culturally defined as more valuable than meat. Neither does it explain the universality of the division of labor observed among hunter-gatherer societies.

3
The Landscape of the Middle Tennessee River Valley

The Tennessee River threads through the northwest corner of Alabama, receiving tributaries that drain three distinct physiographic regions. This rich and varied landscape supports a wide variety of aquatic and terrestrial animals, supplied by a range of plant communities. Combined with local high-quality stone resources, the area had much to offer its early occupants. The regional landscape was far from static, however, particularly during the span between roughly 13,000 and 8,000 years ago with which I am concerned. Dramatic changes associated with the close of the last ice age affected not only the local climate but also the composition of local plant and animal communities. Furthermore, the actions and interactions of early foraging groups shaped the physical and social landscape, as these peoples hunted animal populations, gathered plant resources, quarried stone, traded materials, shared information, and formed kinship bonds in the region beginning over 13,000 years ago.

In this chapter, I describe the physical and cultural setting of the project area. I begin with an overview of the local geology, as well as local forest communities prior to significant Euroamerican impact in the region. I then review the climate changes associated with the close of the Pleistocene and onset of the Holocene and consider the influence of these climatic shifts on the region's plant and animal communities. Finally, I discuss the social landscape of northwest Alabama, particularly as it can be read from the patterning of archaeological sites across the region. After outlining a brief history of archaeological research in the area, I explore the responses of early foraging groups to this changing landscape by examining the distribution of archaeological sites through time.

PHYSICAL LANDSCAPE

The project area, which includes Lauderdale, Colbert, and Franklin counties, encompasses three major physiographic regions: the Highland Rim, com-

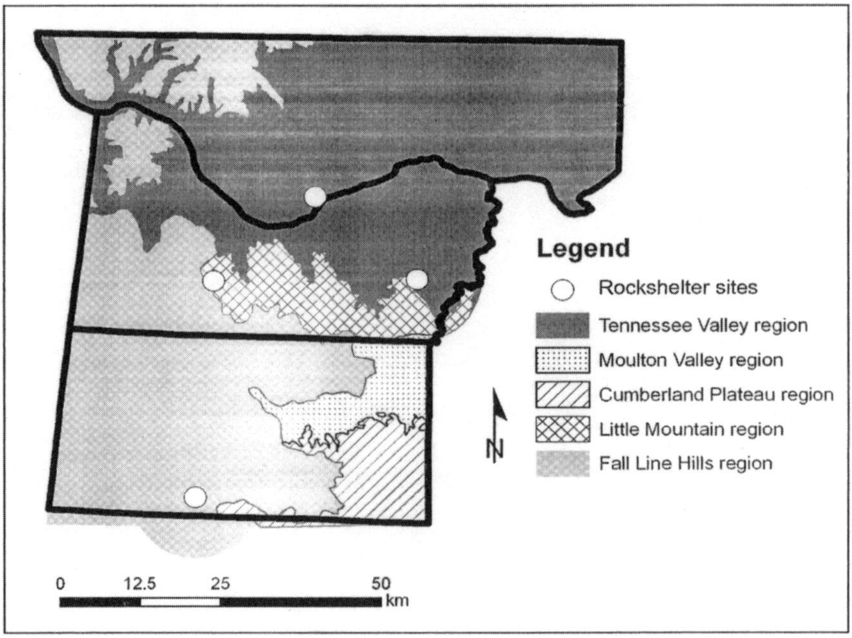

Figure 3.1. Map of the physiographic regions comprising the project area.

prised of the Tennessee Valley, Little Mountain, and Moulton Valley regions; the Cumberland Plateau; and the Fall Line Hills (Figure 3.1). In general, the topography slopes gently westward, with the Tennessee River flowing to the west and turning to the northwest where Alabama meets with Mississippi and Tennessee. The eastern portion of the river in this area is characterized by shoals, called Muscle Shoals, extending approximately 80 km upstream from the present-day city of Florence. Major tributaries to the river include Shoal Creek and Cypress Creek in Lauderdale County; Cane Creek and Spring Creek in Colbert County; and Cedar Creek, Little Bear Creek, and Bear Creek in Franklin County, which drain through Colbert into the Tennessee River.

The three physiographic districts are differentiated by their underlying geology, which in turn dictates the hydrology and the plant and animal communities characteristic of each district. These biological communities and the local hydrology changed in response to climate changes as well as human manipulation. The present landscape of the region has been influenced by Euroamerican settlement that began in earnest by the start of the nineteenth century, but has undoubtedly been most dramatically altered by the construction of dams by the U.S. federal government and the Tennessee Valley Authority (TVA) during the twentieth century. Wilson and Pickwick Landing Dams, completed in 1924 and 1938 respectively, not only powered hydroelectric generators but also made the dangerous Muscle Shoals area navigable (TVA 2005). Prior to the dams, the river dropped over 40 m in elevation along this 80-km stretch of shallow shoals and rapids. The dams submerged the shoals and the surrounding area under some three to four meters of water. The Tennessee Valley Authority also constructed a series of dams along the Bear Creek drainage system to provide flood control as well as a water supply to the region. The first was Bear Creek Dam, finished in 1969, followed by Little Bear Creek in 1975, Upper Bear Creek in 1978, and finally Cedar Creek Dam in 1979 (TVA 2005).

In spite of these significant and relatively recent alterations of the landscape, it is possible to develop a picture of local plant communities by studying the field notes taken by General Land Office (GLO) surveyors in the early 1800s (Bourdo 1956; Delcourt 1975, 1976; Delcourt and Delcourt 1974). As these men laid out townships and ranges in northwest Alabama in 1817–1820 and 1833–1834, they recorded up to four witness trees at the corners of each one-mile-square section, and sometimes two trees at every half section. Furthermore, they briefly noted the quality of the soil, the immediate topography, and the nature of the local vegetation, not only at each corner but also whenever they encountered a significant change in landscape, vegetation, or whenever they crossed a creek (Alabama Secretary of State 2005; Bourdo 1956:758). These notes can be compiled to reconstruct local plant communities, including the relative frequency of particular species on the landscape, the relative density of a species compared to other species present, and the density of trees per acre (Delcourt 1976: 127–128).

In the sections below, I describe the landscapes of the three physiographic districts within the project area. I note the salient characteristics of the topography and underlying geology of each region. These in turn influence local plant communities, as is evident from the notes of GLO surveyors for Lauderdale, Colbert, and Franklin counties. I summarize detailed analyses of these notes (Caddell 1983; Hollenbach 2005; Johnson 1985) and use them to depict forest compositions in different topographic settings within each physiographic region. I also note animal communities and stone resources that are significant to each district.

Highland Rim

The Highland Rim includes all but the western and southeastern portion of the project area. This district can be further subdivided into the Tennessee

Valley, Little Mountain, and Moulton Valley regions (Alabama Maps 2005; Harper 1942).

Tennessee Valley Region

The Tennessee Valley area is characterized by karstic uplands divided by the narrow floodplain of the river, which measures approximately 1.5 to 2.5 km in width. Bluffs of Mississippian-age Tuscumbia limestone flank the floodplain and rise some 20 m above it. These bluffs give way to gently rolling uplands that range between 150 and 200 m above mean sea level. Unlike the other physiographic districts, sinks and springs mark the karstic uplands. Groundwater has also dissolved the underlying limestone to create caves along the bluffs.

At present, oak-hickory forests populate the Tennessee Valley region of the Highland Rim (Bryant et al. 1993). Harper's (1913) description indicates that oak-hickory forests, with relatively few coniferous trees, were present at the turn of the century. The majority of the coniferous trees appear to have been cedar (*Juniperus virginiana*). Cypress (*Taxodium distichum*) trees grew along the creeks west of the shoals, and a wide variety of hardwoods populated the limestone slopes (Harper 1913:43–45).

The notes of GLO surveyors provide further detail for early nineteenth-century forests. Comparing river bottoms, slopes, and uplands, the data suggest that river-bottom communities were the richest in terms of the number of species present. Exclusive to bottomlands were species that thrive in rich deciduous forests, including boxelder (*Acer negundo*), black walnut (*Juglans nigra*), hornbeam (*Carpinus caroliniana*), ironwood (*Ostrya virginiana*), and American basswood (*Tilia americana*). A number of species that prefer moist soils, such as hackberry (*Celtis* spp.) and cypress, as well as fruit trees such as honey locust (*Gleditsia triacanthos*) and mulberry (*Morus* spp.), were also recorded only in the creek bottoms (Hollenbach 2005:280). Oak (*Quercus* spp.) and hickory (*Carya* spp.) were much more dominant in slope and upland communities (Hollenbach 2005:280–284; Johnson 1985:51), but apparently a wider variety of trees grew on slopes than in the uplands. Chestnut (*Castanea dentata*), poplar (*Liriodendron tulipifera* or *Populus* spp.), elm (*Ulmus* sp.), sassafras (*Sassafras albidum*), sweet gum (*Liquidambar styraciflua*), sourwood (*Oxydendrum arboreum*), and pine (*Pinus* spp.) were much better represented in the field notes for Tennessee Valley slopes than uplands (Hollenbach 2005:284). Pine was notably low in the region, generally comprising less than 5 percent of local forests (Hollenbach 2005:284, Table 9.4; Johnson 1985:51).

Local animal communities within oak-hickory forests such as those that populated the Tennessee Valley region tend to differ by animals' preference for edge areas or dense forests. Animals associated with edges between forests and clearings include white-tailed deer (*Odocoileus virginianus*), various rodents, eastern cottontail (*Sylvilagus floridanus*), and wild turkey (*Meleagris gallopavo*). These animals take advantage of the cover and hard mast provided by the forest, the soft mast borne by shrubs and vines along the edges, and the seeds of herbaceous plants in clearings. Carnivores such as red (*Vulpes vulpes*) and gray foxes (*Urocyon cinereoargenteus*) also frequent these edges because of the availability of prey. Gray squirrels (*Sciurus carolinensis*) and flying squirrels (*Glaucomys volans*) prefer densely wooded habitats for mast as well as ease of movement between trees. In contrast, bobwhite quail (*Colins virginiana*) favors openings intermixed with woods (Skeen et al. 1993).

These forest communities can be further divided into upland and lowland habitats. The latter have higher net productivity due to greater available moisture (Bryant et al. 1993:179). As such, the richest diversity of wildlife, particularly bird species, is found in these lowland habitats. Not surprisingly, aquatic species such as wood duck (*Aix sponsa*), snapping turtle (*Chelydra serpentina*), slider (*Trachemys scripta*), painted turtle (*Chrysemys picta*), and herons (Ardeidae) are exclusively associated with the lowlands. This area of the river is also along the Mississippi flyway, an important route for migratory waterfowl, namely ducks and geese, traveling south from Canada in the fall and back north in spring (Walker 1998:150). Muscle Shoals, aptly named but poorly spelled, once provided habitat for some 70 species of freshwater mussels, described as one of the richest arrays in the world (Parmalee 1994: 135). Additional vertebrate species include barred owl (*Strix varia*), screech owl (*Otu asio*), osprey (*Pandion haliaetus*), egrets (Ardeidae), red-shouldered hawk (*Buteo lineatus*), swamp rabbit (*Sylvilagus aquaticus*), cottontail rabbit, fox squirrel (*Sciurus niger*), gray squirrel, flying squirrel, raccoon (*Procyon lotor*), opossum (*Didelphis virginiana*), gray fox, striped skunk (*Mephitis mephitis*), and deer (Bryant et al. 1993; Skeen et al. 1993).

Upland areas do not support aquatic species but offer significant mast resources. As such, they are frequented by a wide range of animals that consume acorns and other nuts, including blue jays (*Cyanocitta cristata*), wild turkeys, gray and flying squirrels, white-tailed deer, and various mice (*Peromyscus* spp.) (Bryant et al. 1993; Skeen et al. 1993). Additional animals associated with the uplands include box turtles (*Terrapene carolina*), gray fox, raccoon, opossum, and striped skunk (Bryant et al. 1993).

The most significant stone resource in the region outcrops along the Tennessee River and its tributaries. The Fort Payne formation, which lies beneath the Tuscumbia limestone, consists primarily of limestone-bearing nodules and beds of blue-gray chert (Osborne et al. 1989). High-quality grades of blue-gray Fort Payne chert served as an important raw material for stone tools throughout human occupation of the region. The tabular beds of the chert located in outcrops of Fort Payne limestone could have been quarried; however, secondary deposits in the form of cobbles, found in nearby rivers and streams, are more easily shaped into tools (Johnson and Meeks 1994).

In addition to blue-gray Fort Payne chert, two other chert types can be found in the Tennessee Valley region. These include other Fort Payne chert, of lower quality than the blue-gray variety, that also outcrops along the Tennessee River. Other Fort Payne is also available both in primary outcrops and in secondary deposits, as cobbles in rivers and streams (Meeks 1998; Randall 2002). The other chert type is Tuscaloosa gravel, which is ubiquitous in the project area. As its name suggests, this chert is found in gravel form in river- and streambeds. Not only is Tuscaloosa gravel generally relatively poor in quality, its smaller size precludes the manufacture of larger tools (Meeks 1998; Randall 2002).

Little Mountain Region

The Little Mountain region lines the southern border of the Tennessee Valley area, in the central and eastern portion of Colbert County. This region corresponds with the Hartselle sandstone formation of Mississippian age (Harper 1942; Osborne et al. 1989). Its boundary with the Tennessee Valley region is sharply demarcated, forming an escarpment roughly 30 m in height. The Little Mountains generally range between 200 m above sea level at their base to nearly 300 m at their highest point. They are highly dissected by streams that cut deep and narrow valleys into the hills. Erosion of the sandstone has formed numerous rockshelters in the hills of the region.

Oak-hickory-pine forests inhabit the Little Mountain region (Harper 1942:68; Skeen et al. 1993). Chestnut appears to have been a significant component of these forests, both in the nineteenth (Hollenbach 2005:285) and early twentieth centuries (Harper 1942:70). Although creek bottoms were poorly represented in the GLO field notes, due in part to the hilly nature of the topography, the available data suggest that bottomlands supported a richer plant community. Recorded bottomland trees include ash (*Fraxinus* sp.), dogwood (*Cornus* sp.), mulberry, poplar, and sugar maple (*Acer saccharum*), but just as important is the relative lack of pines, which are indicative of poorer soils, as compared to slopes and uplands (Hollenbach 2005:285–288).

Other species present on slopes included ash, elm, black gum (*Nyssa sylvatica*), ironwood, sassafras, and sourwood, while elm, maple (*Acer* spp.), persimmon (*Diospyros virginiana*), poplar, sourwood, and sweet gum were recorded among the upland communities (Hollenbach 2005:285).

Animal communities in the Little Mountain region are similar to those found in the oak-hickory forests of the Tennessee Valley region. The major distinction between them is the quantity of wildlife that they support. Because pines comprise a significant portion of the forests in the Little Mountains, these oak-hickory-pine communities generally do not yield the quantity or density of mast resources that oak-hickory forests do. Furthermore, pine forests tend to be associated with lower-quality soils (Harper 1942), suggesting lower productivity in general. Thus although widespread, wildlife in the oak-hickory-pine region is "not necessarily abundant" (Skeen et al. 1993:16).

Aquatic resources also differ between the two regions. Mussels inhabit the Little Mountain springs and streams, but these include different species, and a smaller range of species, than those found in the main channel (Parmalee 1994). Similarly, the variety and quantity of fish and waterfowl differs, primarily reflecting the presence of the Tennessee River in the one region and smaller-order streams in the other.

The Little Mountain region also lacks the stone resources present in the Tennessee Valley. High-quality Fort Payne chert does not outcrop in the region. The only raw material locally available for stone tools is Tuscaloosa gravel, of lower quality and present in smaller packages than blue-gray Fort Payne chert (Meeks 1998; Randall 2002).

Moulton Valley Region

The Moulton Valley region lies south of the Little Mountain region in the northeast corner of Franklin County and extends westward, following Cedar Creek Valley. This region, underlain by Mississippian-age Bangor limestone, has little relief. It is bounded by the hills of the Cumberland Plateau to the south in the eastern portion of Franklin County, and disappears beneath the Fall Line Hills of the Coastal Plain toward the west (Alabama Maps 2005; Harper 1942; Osborne et al. 1989). The lowest elevation of the Moulton Valley region is roughly 180 m above mean sea level in the northeastern corner of the county, increases to roughly 220 m in the upper reaches of Cedar Creek Valley, and falls again to around 140 m at the lower end of the valley.

Due to the underlying limestone, the forests of the Moulton Valley region are more similar to the Tennessee Valley than the sandstone hills of the

Little Mountain region. The oak-hickory forests that cover the region today (Bryant et al. 1993) are reflected in the early nineteenth-century survey notes, which indicate very low numbers of pine. Surveyors also recorded species that prefer rich soils, including ash, elm, ironwood, and mulberry, further suggesting that the forests of the region were highly productive (Hollenbach 2005:292).

These highly productive oak-hickory forests support a wildlife community more similar in quantity to the Tennessee Valley region than the Little Mountains. However, Moulton Valley lacks the main channel resources present in the Tennessee Valley, including the extensive shoals. Stone tool resources are also limited, as Tuscaloosa gravel is the only locally available raw material (Meeks 1998; Randall 2002).

Fall Line Hills

The second major physiographic region in the project area is the Fall Line Hills of the Coastal Plain, which comprises the western portion of the three counties. These hills consist of Cretaceous deposits of sand and gravel, termed the Tuscaloosa formation. Bear Creek and its two major tributaries, Little Bear and Cedar creeks, wind their way westward through the Fall Line Hills. These and other smaller-order streams deeply dissect the hills, exposing the underlying Bangor limestone and Pottsville sandstone formations of the Cumberland Plateau (Harper 1942; Osborne et al. 1989). The lowest elevation in this region is 126 m, the level of the Pickwick Reservoir, but the hills rise sharply from here and are generally over 200 m above mean sea level.

Oak-hickory-pine forests cover the Fall Line Hills at present (Skeen et al. 1993). In the early 1900s, local forests could be described as a mix of the Coastal Plains' southern pines and the Highland Rim's oak-hickory forests. Pines comprised roughly 44 percent of forest trees. The slopes of the region supported more diverse woods, adding beech (*Fagus grandifolia*), sweet gum, and other hardwoods to the pines, oaks, and hickories that covered the uplands (Harper 1913:74–76).

The early nineteenth-century GLO notes similarly depict slopes as supporting a wider variety of species than the uplands, although the majority of the topography in the Fall Line Hills can be classified as "slope" (Hollenbach 2005:291). In addition to a variety of oaks, slope forests included chestnut, black gum, hickory, ash, elm, dogwood, yellow poplar (*Liriodendron tulipifera*), and persimmon (Caddell 1983:336; Hollenbach 2005:291). Bottomland forests appear to have been the richest communities, however, and were comprised of beech, black walnut, cedar, cypress, holly (*Ilex* spp.), hornbeam, ironwood, redbud (*Cercis canadensis*), sugar maple, and willow (*Salix* spp.) (Caddell 1983:336; Hollenbach 2005:291). The comparative richness of creek bottoms is further underlined by the lower frequencies of pine recorded in these settings as compared to slopes (Hollenbach 2005:291).

Animal communities in the Fall Line Hills are similar to those found in the Little Mountain region. The oak-hickory-pine forests of the district support a variety of mammals and birds, but in lesser quantities than in the Tennessee and Moulton Valley regions. The greater quantities of pine in the Fall Line Hills are indicative of poorer soils, lower productivity, and fewer food resources for animals (Skeen et al. 1993:16). The numerous creeks and streams support a variety of aquatic species, but those that prefer larger river channels have little habitat in this physiographic district.

In addition to the ubiquitous Tuscaloosa gravel, a fossiliferous chert derived from nodules in the limestone Bangor formation is available in the Bear Creek watershed area of the Fall Line Hills. Referred to as fossiliferous Bangor, this chert is of comparable quality to Tuscaloosa gravel and is similarly available in small packages (Meeks 1998; Randall 2002).

Cumberland Plateau

The Cumberland Plateau, the third major physiographic region of the research area, reaches into the southeast corner of Franklin County and the upper portions of Bear Creek. This region is defined by the Pottsville formation, a Pennsylvanian-age sandstone. The plateau stands at the highest elevation in the project area, ranging between 290 and 320 m above mean sea level, and is highly dissected by streams. Through erosion of the sandstone, rockshelters have formed in the sides of the hills. Similar to the Highland Rim, the Cumberland Plateau gives way to the Fall Line Hills in the western half of Franklin County (Alabama Maps 2005; Harper 1942; Osborne et al. 1989).

Modern forests on the plateau are characterized as oak-hickory-pine (Skeen et al. 1993). In the early 1900s, the uplands supported forests dominated by short leafpines (*Pinus echinata*) and oaks, with conifers comprising nearly 30 percent of forests. As with the other regions, wider varieties of hardwoods, including beech, poplar, and sweet gum, populated the slopes leading down to the creeks (Harper 1913:49–50). Harper (1913:50–51) further noted that the forests on the richest plateau soils were similar to those on the poorest soils in the Tennessee Valley region, as both included higher percentages of conifers.

The GLO surveys also indicate relatively high quantities of pine (Hollenbach 2005:292–295). In addition to the dominant oak and hickory species, a range of hardwoods populated the slopes, including chestnut, sassafras, sourwood, dogwood, maple, and grape (*Vitis* spp.). Bottomlands are limited in this highly dissected region and are therefore poorly represented in the GLO notes, but the surveyors did record poplar, beech, and chestnut in these settings (Caddell 1983:337; Hollenbach 2005:292–295).

Similar to the other physiographic districts underlain by sandstone, which sustain relatively less productive forests and do not include a large river channel, the quantity of wildlife supported by the Cumberland Plateau is less than that of the richer Tennessee and Moulton Valley regions (Skeen et al. 1993:16). Within the portion of the Cumberland Plateau included in the project area, both Tuscaloosa gravel and fossiliferous Bangor chert are available as local stone resources (Meeks 1998; Randall 2002).

Summary

Although the various physiographic districts differ in a number of regards, the most salient distinguishing characteristic is the nature of the underlying geologic formations. Those that are underlain by sandstone are dominated by highly dissected uplands and poorer soils that support forests with higher percentages of coniferous trees. Areas where limestone serves as bedrock tend to be characterized by gently rolling topography and richer soils. The oak-hickory forests in these areas are more productive, and in turn sustain a greater quantity of wildlife, than the oak-hickory-pine forests in soils derived from sandstone.

Within each physiographic district, there are also important differences in plant and animal communities among the various topographic settings. In addition to a wide range of aquatic animals, bottomlands tended to support the richest forests and generally included the greatest number of species. Fruit trees, such as hackberry, mulberry, and honey locust, were more frequently found in these moist, alluvial settings. Herbaceous weedy taxa also thrive in disturbed bottomlands, and were more likely to occur in quantity within creek bottoms (Hollenbach 2005:297–298). Nut-bearing trees, in contrast, were most abundant in uplands and slopes. As nuts ripened in the fall, the density of animals that rely on mast increased within these topographic settings.

Of further note is the Tennessee Valley region, which is distinguished by access to Muscle Shoals and its rich aquatic resources, as well as outcrops of high-quality blue-gray Fort Payne chert. Available in larger packages than the ubiquitous Tuscaloosa gravels and of higher quality than fossiliferous Bangor, blue-gray Fort Payne chert was the preferred stone tool material in the region.

The fact that the general topography and ecological communities in the project area are largely dictated by local geology, which has not changed significantly over the past 15,000 years, suggests that the relative differences among these communities likely held even as climatic conditions changed. These climatic changes, and their influences on local plant and animal communities, are discussed below.

CLIMATE

Global climatic conditions changed significantly over the last 15,000 years as the last glacial period waned and interglacial weather patterns were established (Figure 3.2). By approximately 14,500 cal B.P., increases in summertime solar radiation and the resulting retreat of glacial ice sheets that covered most of Canada and the northern United States brought significant and relatively rapid shifts in the climate of North America. In general, the colder, drier conditions associated with the last glacial maximum ameliorated. However, the degree to which various regions experienced this trend in warming and shift in rainfall differs based on the varying influence of ice sheets, air masses, and ocean currents (COHMAP Members 1988; Delcourt and Delcourt 1987; Kutzbach et al. 1993; Shuman, Bartlein, Logar, Newby, and Webb 2002; Shuman, Webb, Bartlein, and Williams 2002). A steep temperature gradient likely existed between regions affected by arctic winds blowing off the glaciers, such as the Great Lakes region, and those located below the jet stream. The latter included the Southeast, where the Pacific and Maritime Tropical air masses prevailed (COHMAP Members 1988; Delcourt and Delcourt 1987; Kutzbach et al. 1993). In the southeastern United States, January temperatures were probably between 4° and 8°C cooler than present, and July temperatures probably only 0° to 2°C cooler. Annual precipitation appears to have been approximately 200 mm less than present (Kutzbach et al. 1993; Webb et al. 1993).

This warming trend reversed briefly during the Younger Dryas event (12,900–11,600 cal B.P.). The sudden discharge of cold, freshwater glacial lakes to the north Atlantic Ocean disrupted the circulation of warmer ocean

Calibrated Radiocarbon Years	Global Climate Shifts	Cultural Periods	Plant Communities in the MidSouth // Deep South
7,000	Temperatures similar to present		
		Kirk Stemmed (8,900-7,800 cal B.P.)	Oak-hickory-southern pine forest // southern pine forest
8,000	8.2ka Event (8,200-7,900 cal B.P.)		
		LeCroy/Kanawha Bifurcates (9,800-8,600 cal B.P.)	
9,000	Continuing warming and increase in moisture as glaciers retreated		Deciduous hardwoods // warm temperature broadleaf-evergreen forest
		Kirk Corner-Notched (10,500- 9,800 cal BP)	
10,000		Early Side-Notched (11,200- 10,500 cal BP)	Mixed hardwoods // oak-hickory-southern pine forest
11,000	Preboreal Oscillation (11,400-11,200 cal BP)	Dalton (12,000-11,200 cal BP)	
12,000	Younger Dryas (12,900-11,600 cal BP)	Quad/Beaver Lake (12,900-12,000 cal BP)	
13,000			Non-analog mixed conifers and northern hardwoods // mixed hardwoods
	Continuing retreat of glacial sheets		
14,000			

Figure 3.2. Climatic, cultural, and vegetative changes in the Midsouth between 14,000 and 7,000 cal B.P.

currents. The colder surface seawater brought significant dips in temperatures throughout the north Atlantic, dropping global temperatures by several degrees (Meeks 2001; Shuman, Webb, Bartlein, and Williams 2002; Teller et al. 2002; Yu and Eicher 1998). However, the Younger Dryas also produced varying conditions in different regions. In the southeastern United States, this event brought winter temperatures 4° to 5°C lower than present day, as well as summer temperatures roughly 2°C warmer than present (Shuman, Webb, Bartlein, and Williams 2002). The Younger Dryas ended abruptly, probably as ocean circulation again changed. Moisture levels increased and global temperatures rose an average of 7°C over just several decades (Meeks 2001; Shuman, Webb, Bartlein, and Williams 2002; Taylor et al. 1997; Yu and Eicher 1998).

A second, smaller oscillation, termed the Preboreal Oscillation, occurred roughly between 11,400 and 11,200 cal B.P., apparently triggered by an abrupt discharge of glacial meltwater into the Arctic Ocean (Fisher et al. 2002; Teller et al. 2002). Briefer than the Younger Dryas event, the Preboreal Oscillation brought a drop of approximately 2°C in global temperatures (Meeks 2001; Wagner et al. 1999; Wagner et al. 2004; Yu and Eicher 1998), although the effect may have been less severe in the Southeast. Warming continued as summer solar radiation increased and the ice sheet retreated (Yu and Eicher 1998). By approximately 10,000 cal B.P., the jet stream had moved farther northward, although winds continued to blow across the remaining glaciers onto the Northeast. Winter temperatures in the southeastern United States were only 1° to 4°C cooler than present, while summer temperatures may have been as much as 2°C warmer than present. Annual precipitation appears to have been roughly similar to current values (Kutzbach et al. 1993; Webb et al. 1993), although lake levels indicate that the region was drier relative to the present (Shuman, Bartlein, Logar, Newby, and Webb 2002; Webb et al. 1993). Available moisture in the Southeast increased by 9000 cal B.P., however, as the ice sheet continued to wane and subtropical air masses dominated the region.

A final oscillation, lasting some 300 years, occurred at approximately 8200 cal. B.P. (Shuman, Bartlein, Logar, Newby, and Webb 2002; Wagner et al. 2004; Yu and Eicher 1998) as the vast glacial-meltwater lakes drained completely into the north Atlantic Ocean and the portion of the Laurentide Ice Sheet over the Hudson Bay collapsed (Shuman, Bartlein, Logar, Newby and Webb 2002; Teller et al. 2002). Again, the northeastern United States and eastern Canada, particularly those areas near the ice sheet, were most significantly affected by this "8.2 ka Event." However, the disappearance of the cooler air mass associated with the ice sheet gave greater influence to warm, moist, subtropical air masses, bringing even wetter conditions to the Southeast (Shuman, Bartlein, Logar, Newby, and Webb 2002). By roughly 7000 cal B.P., annual precipitation appears to have increased to around 200 mm greater than present, particularly in the Coastal Plain of the Carolinas, Georgia, and Florida. Winter temperatures may have been slightly cooler than present, but summer temperatures were apparently comparable with modern values (Webb et al. 1993).

Local Climatic Conditions

At the request of Lara Homsey (2004), Reid Bryson of the Center for Climate Research at the University of Wisconsin created a model of the climatic conditions for the area around Dust Cave, using the nearby city of Muscle

Shoals, Alabama, as a proxy. The model includes variables such as solar radiation, the global extent of continental ice sheets, the absorption and reflection of heat by the earth's surface, and circulation of air masses (Homsey 2004:44). The outputs are graphs of mean annual temperature, as well as annual, winter, and summer precipitation.

Bryson's (1999a, 1999b in Homsey 2004:316) model indicates that annual mean temperatures around 14,000 cal B.P. for northwest Alabama were as low as 12°C, approximately 4°C cooler than present. Annual precipitation measured just above 2,000 mm, significantly higher than the 1,250 mm seen today and apparently driven by higher winter precipitation. Temperatures steadily increased through approximately 11,000 cal B.P. (or roughly 10,000 radiocarbon years before present), with the exception of two downward spikes that likely correspond to the Younger Dryas event and Preboreal Oscillation. Both events apparently dropped annual mean temperatures for the area by roughly 1°C. They are also associated with upward spikes in winter precipitation, which otherwise decreased steadily.

Annual mean temperature and precipitation were comparatively stable for the next 2,000 years or so, hovering around 15°C and approximately 1,500 mm annually in precipitation. This contrasts markedly to the interval between 8900 and 7900 cal B.P, when annual mean temperature increased to nearly 17°C and annual precipitation fell to roughly 1,300 mm. The latter was influenced both by a drop in winter precipitation and a slight increase in summer rain. A final significant increase in temperature is likely related to the collapse of the Laurentide Ice Sheet, when glacial air masses no longer dominated circulation patterns over the northern United States. Although winter precipitation decreased further and summer rain rose slightly after 7900 cal B.P., these climatic conditions generally prevailed through the present (Bryson 1999a, 1999b in Homsey 2004:316).

While the annual mean temperature near Muscle Shoals shifted relatively little over the Pleistocene/Holocene transition, there may well have been more dramatic differences between winter and summer temperatures. This is suggested by regional climatic reconstructions (Kutzbach et al. 1993; Shuman, Bartlein, Logar, Newby, and Webb 2002; Webb et al. 1993).

Interestingly, Bryson's (1999a, 1999b) reconstructions differ significantly in terms of available moisture from the larger regional models (e.g., Kutzbach et al. 1993; Shuman, Bartlein, Logar, Newby, and Webb 2002; Webb et al. 1993). The latter suggest drier conditions than present for the Southeast during the Pleistocene/Holocene transition, with a trend toward increasing moisture. In contrast, Bryson's (1999a, 1999b) local model for Muscle

Shoals suggests significantly wetter conditions during the last ice age than at present.

CLIMATIC INFLUENCES ON ECOLOGICAL COMMUNITIES

An understanding of local climatic conditions and changes is important because they directly affect the local vegetation and the wildlife that it supports. Plants are sensitive not only to soil quality and moisture balance but also to the length of growing seasons and temperature extremes. Animals, in turn, may depend on particular vegetation structures, but also may respond to temperature shifts. For example, some species of mollusks, mice, and voles (*Microtus* spp.), among others, are quite sensitive to climatic conditions. Possible shifts in local habitat structures are important to understand because they shape the resources available to hunter-gatherers and the strategies these groups employ to exploit those resources.

Plant Communities

Current reconstructions of paleoenvironments are based on pollen studies of lake cores. Relatively few pollen cores have been analyzed from the Southeast, making paleoenvironmental reconstructions broad in nature. Several cores are located relatively near the study area. These include Anderson Pond in eastern Tennessee; B. L. Bigbee Oxbow in eastern Mississippi; Cahaba Pond in eastern Alabama; and Pigeon Marsh and Quicksand, both in northwest Georgia (Figure 3.3; Delcourt and Delcourt 1987; Webb et al. 1993). Spanning the last 20,000 years, the cores from these sites indicate changes in vegetation in the region during the Pleistocene/Holocene transition and the presence of plant communities that lack modern analogs.

It is difficult, however, to extrapolate from these broad reconstructions to develop an understanding of local environments within the study area, largely because it includes three major physiographic regions. As is evident from the GLO survey notes and more recent studies, the Highland Rim, Fall Line Hills, and Cumberland Plateau comprise distinct communities today, and likely did in prehistory as well. Inasmuch as plant communities are structured by the local geology and topography, differences in richness and productivity between the various physiographic regions and topographic zones may be applied to past landscapes as well. Here I consider these relative differences in tandem with reconstructions of the regional environment developed from pollen analyses. Viewed together, these two sets of information

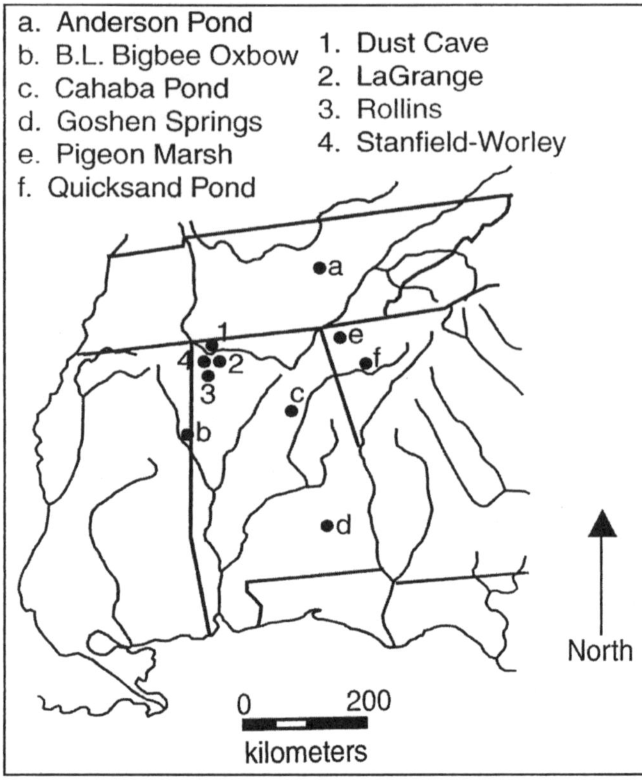

Figure 3.3. Map of pollen cores nearest to the project area.

may supply a reasonable estimation of local plant communities until finer-grained environmental reconstructions are available for the project area.

Paleovegetation reconstructions suggest that northwest Alabama might have been near the confluence of three vegetation communities around 14,000 cal B.P. Deciduous forests apparently covered the Coastal Plain and Fall Line Hills, while mixed forests dominated plant communities of the Ridge and Valley province to the east. Nonanalog communities, comprised primarily of spruce woodlands, characterized the Highland Rim (Delcourt and Delcourt 1981; Overpeck et al. 1992). Shortly after the close of the Younger Dryas event, around 11,200 cal B.P., mixed hardwoods typical of cold-temperate forests dominated the local vegetation (Adams 2002; Delcourt and Delcourt 1981). These deciduous forests apparently persisted in the project area through 7000 cal B.P. (Adams 2002; Adams and Faure 1997; Overpeck et al. 1992), although forests dominated by oak, hickory, and southern pines increasingly encroached from the south (Adams 2002; Delcourt and Delcourt 1981). Indeed, by 10,000 cal B.P. the boundary between the two biomes appears to be close to the research area (Adams 2002; Adams and Faure 2002; Delcourt and Delcourt 1981). This may be related to the physiographic regions encompassed in the research area; as it does presently, the Highland Rim north of the Tennessee River might well have supported different vegetation from the Fall Line Hills and Cumberland Plateau to the south.

Analyses of individual taxa in pollen cores suggest more specific changes (Table 3.1). Around 13,000 years ago, just prior to the adoption of Quad/Beaver Lake points (12,900–12,000 cal B.P.), trees associated with cooler conditions were in the process of migrating northward. These include spruce (*Picea* spp.), which at one point comprised nearly 20 percent of regional forests, as well as birch (*Betula* spp.), fir (*Abies* spp.), hemlock (*Tsuga* spp.), and alder (*Alnus* spp.). Southern pines might have begun to encroach on the area from the south. Oaks constituted some 20–40 percent of forests, and hickory between 5 and 20 percent. Other hardwoods, including maple, hackberry, beech, ash, walnut, aspen/cottonwood (*Populus* spp.), tupelo (*Nyssa* spp.), and willow, accounted for less than 5 percent of forest trees (Delcourt and Delcourt 1987; Shuman, Webb, Bartlein, and Williams 2002; Webb et al. 1993).

By 12,000 years ago, during the cooler Younger Dryas and as peoples began to use Dalton toolkits (12,000–11,200 cal B.P.), spruce comprised less than 20 percent of regional forests. The presence of sedges (Cyperaceae) at more than 5 percent of regional assemblages indicates the cooler weather associated with this climatic oscillation. The increase of ash to over 5 percent may also suggest colder temperatures. However, although annual temperatures were colder, warmer summers continued to push trees that prefer cooler conditions northward (Delcourt and Delcourt 1987; Shuman, Webb, Bartlein, and Williams 2002).

Just after local peoples began to fashion Early Side-Notched points (11,200–10,500 cal B.P.), forests of the region could be characterized as mixed hardwood communities. By 11,000 years ago, oaks increased to 40–60 percent of area forests, elms and maples to roughly 10 percent, and pine to as much as 20 percent. Spruce and birch, as well as ash, continued to decrease. Hickory, beech, walnut, hackberry, tupelo, and other hardwoods demonstrated little change (Delcourt and Delcourt 1987; Shuman, Webb, Bartlein, and Williams 2002).

By 10,000 years ago, well into the time that peoples made Kirk Corner-

Table 3.1. Proportional Representation of Various Taxa in Regional Pollen Assemblages during the Pleistocene-Holocene Transition.*

Category: Taxon	14,000 cal B.P. (%)	13,000 cal B.P. (%)	11,000 cal B.P. (%)	10,000 cal B.P. (%)	9,000 cal B.P. (%)	7,000 cal B.P. (%)
Major constituents:						
Oak (*Quercus* spp.)	20–40		40–60	40–60	40–60	60
Hickory (*Carya* spp.)	5–20		10–20	> 5	10	10–20
Pine (*Pinus* spp.)	5–20	< 20	0–20	5	0–20	0–20
Northern species:						
Spruce (*Picea* spp.)	1–20	< 20	0–20	1–5	0	0–5
Fir (*Abies* spp.)	< 0.5–1			< 0.5		< 0.5
Hemlock (*Tsuga* spp.)	< 0.5		< 1–10	< 0.5–1	0	< 0.5
Alder (*Alnus* spp.)	< 1–5			< 1–5		< 1–5
Birch (*Betula* spp.)	1–5		0–10	1	0	0–5
Minor constituents:						
Ash (*Fraxinus* spp.)	0–10	> 5	0–10		0–10	0–10
Aspen/cottonwood (*Populus* spp.)	0–20		< 1		< 1	
Basswood (*Tilia* spp.)	0		< 1–5		0	
Beech (*Fagus* spp.)	0–5		0–5	1–5	0–5	0–5
Cedar/Cypress (Cupressaceae)	0–10		0		0	0
Elm (*Ulmus* spp.)	1–5		10–15	1–5	5–10	0–5
Hackberry (*Celtis* spp.)	0–5		5		0–5	0–5
Maple (*Acer* spp.)	0–10		10			10–20
Tupelo (*Nyssa* spp.)	0		< 1		0–10	0–20
Walnut (*Juglans* sp.)	1		0–1		0	1
Willow (*Salix* spp.)	0–5		0		0–5	0–5
Other:						
Sedges (Cyperaceae)	1–10	> 5		1–5		5–10

*Data derived from pollen maps developed by Delcourt and Delcourt (1987), Shuman, Bartlein, Logar, Newby, and Webb (2002), Shuman, Webb, Bartlein, and Williams (2002), and Webb and colleagues (1993).

Notched points (10,500–9800 cal B.P.), trees associated with colder climates had little presence in the area. Spruce and alder comprised less than 5 percent of regional forests, and birch and hemlock less than 1 percent (Webb et al. 1993). By 9,000 years ago, during the time that groups used bifurcate points (9800–8600 cal B.P.), these northern trees disappeared from local forests completely. Oaks remained dominant at 40–60 percent, but hickories may have decreased to around 10 percent of the trees in area forests. Maple and tupelo increased slightly, but other hardwoods, including ash, hackberry, and walnut, demonstrate little change. Southern pines may have been pushed slightly southward, perhaps retreating from the Highland Rim and taking up their position in the Fall Line Hills (Delcourt and Delcourt 1987; Shuman, Webb, Bartlein, and Williams 2002).

Well into and after the use of Kirk Stemmed points (8900–7800 cal B.P.), by at least 7,000 years ago, regional plant communities may reflect drier conditions. Sedges and forbs constituted roughly 5 percent of regional assemblages, suggesting drier weather. Oaks increased to 60 percent of area forests, and hickory appears to have rebounded to 10–20 percent. Pines, ash, beech, hackberry, tupelo, and walnut demonstrate little change (Delcourt and Delcourt 1987; Shuman, Bartlein, Logar, Newby, and Webb 2002; Webb et al. 1993).

These shifts in regional plant communities would have in turn affected the animal and human communities that subsisted on foodstuffs gathered from them. As acorn-bearing oaks in particular replaced spruces and other cooler-climate species, the productivity of regional forests—in terms of plant foods available to both people and animals—certainly increased. Other members of mixed hardwood communities, including walnut and hackberry, appear to have changed relatively little over this span. Hickory also demonstrated less of a shift than oak, apparently decreasing around 9,000 years ago before rebounding to 10–20 percent of regional forests roughly 7,000 years ago, suggesting a possible decrease in productivity during this span.

Relative differences in plant communities within the various physiographic and topographic districts presumably changed little over this course. The creek bottoms likely supported rich hardwood communities throughout. Differences between the uplands and slopes of the Tennessee Valley, Little Mountain, and Fall Line Hills regions might have been less distinct in the Late Pleistocene, particularly if spruce woodlands covered the Highland Rim and more productive deciduous forests occupied the Fall Line Hills. As spruces retreated from the Highland Rim and southern pines moved into the Fall Line Hills between 11,000 and 9,000 years ago, the current distinctions between the limestone uplands and sandstone hills might have been established.

In general, I assume that the differences in productivity of the physiographic regions may have been minimal in the Late Paleoindian period but became more apparent during the Early Archaic period as southern pines moved into the Fall Line Hills. Among topographic zones, river and creek bottoms were likely the richest communities in terms of number of species present, regardless of time period, while uplands and slopes yielded the highest nut productivity. These assumptions are subject to review as more fine-grained information about local paleoenvironments becomes available.

Animal Communities

Largely in response to shifting plant communities, animal communities in the Southeast also changed substantially between 14,500 and 7000 cal B.P. The most significant change was the extinction of 35 genera of Pleistocene fauna and megafauna, which had fully occurred in North America by approximately 12,200 cal B.P. (Beck 1996; Grayson and Meltzer 2003). The relatively abrupt disappearance of animals such as mammoths (*Mammuthus primigenius*) and mastodons (*Mammut americanum*), which greatly influenced local ecosystems through trampling, grazing, and browsing, might well have been an important factor in changing plant and animal communities, in addition to climate change (Haynes 2002). Because of these extinctions and their ripple effects on ecological communities, as well as the fact that different species responded at different rates and in different manners to changing climates and habitats, Late Pleistocene animal communities often do not have modern analogs (FAUNMAP Working Group 1996). This is not surprising given the lack of modern analogs for Late Pleistocene plant communities.

Using a hierarchical clustering technique to analyze possible associations among faunal assemblages from nearly 3,000 sites, the FAUNMAP Working Group (1996) mapped distinct animal communities in the Late Pleistocene (approximately 17,000–11,200 cal B.P.). The results suggest that the indicator species for northwest Alabama include white-tailed deer, short-tailed shrew (*Blarina* spp.), masked shrew (*Sorex cinereus*), pygmy shrew (*Sorex hoyi*), arctic shrew (*Sorex arcticus*), water shrew (*Sorex palustris*), southern bog lemming (*Synaptomys cooperi*), northern bog lemming (*Mictomys borealis*), eastern chipmunk (*Tamias striatus*), thirteen-lined ground squirrel (*Spermophilus tridecemlineatus*), yellow-cheeked vole (*Microtus xanthognathus*), and meadow jumping mouse (*Zapus hudsonius*) (FAUNMAP 1996:Figure 3). Of these, southern bog lemming and thirteen-lined ground squirrel are today associated with prairie habitats (FAUNMAP 1996); the masked shrew (Lee 2001), arctic shrew (Rose 1999), and water shrew (Carmen 2001) are found in Canada and the northern United States; and the northern bog lemming (Nicholas 2001) and yellow-cheeked vole (Kroenig 2004) are specifically associated with boreal forests. These suggest cooler and drier conditions in the research area at the close of the Pleistocene, and different availabilities of animal species, than at present.

Southeastern Pleistocene fauna also included extinct species, such as mammoth, mastodon, giant armadillo (*Glyptodon* sp.), sloth (*Eremotherium* sp.), dire wolf (*Canis dirus*), saber-tooth cat (*Smilodon fatalis*), tapir (*Tapirus veroensis*), flat-headed (*Platygonus* sp.) and long-nosed peccary (*Mylohyus* sp.), jaguar (*Panthera* sp.), fugitive deer (*Sangamona* sp.), giant tortoise (*Geochelone* sp.), and giant beaver (*Castoroides* sp.) (Clausen et al. 1979; Walker 1998). The extent to which early inhabitants of the region exploited them is a topic of debate (Anderson 1995; Grayson and Meltzer 2003). However, remains of dire wolf and giant beaver recovered from Dust Cave and tapir or peccary from neighboring Basket Cave (Cobb et al. 1995:227; Sherwood 2001:70; Walker 2007:109) are associated with deposits that predate the Late Paleoindian (Quad) occupation at Dust Cave. Possible human use of extinct megafauna are thus beyond the scope of this project.

By the Late Holocene (approximately 4500 cal B.P.), indicator species of the research area derived by FAUNMAP include more familiar southeastern animals, such as the eastern gray squirrel, common opossum, marsh rice rat (*Oryzomys palustris*), swamp rabbit, and eastern woodrat (*Neotoma floridana*) (FAUNMAP 1996:Figure 2). These animal communities are generally similar to those observed in the region today, although historic land clearing has shaped the landscape and therefore the distribution and frequency of animal populations (Bryant et al. 1993; Skeen et al. 1993).

In general, the research area supports a wide variety of wildlife. The Tennessee River and its tributaries provide habitat for waterfowl, aquatic mammals, amphibians, reptiles, fishes, and at one time a remarkably diverse community of freshwater mollusks. Over 250 species of birds populate the canopy and understory of the oak-hickory-pine and oak-hickory forests of the region. Mast from these trees feed various animals, including squirrels, mice, deer, turkeys, blue jays, and woodpeckers (Picidae); seeds of herbaceous plants also provide food for a remarkable range of birds and small animals (Bryant et al. 1993; Skeen et al. 1993). As discussed previously, although the animal communities found within the oak-hickory and oak-hickory-pine forests are similar in the species they include, the density of animals, particularly small mammals, is somewhat lower in the latter, primarily due to differences in the availability of food resources between the two (Skeen et al. 1993:22).

Summary

Plant and animal communities in the Southeast have changed dramatically over the last 15,000 years, particularly as climate changed at the close of the last ice age. Oak-hickory and oak-hickory-southern pine forests replaced boreal species, while Pleistocene megafauna became extinct and animals that prefer cooler conditions moved northward. Different species of both plants and animals migrated at different rates and in different directions, resulting in communities that do not have analogs in the present. However, these communities were likely shaped largely by local physiography in the past as they are today. Thus lowland communities along the rivers were likely more productive than the uplands, in terms of both plant and animal resources, and the karstic uplands of the Highland Rim richer than the sandstone uplands of the Fall Line Hills and Cumberland Plateau.

It is also important to note the interactions between plant and animal communities, and also between these and human populations. Just as animals affect the range of particular plants through seed dispersal and encourage growth of other species by browsing and foraging, humans also actively shape plant and, by extension, animal communities. People may manage forests and clearings through pruning, coppicing, and burning undergrowth (Delcourt et al. 1998; Fowler 1996; Munson 1986). As such, hunter-gatherers enhance the productivity of plant resources, not just for themselves but also for animals, including prey species. They can thus maintain stands and clearings that provide plant foods and at the same time attract game.

Whether Late Paleoindian and Early Archaic hunter-gatherers were actively managing ecological communities through the use of fire and other methods is debatable, although I suspect they were. Regardless, these groups were agents on the landscape, affecting the animal populations that they hunted, fished, and collected; competing for nuts, berries, and seeds with birds, deer, and small mammals; and disturbing plant communities with their trails and base camps. The landscape cannot be viewed simply as a backdrop on which early foragers went about their daily lives, but instead early foragers must be seen as active components within an ever-changing and meaningful landscape. Traces of their activities on this landscape, manifest as archaeological sites, are examined in further detail in the next section.

THE CULTURAL LANDSCAPE OF THE MIDDLE TENNESSEE VALLEY

Northwest Alabama claims one of the richest archaeological records of early hunter-gatherers in the United States; more fluted Paleoindian points have been found in each of Lauderdale and Colbert counties than in most states (Futato 1982). This is in part due to the abundance of resources available within the area to early occupants, but also is related to the extent of archaeological research performed there. In this section I present an overview of research performed in Lauderdale, Colbert, and Franklin counties over the past 70 years. I highlight several important sites in the region that have significantly shaped our understanding of early occupations in the area. Finally, I explore site patterning within the region and what it suggests about the relationship between early foragers and the local landscape.

Previous Archaeological Research

The Middle Tennessee River Valley has received much attention over the last century from people interested in Native American artifacts. Many are not professional archaeologists, which can be problematic. Collecting is apparently a favorite pastime of many of the locals, and looting of sites is rampant (Futato 1996; Goldman-Finn 1995a; Oakley and Futato 1975; personal observation[1]). However, the interest of nonarchaeologists has also been positive. Avocational archaeologists such as Frank Soday, Jack Cambron, and David Hulse have added significantly to the body of knowledge regarding prehistoric occupation of Alabama through the discovery, recording, and sometimes the excavation of sites, as well as cataloging and describing artifacts. Numerous sites have been documented and reported by collectors and members of archaeological societies that might otherwise have gone unnoticed (Cobb et al. 1995; Hubbert 2004; Walthall 1980). Local chapters of the Alabama Archaeological Society have provided venues for archaeologists to present their work to interested people and also have supplied funding and invaluable volunteer labor for surveys and excavation projects, including Stanfield-Worley and Dust Cave (DeJarnette et al. 1962; Driskell 1996; Goldman-Finn 1995a; Walthall 1980).

Perhaps the first avocational archaeologists to do research in the Middle Tennessee Valley were Squier and Davis, who mapped the Florence mound in their studies in the 1840s (Figure 3.4). Not until the late 1800s were the first archaeological excavations performed in the area, when Cyrus Thomas and his crew recorded and dug two mound sites in Lauderdale County. Mounds also interested Clarence B. Moore, who traveled down the Tennessee River in the early 1900s in his houseboat, the *Gopher*. He documented some eleven sites and site complexes in Colbert and Lauderdale counties, including mounds and "dwelling sites" (Goldman-Finn 1995b:17–20).

Walter B. Jones and David L. DeJarnette of the Alabama Museum of Natural History initiated a more comprehensive survey of archaeological sites in the Tennessee River Valley in 1932 (Walthall 1980:2). The museum also excavated Reeder Mound, at the mouth of Mulberry Creek in Colbert

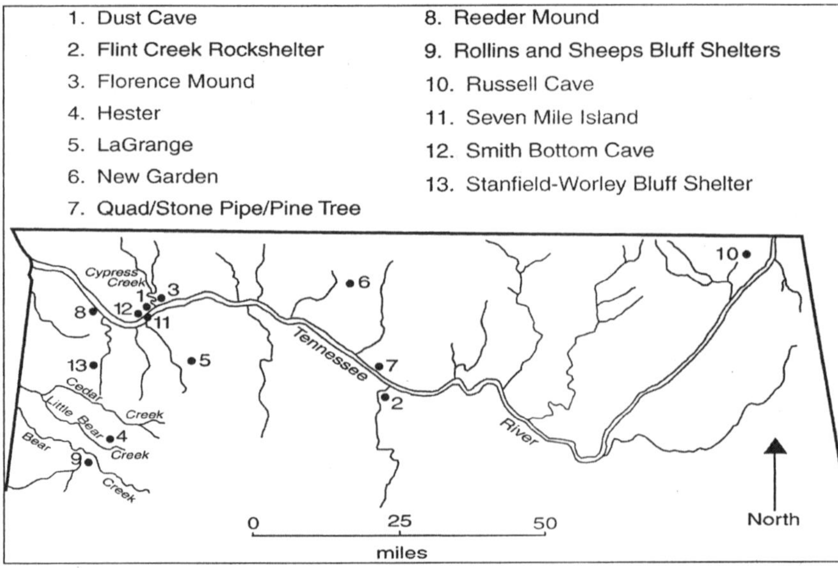

Figure 3.4. Map of Late Paleoindian and Early Archaic sites in north Alabama discussed in text.

County, and a cave site on Little Bear Creek in the early 1930s (Goldman-Finn 1995b:21). Intensive investigation of the valley began in 1934 as salvage archaeological work commenced in light of the impending construction of Pickwick Landing and Wheeler dams by the TVA and resulting inundation of a considerable portion of the floodplain in Colbert and Lauderdale counties.[2] These efforts were supervised by William S. Webb, with DeJarnette directing fieldwork. Supplied with extensive labor by the Civil Works Administration and later the Works Progress Administration, the crews surveyed, mapped, and described some 323 sites in the Pickwick Basin. Excavation began in 1936 and focused on the largest sites, namely mounds and shell mounds. With little time and water rising, nineteen sites were hurriedly, but systematically, excavated and documented (Goldman-Finn 1995b; Walthall 1980:3; Webb and DeJarnette 1942).

Little archaeology was performed in the Pickwick Basin during the 1940s and 1950s, although farther upstream, avocational and professional archaeologists surface collected and excavated a number of sites, searching for evidence of Paleoindian occupations. These include the Quad site (Cambron and Hulse 1960; Soday 1954), Stone Pipe (Cambron 1955), Pine Tree (Cambron 1956), Flint Creek Rockshelter (Cambron and Waters 1959), and Russell Cave (Miller 1956), among others (Futato 1996:299; Goldman-Finn 1995b:25). With the aim of developing a chronology of these earliest occupations, the Archaeological Research Association of Alabama and the University of Alabama, under the direction of DeJarnette, began a program in the 1960s to test rockshelters in Colbert and Franklin counties for stratified cultural deposits (Futato 1996:299). Stanfield-Worley Bluff Shelter in Colbert County (DeJarnette et al. 1962) was the first of these sites to yield significant evidence of early occupations, associated with Dalton and Early Side-Notched points. Additional sites excavated under this program include Rollins and Sheeps Bluff Shelters in Franklin County (Hollingsworth 1989; Stowe 1970), and LaGrange in Colbert County (DeJarnette and Knight 1976).

In the latter part of the 1960s and in the 1970s, archaeology throughout the state reorganized around cultural resource management. Large-scale surveys and more limited testing programs provided valuable information for areas that had previously received little attention (Futato 1996:302). A series of surveys and limited excavations was conducted in the Bear Creek drainage from 1967 through 1977, prior to the construction of dams on the Little Bear Creek (completed in 1975), Upper Bear Creek (completed in 1978), and Cedar Creek (completed in 1979) (Futato 1983; Oakley and Futato 1975; TVA 2005). These surveys and excavations were conducted by the University of Alabama Department of Anthropology and Office of Archaeological Research, and were funded primarily by the TVA and partially by the National Park Service. Additional survey projects in Lauderdale County included one focusing on Cypress Creek conducted by the University of Alabama in the early 1970s (O'Hear and DeJarnette 1974), and a survey of Seven Mile Island performed by Auburn University in the early 1980s (Waselkov and Morgan 1983). Waselkov returned to Lauderdale County in 1986 to survey areas surrounding the upland sinks (Waselkov and Hite 1987). Beginning in the late 1980s, the University of Alabama Division of Archaeology conducted a survey of TVA property in the Pickwick Basin, which included over 800 archaeological sites in Alabama, Mississippi, and Tennessee (Meyer 1995). Goldman-Finn (1995a) also directed a smaller survey project in 1994, crosscutting the Tennessee River floodplain and upland hills in Colbert and Lauderdale counties.

Interest in cave and rockshelter sites resumed in the early 1980s, when Richard Cobb, a local spelunker, brought several cave sites in the Pickwick Basin to the attention of University of Alabama archaeologists (Cobb et al. 1995). Excavation of Smith Bottom Cave began in 1984, and in 1988 the Di-

Table 3.2. Archaeological Sites Recorded to Date in Lauderdale, Colbert, and Franklin Counties.

	Lauderdale County	Colbert County	Franklin County
Early Archaic sites	106	60	28
Late Paleoindian sites	48	20	11
Late Paleoindian and Early Archaic sites	117	62	32
Total recorded sites	668	536	695

vision of Archaeology began a survey and testing program of twenty caves, thirteen of which are listed as archaeological sites. One of these sites, Dust Cave, yielded significant cultural deposits and was further excavated from 1989 through 2002 (Driskell 1996, 2001; Sherwood and Driskell 2003).

Archaeological investigations continue in the area today, primarily under the auspices of cultural resource management. Through the numerous survey and excavation projects conducted over the years, some 668 sites have been recorded in Lauderdale County, 536 in Colbert County, and 695 in Franklin County. Of these, 117 sites in Lauderdale, 62 in Colbert, and 32 in Franklin County include a Late Paleoindian and/or Early Archaic component (Alabama State Site File 2005) (Table 3.2).

Key Late Paleoindian and Early Archaic Sites

The vast majority of Late Paleoindian and Early Archaic sites recorded by surveys in northwest Alabama are represented by lithic scatters and few diagnostic artifacts. However, several of the sites include much larger concentrations of artifacts, sometimes within the context of stratified deposits. These provide valuable information regarding early occupation of the region, giving broader context to early foragers' relationship with the landscape. I discuss several of these sites that have substantially shaped our understanding of Late Paleoindian and Early Archaic peoples in the Middle Tennessee Valley below.

Quad Site

The Quad site is located on the north bank of the Tennessee River in Limestone County. Consisting of clusters of chipped stone artifacts, debris, and fire-cracked rock, the site may actually be thought of as a complex of sites stretching some three miles along the riverbank (Futato 1996:309; Hubbert

1989). Hubbert (1989:148) considers the Pine Tree site (Cambron 1956) and Stone Pipe site (Cambron 1955) to be within this complex. The Quad site is presently under the waters of Wheeler Lake, but while the water level was lowered during maintenance of Wheeler Dam in the early 1950s, the site received much attention from local amateur archaeologists. Frank Soday (1954) discovered the site in 1951 and performed extensive surface collections. In 1959, Cambron and Hulse (1960) excavated 21 5-by-5-ft units between 9 and 12 inches in depth. Unfortunately, the site has now largely eroded away, is apparently deflated, and has been intensively collected, leaving little promise for future systematic excavation (Futato 1996:309; Hubbert 1989).

The materials recovered indicate that the locale contains multiple components. Diagnostic Paleoindian artifacts include Clovis, Cumberland, Quad, Beaver Lake, and Dalton points; Early Archaic points include Early Side-Notched, Kirk Corner-Notched, and bifurcate forms (Cambron 1956; Cambron and Hulse 1960; Soday 1954). The Early Archaic occupation appears to be more extensive (Walthall 1980:51): while over 200 fluted points have been found at the site (Futato 1996:309), Early Side-Notched points from the Quad locale number near 3,100 (Randall 2002:60). A wide range of tools other than hafted bifaces were also recovered, including numerous scrapers, unifacial and bifacial knives, gravers, drills, hammerstones, and at least one mortar and one greenstone bead (Cambron and Hulse 1960). The majority of tools appear to have been made on locally available Bangor chert, although blue-gray Fort Payne chert also comprised "a considerable amount" of the stone artifacts (Cambron and Hulse 1960:26). Cambron and Hulse (1960:24) also encountered one feature, which contained fragments of raccoon bone.

The diversity of the toolkit suggests use of the site as a base camp. Some have further suggested that the spatial clustering of artifacts represents repeated use of the Quad locale by small groups, due to its favorable location along the river (Soday 1954; Walthall 1980:33–34). However, Hubbert (1989:157) and Futato (1996:309) envision the Quad site as a locus of seasonal aggregation. Each cluster can then be thought of as representing the base camp of a single band, and the entire complex of clusters as the co-occupation of several related bands—or a macroband—that have coordinated their seasonal rounds to live along this section of the river at the same time.

New Garden

Located in the uplands of Limestone County, north of the Quad locale, the New Garden site is the only single component Early Side-Notched site recognized in the Middle Tennessee Valley to date (Randall 2002:58). Also collected by an avid amateur, Gene Lenser, the site's artifact assemblage includes a wide variety of tool forms, including uniface endscrapers and blades, stage bifaces, drills, and flake tools, apparently made from chert available as cobbles in a nearby stream. Some 42 Early Side-Notched points were also collected (Randall 2002:58; Walthall 1980:51). Based on the site's proximity to a chert source, the various stages of tool manufacture and use present within the lithic assemblage, and "a high percentage of workshop debris," Walthall (1980:51) suggests that the site served primarily as a stone-tool workshop and is therefore an example of a "limited activity work camp." Randall (2002:58–59) disagrees, however, arguing that the range of tool types from the site indicates that various activities were performed at the site.

Hester Site (1FR311)

Located at the confluence of Lost Creek and Cedar Creek in the Fall Line Hills of Franklin County, the Hester site is now under the waters of Cedar Creek Reservoir. Investigations of the site by archaeologists in the 1970s recovered several Dalton and 26 Early Side-Notched points (Randall 2002:61), although previous efforts by local collectors apparently produced over 200 Dalton points (Futato 1996:312). The Early Side-Notched points are made primarily from locally available Tuscaloosa gravel and fossiliferous Bangor, although some 30 percent are made from blue-gray Fort Payne chert (Randall 2002:78). Randall (2002:87–88) also notes that the majority of these hafted bifaces (over 85 percent) are in the early stages of reduction, and suggests that tool production and replacement were more important to the site's occupants than tool conservation (Randall 2002:104).

Because of extensive collecting, historic cultivation, and prehistoric construction of a Middle Woodland burial mound, no intact early deposits remain at the Hester site, but Futato (1996:312) suggests that it was intensively occupied during the Early Archaic period. The wide range of bifacial and unifacial tools, as well as expedient flake tools, recovered from the site supports a base camp interpretation (Randall 2002:61–62).

Seven Mile Island Archaeological District

An area encompassing Seven Mile Island and Coffee Slough has been designated as an archaeological district on the National Register of Historic Places. This complex of islands and riverbank floodplains immediately downstream from the Muscle Shoals has been surveyed by Waselkov and Morgan (1983), as well as the University of Alabama's Office of Archaeological Services (Meyer 1995). The boundaries of the district are somewhat arbitrary, such that 159 sites are located within the immediate area, although only 122 are technically within the district's bounds. Of these 159 sites, 29 have Paleoindian and/or Early Archaic components (Meyer 1995:117–125). Two are cave sites: Smith Bottom Cave, which will be discussed further below; and Dust Cave, which I use in my analysis. Most of the sites have only been surface collected (Alabama Online Cultural Resources Database 2005), although test excavations have been conducted at several. Among these is the Refuge Site (1LU356), a stratified open-air site at the mouth of Cypress Creek. This site contains a Kirk Corner-Notched component, which Meeks (1997:75) interprets as a residential base camp that may have been occupied in fall or winter. A deeper stratum, from which a uniface blade was recovered, may represent a Late Paleoindian component (Meeks 1997:75).

With numerous sites lining the rises of the islands and creek banks, the Seven Mile Island Archaeological District is reminiscent of the Quad locale. Located in a similarly rich environment, or perhaps more so given the proximity of the shoals, Seven Mile Island also may well have served as a seasonal aggregation site for early macrobands (Randall 2002). Unfortunately, similar to the Quad locale, many of the sites are under water and/or significantly eroded by the river and cultivation.

Rockshelter and Cave Sites

Numerous caves and rockshelters located in the limestone and sandstone bluffs of Lauderdale, Colbert, and Franklin counties have been recorded in the Alabama State Site File (2005). Fourteen caves and/or rockshelters are listed in Lauderdale County, two of which (Smith Bottom Cave [1LU131] and Dust Cave [1LU496]) contain deposits of early human occupation. In Colbert County, 40 caves and/or rockshelters are included in the site file; Stanfield-Worley (1CT125) and LaGrange (1CT90) are the only two known to contain Late Paleoindian or Early Archaic deposits. Fifty-six rockshelters and one cave with an associated rockshelter were recorded in Franklin County, in which sandstone dominates the surface geology. Of these, only Rollins Bluff Shelter (1FR323) is known to possess Late Paleoindian and Early Archaic deposits; two additional sites (1FR324 [Sheeps Bluff Shelter] and 1FR593) contain Early Archaic components (Alabama State Site File 2005; Hollingsworth 1989). Note that other rockshelter and cave sites may also hold evidence of early occupation in the region; many have yet to be systematically tested.

Four of these cave and rockshelter sites with Late Paleoindian and Early

Archaic deposits form the backbone of this study (Dust Cave, Stanfield-Worley, LaGrange, and Rollins), and I discuss the investigations performed at these sites in detail in Chapter 5. Smith Bottom Cave was also systematically investigated, but unfortunately I could not locate floatation samples unequivocally associated with the Early Archaic and Late Paleoindian components at the site, and thus could not include it in my paleoethnobotanical analysis. The results of other analyses at the site, particularly faunal analyses, bear mentioning.

Smith Bottom Cave. Dr. Richard Cobb, a local teacher and avid speleologist, mapped a series of caves in the Pickwick Basin for the Alabama Cave Survey, and in 1984 submitted an archaeological site form to the Alabama State Site File for Smith Bottom and other caves in which he found cultural materials (Cobb et al. 1995:220). Subsequent excavations at the site were initiated by field schools from the University of Alabama and University of North Alabama in 1984 and 1987 through 1989 (Cobb et al. 1995). This work revealed cultural deposits over three meters in depth, both within the cave as well as the adjoining shelter area and talus slope. These deposits include a Late Paleoindian component represented by Quad and Dalton points, as well as uniface tools. Both an Early Side-Notched and Kirk Corner-Notched component are also present (Cobb et al. 1995:252–255).

Few interpretations about the nature of occupation at Smith Bottom Cave were made in the preliminary site report. Cobb and colleagues (1995:260) describe it as a habitation site, but do not venture further about the character of this habitation. Analyses of the extensive, well-preserved faunal remains found within the cave (Parmalee 1994; Snyder and Parmalee 1992) suggest that the site's early occupants exploited a variety of habitats, collecting mussels, fishing, and hunting waterfowl along the river and its tributaries; hunting and/or trapping small mammals, turkeys, and deer in wooded and ecotone areas; and hunting birds in grassland areas that likely spotted the level uplands above the bluff line. The presence of waterfowl in the deposits indicates that Smith Bottom was occupied at least during the spring and/or autumn, although use of the site during other seasons is not precluded. These faunal analyses provide valuable insight to hunting and fishing pursuits of early occupants of the region, as faunal remains are poorly preserved at open-air sites.

Site Patterns in the Middle Tennessee Valley

The various surveys, testing programs, and excavations performed over the last 70 years in the Middle Tennessee Valley provide a significant body of information for the nearly 1,900 sites recorded in the three counties considered here. Several researchers have explored the site file data for patterning in site use through time, to draw conclusions about changes in mobility and settlement systems.

Focusing on sites in the Pickwick Basin of the Tennessee River, Futato (1995:273) notes that Paleoindian sites tend to be located on older levees or at the rear of the floodplain, where it meets the upland slopes. Sites are also not as strongly associated with the river as they are in later periods, but instead cluster 100 to 200 m from first- or second-order streams. Early Archaic sites demonstrate slightly greater ties with the river, although still not as great as those seen during later periods (Futato 1995:272–273). Futato (1995) makes few interpretations from the data, simply noting that Paleoindian sites are more frequently found on older levees largely because modern levees postdate, and therefore obscure, these occupations.

Goldman-Finn (1994:222–223) compares the distribution of Early and Middle Archaic sites in five counties in northwest Alabama (Colbert, Franklin, Lauderdale, Lawrence, and Limestone), although she apparently lumps Dalton sites into the Early Archaic period. Similar to Futato, she notes that Early Archaic sites are much less likely to be found in the lower elevations of the floodplain than Middle Archaic sites, and instead are located in the uplands. Perhaps not surprisingly, Dalton/Early Archaic sites are highly associated with sinks, which are common in the karstic uplands of the region. In contrast, Middle Archaic sites show a greater association with the Tennessee River and first-order streams than do Early Archaic sites. Goldman-Finn (1994:223) suggests that these patterns represent coping mechanisms as peoples adjusted to drier and warmer environmental conditions during the Holocene.

Meeks (2001) compares Clovis through Bifurcate sites in the Highland Rim region of Alabama. His use of finer time intervals (Clovis, Cumberland, Quad, Dalton, Early Side-Notched, Kirk Corner-Notched, and Bifurcate) produces slightly different patterns. While sites for all time periods tend to be associated with higher elevations, Dalton, Early Side-Notched, and Kirk Corner-Notched sites are more frequently found in riverine settings. Notably, less than 15 percent of Quad sites are located near the river. As seen in the other studies, Paleoindian sites are primarily associated with upland sinks, but Bifurcate sites show a similar correlation. Quad, Dalton, and to a lesser extent Kirk Corner-Notched sites were more frequently reoccupied in subsequent cultural phases. Meeks suggests that the larger size of Quad sites may be related to frequent reoccupation by Quad peoples. Taking the span of years encompassed by each cultural phase into account, he notes that Quad sites are relatively infrequent, but also striking is a dramatic drop in the number of Bifurcate sites per hundred years.

Like Goldman-Finn, Meeks (2001) draws upon changing climatic conditions to explain these differences. He links the Quad phase with the Younger Dryas event (12,900–11,600 cal B.P.), associated with a sudden drop in temperatures, particularly winter temperatures, and likely with a drop in resource availability as well. Meeks suggests that Quad groups reoccupied these sites frequently during this time of resource stress because they were advantageously located. The orientation of these sites away from the river was probably related to instability of waterways during this climatic oscillation. Dalton and later peoples reoccupied them because of their favorable locations. Interestingly, Dalton and Early Side-Notched sites displayed similar patterns, suggesting little difference in settlement strategies for these time periods. Finally, Meeks hypothesizes that the decline in Bifurcate sites, and perhaps in population, may be related to the "8.2 ka" cooling event.

Of note is the fact that each of these researchers ties site distributions to the stability of the river, and often to changes in environmental conditions. The recurrence of this theme begs the question whether changes in river morphology have simply washed away evidence of occupation along banks and levees that are now inundated, silted over by new banks, or eroded by changing stream positions (Collins et al. 1994). Instability of rivers may have been less of a factor for relatively mobile groups with little investment in shelter or preparation of land, unlike more sedentary horticultural groups. The possibility that early sites are no longer visible because of fluvial activities must be kept in mind while reviewing such patterns.

Patterning in the Site File Data for the Project Area

Although Futato (1995), Goldman-Finn (1994), and Meeks (2001) have mined the Alabama Site File Database for patterning in early settlements within the region, their research addressed different time spans or different geographic regions than those I consider here. I examine the site file data by phase, from the Early Paleoindian Clovis through the Middle Archaic Eva/Morrow Mountain phases (Table 3.3; Hollenbach 2005). I frame the Late Paleoindian and Early Archaic data with these earlier and later phases to provide a broader context of landscape use in the region. It is important to note that Beaver Lake occupations are included in the Cumberland phase (Middle Paleoindian) in the database rather than the Quad phase (Middle/Late Paleoindian), as would be more consistent with current understandings

Table 3.3. Paleoindian, Early Archaic, and Middle Archaic Sites within Lauderdale, Colbert, and Franklin Counties.

Period	Phase	Number of Sites
Middle Archaic	Eva/Morrow Mountain	58*
Early/Middle Archaic	Kirk Stemmed	24
Early Archaic	Bifurcate	40
	Kirk Corner-Notched	165
	Early Side-Notched (Big Sandy)	91
Late Paleoindian	Greenbrier	26
	Dalton	55
Middle/Late Paleoindian	Quad	36
Middle Paleoindian	Cumberland (Beaver Lake)	55
Early Paleoindian	Clovis	43

*30 are Eva, 42 are Morrow Mountain; 14 sites have both components.

of regional chronology (Sherwood et al. 2004). This should be kept in mind as the two phases are compared.

The influence of formal archaeological testing on the structure of the database must also be noted. The vast majority of the surveys performed in the project area have concentrated on lands owned and/or affected by the TVA and its damming activities. As such, most of the sites are located within the Cedar Creek, Bear Creek, and Little Bear Creek valleys, and of course the Tennessee River Valley (Figure 3.5). The karstic uplands, particularly the sinkholes, of the latter have also received much archaeological attention. These certainly introduce biases to the data, particularly with respect to the use of uplands in the remaining physiographic regions, for which comparatively little data is available. The absolute number of sites located in each physiographic region is therefore not necessarily meaningful. However, as long as surveyors systematically recorded all sites from all time periods that they came across within the surveyed areas, and there is no reason to think otherwise, the data can be used to discern trends through time within each physiographic region.

This also rests on the assumption that sites from all time periods have equal chances of being discovered and recorded. Paleoindian toolkits, with their unifacial technology, may be more easily recognized than more expedient Early Archaic toolkits, regardless of whether diagnostic points are present. However, hafted bifaces are key components of all Paleoindian and

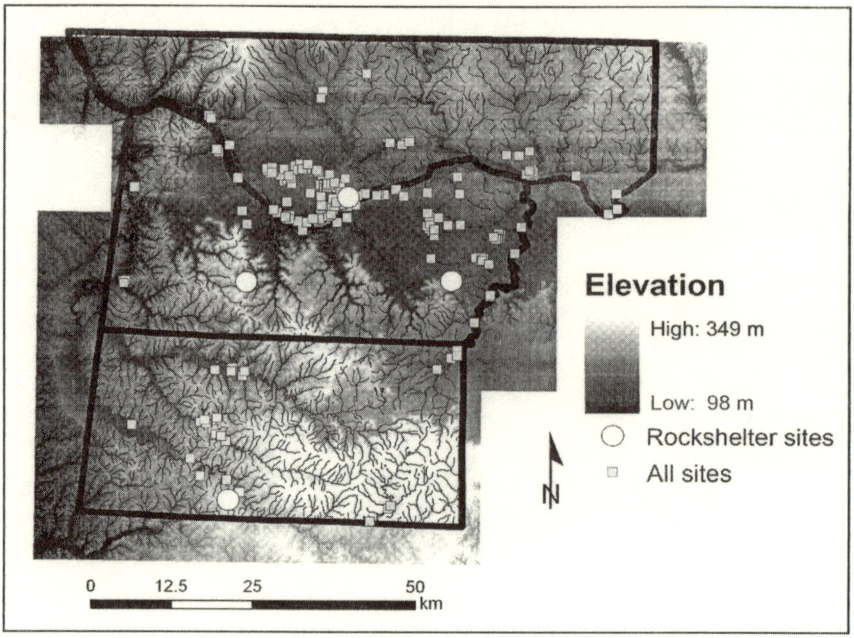

Figure 3.5. Paleoindian, Early Archaic, and Middle Archaic sites in the project area.

Early Archaic toolkits, so that significant differences between the visibility of the various periods and phases are unlikely. Perhaps of greater concern is whether Paleoindian sites located along waterways may be covered by alluvial deposits or scoured away by the meandering of rivers and streams, as I noted earlier. Indeed, Collins and colleagues (1994) argue that the Tennessee River significantly incised the valley between roughly 18,000 cal B.P. and 12,500 cal B.P., making the possibility of finding intact sites that predate the leveling of the river extremely low. This should be kept in mind, particularly when comparing Clovis and Cumberland site frequencies with later phases.

The Alabama Site File Database includes quantitative information regarding the elevation, distance to water, and the length of the major and minor axes of the sites, as well as qualitative information about the nature of the nearest water source, the topographic setting, and the physiographic district in which each site is located. I found few quantitative differences among the sites (Hollenbach 2005:341, Figures 9.25–27). There are no significant differences between the phases for distance to water. Cumberland sites have significantly lower elevations, but the remaining phases overlap considerably in the range of their elevation values. Subtle differences in site size[3] may be present. Early Side-Notched (or Big Sandy) sites, and to some extent Kirk Corner-Notched sites, appear to be slightly smaller in size than those associated with earlier phases, with the exception of Greenbrier sites.

Qualitative differences among the sites are more pronounced. In terms of the nearest water source, all Paleoindian sites show a distinct preference for sinks, which are located in the karstic uplands of the Tennessee Valley region (Figure 3.6). This is not surprising, given that a number of surveys have specifically targeted these upland sink areas (Futato 1996; Goldman-Finn 1995a; Waselkov and Hite 1987). However, the percentage of sites located near sinks decreases over time, falling below 30 percent in the Early Side-Notched phase. This percentage rises again through the Bifurcate phase, displaying values similar to earlier Paleoindian sites, but then drops dramatically in the Kirk Stemmed phase. In both the Kirk Stemmed and subsequent Eva/Morrow Mountain phases, sites are much more evenly distributed among water sources, with higher percentages located near rivers and major tributaries than in previous phases. As suggested by Futato (1995) and Goldman-Finn (1994), this may be related to stabilization of the rivers and/or drier and warmer conditions during the Holocene. People might have been adapting to these changes, or deposits simply might not have continued to be obscured by movements of the river.

These trends coincide with patterning in sites by topographic zone (Figure 3.7). Most Paleoindian sites are located in the uplands, where sinks are also found. This may be related to the changing morphology of the Tennessee River, which might well have scoured away evidence of early sites (Collins et al. 1994) and/or covered them in alluvial deposits. Perhaps not surprisingly, use of floodplains remains low until the Greenbrier phase and then decreases again through the Kirk Corner-Notched and Bifurcate phases to values similar to Paleoindian sites. The percentage of floodplain sites increases dramatically in the Kirk Stemmed phase, however, nearly doubling the value for Greenbrier sites. This preference for floodplain sites and decrease in use of upland areas continues through the Eva/Morrow Mountain phase, and again may be related to stabilization of major waterways during the Holocene.

Similar patterning is seen among use of physiographic districts (Figure 3.8). The vast majority of sites from all phases are located in the Tennessee Valley region. However, the placement of sites in other regions increases steadily through time. The percentage of Fall Line Hills sites increases through the Greenbrier phase, and then decreases again through the Bifurcate phase. In contrast with the Paleoindian sites, however, Early Archaic sites are regularly located in Moulton Valley and Cumberland Plateau as

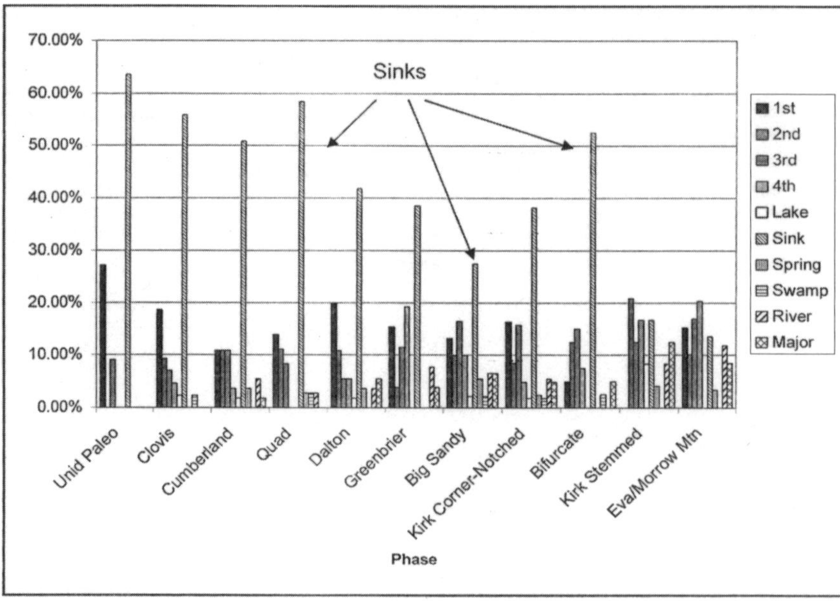

Figure 3.6. Bar graph comparing the percent of sites associated with each water source by phase.

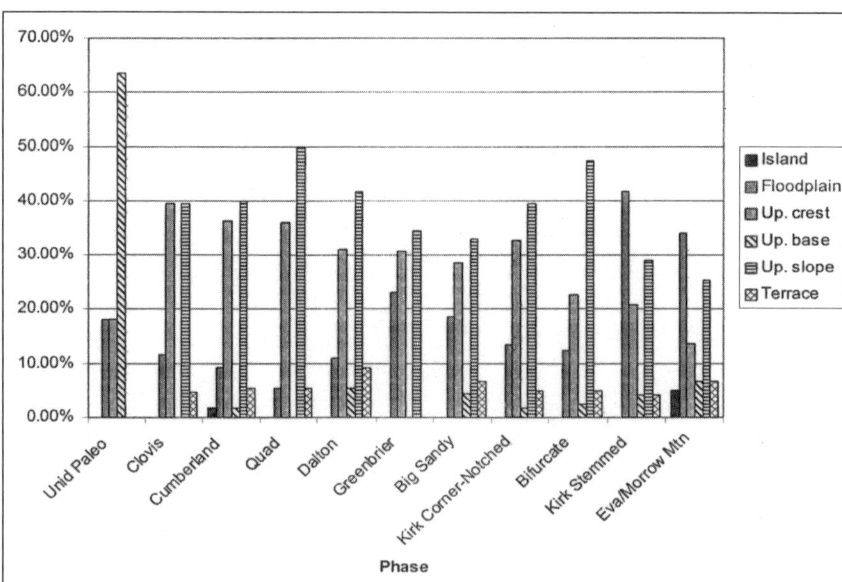

Figure 3.7. Bar graph comparing the percent of sites associated with each topographic zone by phase.

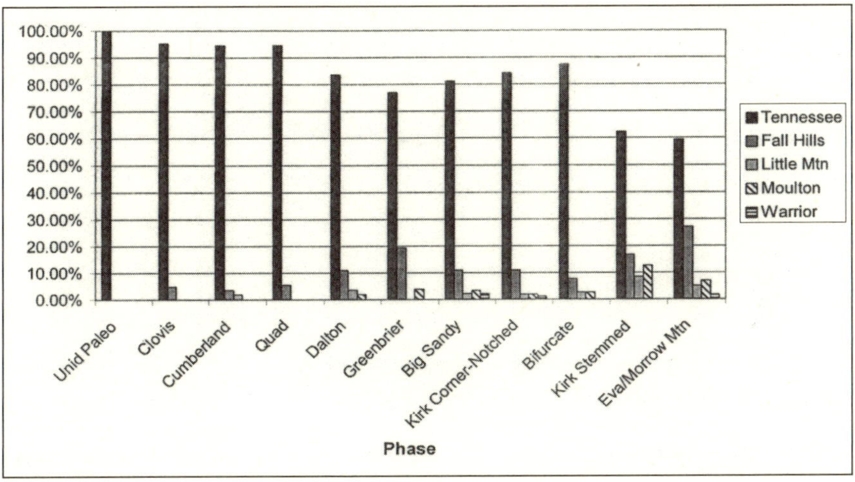

Figure 3.8. Bar graph comparing the percent of sites associated with each physiographic district by phase.

well. Again, the most dramatic difference is seen in the Kirk Stemmed and Eva/Morrow Mountain phases, when roughly 40 percent of sites occur outside of the Tennessee Valley region for the first time. Unlike trends in nearest water source and topographic setting, this pattern is not likely related directly to stabilization of rivers and hints at more complex shifts in landscape use by the close of the Early Archaic period and the subsequent Middle Archaic.

The frequency of sites per hundred years also demonstrates interesting trends (Table 3.4). The frequency of Quad sites may drop slightly, which Meeks (2001) suggests is related to repeated use of particularly favorable sites, which tend to be somewhat larger in size. However, the general picture is one of stability until the Early Side-Notched and particularly the Kirk Corner-Notched phase, when the number of sites per century increases by an order of magnitude. In the succeeding Bifurcate phase, the frequency of sites drops just as dramatically. By the Eva/Morrow Mountain phase, the number of sites per century returns to values seen in earlier Paleoindian phases.

The reoccupation of sites demonstrates somewhat greater stability, however (Table 3.4). Roughly 40 percent of the sites in the Paleoindian and Early Archaic periods are ones that were occupied in the immediately preceding phase. The value is slightly higher for the Quad phase and lower for the Early Side-Notched phase, although if Dalton and Greenbrier sites are collapsed into a single category, reoccupation in the Early Side-Notched is much more comparable to other phases.

Table 3.4. Site Frequency and Reoccupation.

Phase	Sites (N)	Time Span[a]	# Sites/100 yrs	# Reoccupied Sites	% Reoccupied Sites
Clovis	43	600	7.17		
Cumberland	55	900	6.11	22	40%
Quad	36	900	4.00	16	44%
Dalton	55	800	6.88	23	42%
Greenbrier	26	800	3.25	27	100%
Early Side-Notched	91	700	13.00	15	30%
Kirk Corner-Notched	165	700	23.57	66	40%
Bifurcate	40	1200	3.33	35	88%
Kirk Stemmed	24	1100[b]	2.18[b]	3	13%
Eva/Morrow Mountain	58	900	6.56	11	19%

[a] Given in calibrated radiocarbon years, following Sherwood et al. 2004.

[b] The span associated with Kirk Stemmed may be truncated to 600 years (Sherwood et al. 2004); this gives a frequency of 4.00 sites per 100 yrs.

Bifurcate sites are significantly different, however: 88 percent of the sites represent reoccupations. Along with the drop in frequency of sites, this may represent significant conservatism in landscape use. As noted above, Meeks (2001) speculates that this significant Bifurcate shift may be related to stresses brought by the 8.2 ka cooling event. Coupled with the similarity among the placement of these sites and earlier Paleoindian sites in terms of nearest water source, topographic zone, and to some extent physiographic district, Bifurcate peoples might have faced constraints similar to these earlier groups.

Just as significant is the dramatic decrease in reoccupation of sites in the subsequent Kirk Stemmed and Eva/Morrow Mountain phases. Although there are relatively few Kirk Stemmed sites in the project area, only three represent reoccupations. Similarly, Eva/Morrow Mountain groups appear to be establishing new sites. Viewed in concert with the significant differences among these and earlier phases in terms of nearest water source, topographic zone, and physiographic district, Kirk Stemmed and Eva/Morrow Mountain peoples organized their landscape settlement in much different manners than did preceding occupants of the region.

In general, there appear to be subtle as well as more definitive differences in regional site distribution through time. The first of these begins in the

Dalton phase and continues into the Early Archaic period. The number of sites in regions other than the Tennessee Valley increases, along with the use of floodplain areas and a decrease in use of sites near sinks. The number of sites, particularly those associated with the Kirk Corner-Notched phase, also increases markedly. In the Bifurcate phase, however, these trends are reversed. Bifurcate peoples appear to prefer sites more similar to those used by Paleoindian peoples, near sinks and away from floodplains. Landscape use shifts dramatically at the start of the Kirk Stemmed phase, however, and continues into the subsequent Eva/Morrow Mountain phase. Kirk Stemmed peoples reoccupy few of the sites used by their Bifurcate predecessors, opting for more floodplain locales and a larger percentage of sites in regions other than the Tennessee Valley.

These trends largely speak to continuity in Late Paleoindian and Early Archaic peoples' use of the landscape in the study area. Their expansion into areas beyond sinks, uplands, and the Tennessee Valley may be related in part to climatic shifts and the subsequent responses of plant and animal communities. Peoples using bifurcate points may have reversed this expansion, perhaps as the 8.2 ka climatic oscillation brought cooler winter temperatures to the region, as suggested by Meeks (2001). The subsequent warmer and drier conditions are associated with a dramatic shift in landscape use by Kirk Stemmed peoples. As we will see, this corresponds with the absence of unifacial blades in toolkits, a possible intensification of hickory nut use, and a shift toward use of animals found in closed habitats (Hollenbach 2005; Meeks 1994; Walker 1998). Whether this break in continuity in site use, toolkits, and subsistence patterns represents a significant shift in local peoples' interactions with the landscape, or whether it reflects the influx of a new population in the region, remains to be seen.

SUMMARY

There are several trends in early foragers' use of the landscape that are of interest. The first is the apparent preference of Clovis, Cumberland, and Quad peoples for sites outside of the floodplain, as well as sites within the Tennessee Valley region. The succeeding expansion of Dalton and Early Archaic peoples into other topographic and physiographic regions is also of interest. The third trend of note is the marked shift in site use that begins with the Kirk Stemmed phase.

These trends are related in large part to changes in the nature and distribution of local resources. These shifts in local plant and animal communities were driven largely by climatic changes associated with the close of the last ice age. Broad descriptions of these changes have been developed from regional pollen and faunal studies. Until local pollen analyses have been undertaken, a more nuanced picture of local communities may be derived by combining regional data with the GLO survey notes collected in the early 1800s. These indicate that there are notable differences in plant communities related both to topographic setting and local bedrock. The most productive communities, for both animals and human foragers, are creek bottoms and areas underlain by limestone rather than sandstone. Because neither the general topography nor the local bedrock changed significantly over the past 14,000 years, these differences likely held in the past as well.

In order to address the relationship between the nature of local plant and animal communities and trends in early foragers' use of the northwest Alabama landscape, I turn to central place foraging theory. This concept models the costs and benefits of procuring particular resources and bringing them back to camp. Stated in another way, it can be used to explore the economic impetus behind why a group might set up camp in the floodplains versus the uplands, or the Tennessee Valley versus the Fall Line Hills. I directly apply central place foraging theory to the project area in the next chapter.

NOTES

1. The number of people who approached our vehicles marked with "University of Alabama Division of Archaeology" to tell us about the fields they recently walked, or used to walk with their dads and granddads, is striking and sometimes disheartening.

2. Wilson Dam also significantly impacted the floodplain in these counties; it was completed in 1924, prior to significant archaeological investigation.

3. Site size is defined as the site area, which is computed by treating the site as an ellipse. For an ellipse, area = pi * radius a * radius b, where radius a is the major axis of the site and radius b is the minor axis of the site. Measurements of both axes are included in the Alabama Site File Database for a number of sites.

4
Modeling Resource Procurement in the Middle Tennessee River Valley

With an understanding of the local landscape in hand, and how plants, animals, and early foraging groups populated the project area, I now turn to central place foraging theory to model the ways in which early peoples might have hunted and gathered on this landscape. More specifically, I evaluate the costs that the regional topography imposes on foragers as they procure various subsistence resources and return with their proceeds to a base camp.

I use a geographic information system (GIS) to directly compare the costs and benefits of procuring various subsistence resources, including animals, plants, and stone, available to early foraging groups in northwest Alabama. I also consider differences in these costs and benefits according to season and topographic setting. I use these comparisons to discuss the mobility patterns we might expect gatherers and hunters to display on this particular landscape in order to most efficiently exploit these various resources.

MODELING RESOURCE PROCUREMENT AND TRANSPORT

Among the various factors, such as availability of water, firewood, and the presence of other groups, that affect decisions about where and when to move a campsite, one of the most salient is the structure of food resources (Kelly 1983, 1995:121, 126). As noted in Chapter 2, central place foraging theory contends that foragers should locate their campsites in order to minimize the costs of transporting food items to the site (Orians and Pearson 1979; Zeanah 2000). Stated slightly differently, foragers should choose campsites that maximize their return rates for procuring food items. Return rates are measured as the energy obtained from an item minus the energy expended in procuring that item, divided by the time required to procure the item. This is described by the following equation (after Zeanah: 2000:Table 1.4):

$$r = \frac{e_{obt} - [H_t * H_c + (\sum_{s=1}^{n} D_s * W_s) + (\sum_{f=1}^{n} D_f * L * U_f)]}{H_t + \frac{\sum_{s=1}^{n} D_s}{V}}$$

r = return rate (kcal/hr)
e_{obt} = energy obtained per load (kcal)
H_t = handling time per load (hr)
H_c = handling costs per load (kcal/hr)
D_s = distance of slope s traveled to and from the nearest patch of the resource (km)
W_s = cost of walking across slope s (kcal/km)
D_f = distance of slope f from the nearest patch of the resource to camp (km)
L = weight of one load of the resource (kg)
U_f = cost of carrying one load across slope f (kcal/kg/km)
and V = walking speed (km/hr).

Here the energetic costs of procuring the item include handling costs, or the energy required to obtain and process a food item; the costs of walking to and from the patch where the food item can be found; and the cost of carrying the food item back to camp. Similarly, the time component includes the time required to obtain and process the item, as well as the time to walk to and from the patch where it can be found.

In determining the relation of a site location to food procurement, the costs associated with travel to patches where food can be obtained are of particular interest. In practice, most researchers estimate these costs by approximating the distance associated with various slopes along a path between a central place and a resource patch (e.g., Gremillion 2006; Zeanah 2000). Here I use a geographic information system (GIS) to evaluate the slopes of the project landscape. This technique has several advantages. First, using elevations and slope values stored in the GIS, one can rapidly calculate the costs not only of a single path between two points but also the costs of traveling in any direction from a particular point. In other words, the GIS program can simultaneously calculate and compare the costs of traveling from a campsite to numerous resource patches. Furthermore, one can calculate and compare the return rates associated with exploiting particular resources from various points on the landscape.

Second, geographic information systems organize and display landscape information, facilitating the recognition of patterning within and associations among various landscape characteristics (Environmental Systems Research Institute [ESRI] 1998). These include characteristics that affect site location, such as distance to water sources, slope, and aspect (Kvamme 1999). Thus one can calculate return rates for various resources from various points on the landscape as well as relate these points and return rates to archaeological sites, physiographic regions, topographic locales, and any other landscape characteristics that can be mapped.

Calculating and Mapping Return Rates

In order to determine the return rate of a resource, values must be assigned to the different variables of the equation. These values are listed in Table 4.1 for the various food items considered here. The energy obtained (e_{obt}) from each load is relatively easy to determine: it is the caloric value of a given amount of a resource, which can be found for a surprising variety of foods (USDA NDL 2004). In keeping with Zeanah (2000), I use load sizes (L) of 15 kg and 30 kg, which are in line with ethnographic observations (Bettinger et al. 1997:892). Most food items include inedible portions that can either be removed in the field or at a campsite (Bettinger et al. 1997; Metcalfe and Barlow 1992). If processing occurs in the field, then the entirety (or some greater portion) of the load is presumably edible and the caloric value can be directly calculated; otherwise, the edible portion of the load must first be determined.

Handling time (H_t) includes collection and processing. For hunted animal resources, it also includes stalking. These times are variously observed, estimated from historic accounts, or determined experimentally. The latter two categories are somewhat problematic. Estimates are often at best educated guesses. Experiments are primarily conducted by inexperienced gatherers, collectors, fishers, and hunters, and/or employ tools unavailable to prehistoric groups. However, they do provide an indication of the costs associated with various resources and may be used for broad comparisons between resources. I calculate handling costs (H_c) by multiplying the handling time by 360 kcal/hr, in keeping with Winterhalder and colleagues (1998). Admittedly, using a fixed rate does not account for variation between tasks; grinding seeds is presumably more energy intensive than winnowing. Largely because I could not find more detailed information about the caloric costs associated with various activities, I presume that the assumed value provides an average of these costs.

I derived the costs associated with walking and transporting items across

Table 4.1. Values of Variables Used in Equation for Return Rates of Resources.

Resources	Load size, L (kg)	Edible portion (kg)	Caloric content (kcal/kg)	Calories in load, e_{obt} (kcal)	Handling time, H_t (hr)	Handling costs, H_c (kcal)
Animal Resources						
Deer, fall, uplands	30	21	2560	53760	9[a]	3240
Deer, fall, bottoms	30	21	2560	53760	11[a]	3960
Deer, spring, uplands	30	21	1260	26460	13[a]	4680
Deer, spring, bottoms	30	21	1260	26460	11[a]	3960
Deer, fall, uplands, 2 hunters	30	21	2560	53760	6.4[a]	2304
Squirrel, spring	30	21	3360	70560	54.3[b]	19548
Squirrel, fall	30	21	4440	93240	46.6[b]	16776
Turkey, fall, uplands	30	21	3430	72030	17.5[b]	6300
Turkey, fall, bottoms	30	21	3430	72030	23.5[b]	8460
Turkey, spring, uplands	30	21	2260	47460	51[b]	18360
Turkey, spring, bottoms	30	21	2260	47460	36[b]	12960
Waterfowl	30	21	3050	64050	20.3[b]	7308
Fish, spawning, slough	30	21	1540	32340	2.4[b]	864
Fish, spawning, stream	30	21	1540	32340	3.9[b]	1404
Fish, stream	30	21	1540	32340	8.1[b]	2916
Mussels, pristine	30	2.4	1720	4128	5[c]	1800
Mussels, depleted	30	8.1	1720	13932	63.8[c]	22968
Mussels, pristine, field process	30	30	1720	51600	6.2[c]	2232
Mussels, depleted, field process	30	30	1720	51600	22.9[c]	8244

Plant Resources						
Grapes	15	12.75	670	8542.5	3.3[b]	1188
Mulberries	15	14.55	430	6256.5	0.75[b]	270
Chenopod greens	15	6	430	2580	2.5[b]	900
Other greens	15	6	230	1380	2.5[b]	900
Amaranth, strip	15	15	3740	56100	41.5[d]	14938
Amaranth, cut	15	2.1	3740	7854	4.9[d]	1764
Chenopod, strip	15	15	4140	62100	64.4[e]	23184
Chenopod, cut	15	2.1	4140	8694	6.9[e]	2484
Acorns	15	4.7	5050	23735	26.0[c]	9351
Black walnut	15	2.91	6180	17983.8	30.6[f]	11016
Hazelnut	15	5.04	6280	31651.2	57.9[f]	20844
Hickory, crack and pick	15	5.57	6570	36594.9	242.3[f]	87228
Hickory, smash and boil	15	5.57	6570	36594.9	11.3[f]	4068

[a] Value calculated by assuming a density of 15 deer/km^2 for fall uplands, 10 deer/km^2 for fall and spring bottoms, 8 deer/km^2 for fall bottoms; .5 km/hr for search speed, 35m search radius, 4 hrs pursuit upon encounter, and 1 hr butchering (all but density derived from Winterhalder et al. 1988).

[b] From Reidhead 1981.

[c] From Bettinger et al. 1997.

[d] From Peterson and Munson 1984.

[e] From Seeman and Wilson 1984

[f] From Talalay et al. 1984.

Table 4.2. Costs Associated with Walking and Carrying a Load at a Speed of 3 km/hr.

Slope (%)	Walking Cost (kcal/km)	Carrying Costs (kcal/kg)
−40	88.4	2.78
−35	76.8	
−30	72.6	1.85
−25	69.2	
−20	60.0	1.11
−15	39.6	
−10	36.6	.42
−5	39.8	
0	50.6	.40
5	75.4	.74
10	115.2	1.32
15	140.2	2.10
20	169.4	3.13
25	202.8	4.46
30	239.8	6.11
35	281.2	8.01
40	325.2	10.24

a landscape from values of the calories (kcal) per kilometer associated with walking various slopes at a given speed provided by Brannan (1992) and Zeanah (2000) (Table 4.2). I fit a regression line to a plot of kcal/km versus slope (defined as percent grade), which yielded the following equation:

$$W_s = (-2 * 10^5 * (\text{slope})^3) + (.0933 * (\text{slope})^2) + (2.9297 * \text{slope}) + 66.534$$

which has an associated R^2 of .987. Unfortunately, the regression equation overestimates the costs of lower-grade slopes, namely those between -10 and 10 percent. While fourth- and fifth-order polynomial lines more adequately estimated costs associated with smaller slopes, they produced much larger errors for slopes with high values. As the project area includes many locales with steep slopes, I chose the second-order polynomial equation given above.

I similarly derived the costs associated with carrying a load across a given slope from values given in Brannon (1992) and Zeanah (2000) (Table 4.2). The regression line fit to a plot of kcal/km versus slope is described by the equation:

$$U_f = (3 * 10^5 * [\text{slope}]^3) + (.0038 * [\text{slope}]^2) + (.0401 * \text{slope}) + .5164$$

which has an R^2 of .9994. In keeping with Jones and Madsen (1989), Barlow and Metcalfe (1996), and Zeanah (2000), I assume a walking speed (V) of 3 km/hr. Bettinger and colleagues (1997:895) note that while faster walking speeds have greater caloric costs, they also allow foragers to transport resources at a faster rate, thus increasing the return rate. Adjustments in walking speed, as well as walking costs, are therefore ways in which the model can be further refined.

The distance and associated slopes over which foragers walk were obtained using the ArcView component of ArcGIS 8.1. I downloaded 7.5-minute digital elevation maps (DEMs) from the U.S. Geological Survey National Mapping Program (USGS NMP) that cover the three counties within the project area. These DEMs provide elevation data for 30-by-30-m cells within a grid (USGS NMP 1997). With this data, ArcView develops a topographical map of the area and calculates the slopes associated with each cell, as well as the aspect of these slopes.

I plotted the four rockshelter sites on the map, and used the Spatial Analyst extension of the program to derive the distance and direction to each site. Each 30-m grid cell is assigned a distance to a particular site, and a direction to that site. A person standing in a grid cell 5 km south of a site would have to travel 5 km north to reach it.

The Spatial Analyst extension can also be used to calculate a cost-weighted distance to a particular point. It is possible to assign a caloric cost to traversing each 30-m cell and sum up these costs to a given locale. Unfortunately, the program does not recognize uphill and downhill slopes: all slopes are assumed to be positive, or uphill. Using the "raster calculator" function in ArcGIS, which performs arithmetic functions on each cell, I created a map that assigned positive or negative values to slopes based on the following equation (suggested by Thomas F. Detwiler, personal communication 2005):

Slope Multiplier = cos ([direction to site] - [aspect of slope])[1]

in which both are described between 0 and 360 degrees.[2] For travel toward the site, the equation is positive; for travel away from the site, the equation is multiplied by negative one. Thus if a person is south of the site and walking north toward it (180 degrees) and encounters a slope with a northern aspect (0 degrees), then the downhill slope is assigned a value of -1. The equa-

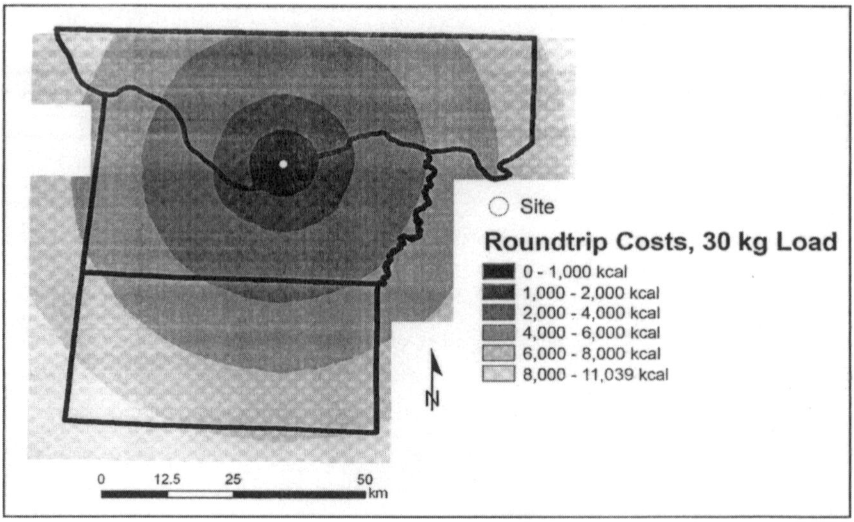

Figure 4.1. Roundtrip travel cost (kcal) at any given distance from the site.

tion assigns a value of zero to east- and west-facing slopes for this traveler, as no additional costs should be associated with traversing these slopes sideways (neither up nor down). All aspects in between are weighted accordingly by a value between 1 (or -1) and zero. These multipliers are then applied to the slopes, and the resulting weighted slopes can then be used in a raster calculation to compute the caloric cost of traversing each 30-m cell (W_s). Travel toward the site includes the additional equation (U_f) for the cost of carrying a load across each cell.

With these values assigned to each cell, the Spatial Analyst can then be used to calculate the cost-weighted distance—here, the cost of travel in kcal—to a given point on the map. From each cell, the program chooses the adjacent cell with the lowest cost. It then adds the cost of traveling from a given point to each cell, resulting in a "least-cost route." In other words, each cell is assigned the lowest total cost of traveling to the site from that cell, resulting in a map that displays these additive costs. The two sums, calculated both to and from the site, without and then with a load, can then be added to give a round-trip total (Figure 4.1).

One of the interesting characteristics of these maps of the project area is that they display more or less concentric circles of costs. It appears that the local topography does not significantly affect the costs of traversing the land-

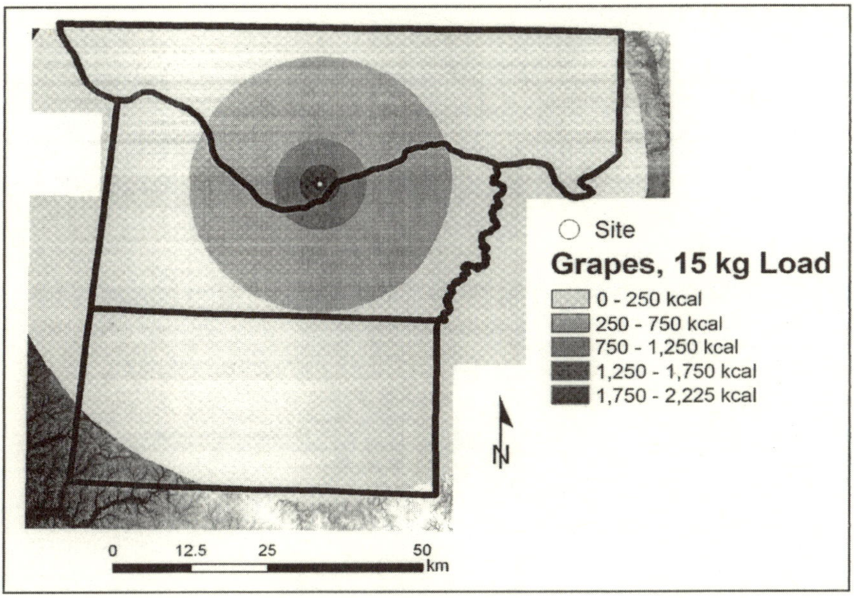

Figure 4.2. Return rate map for 15-kg load of grapes.

scape. Indeed, the northwest Alabama landscape is generally hilly, such that a person who travels uphill is likely to travel downhill shortly. So although there is some variability in the map at smaller scales, the larger picture is one of relatively similar travel costs regardless of the direction of travel. Due to this fact, there are relatively small differences in the costs of traveling to and from each of the four sites, even though they are in different topographic settings. Costs are slightly greater at Rollins Bluff Shelter due to the very hilly local landscape, but again, these differences are slight. As such, I present the results of round-trip travel from Dust Cave and consider them to be generally representative of travel to and from the remaining three sites.

Employing the raster calculator once more, the return rate of exploiting a 15-kg or 30-kg load of a particular resource at each cell can be determined. Using defined values for e_{obt}, H_c, H_t, and V, the summed costs of travel to and from each point are input, as well as the distance from the site to each cell. The resulting map defines the return rate of the resource for each cell (e.g., Figure 4.2, which depicts the return rate map for a 15-kg load of grapes), allowing the viewer to readily evaluate the costs and benefits of exploiting the resource in a given landscape.

Comparing Animal and Plant Resource Procurement

Using the above process, I created return rate maps for the animal and plant resources listed in Table 4.1. These taxa were chosen in part because they occurred repeatedly in the organic assemblages from the four rockshelter sites (see Chapters 5 and 6), and also because I was able to obtain the necessary information for the return rate equation for each. The results are informative, and in some instances rather surprising. I begin with the animal resources, and then discuss the various plant taxa. I also explore the advantages of hunting or gathering in groups of various sizes. To better facilitate comparison among the different resources, I plot the values for return rates at various distances from the site. This gives a two-dimensional picture that illustrates how rapidly return rates fall as foragers travel farther distances to obtain resources.

Animal Resources

In general, animal foodstuffs provide large packages of calories with low processing costs, particularly compared to plant foods. However, most are mobile, and thus often require a significant time investment for stalking and hunting. The various taxa are notably similar in caloric content, generally ranging between 125 and 250 kcal per 100 g, although seasonal differences in fat may significantly increase these values to above 300 kcal per 100 g (Table 4.1). The greatest difference among the animal taxa is the size, and thus the corresponding amount of time required to obtain a load of 15 or 30 kg. A single deer provides at least two 30 kg loads, while 41 squirrels are required to reach 30 kg. Not surprisingly, it takes a forager roughly ten times as long to obtain 30 kg of squirrels than 30 kg of deer. Accordingly, these differences in handling time and associated costs largely account for the differences among the animal taxa.

The return rate values for deer in autumn in the uplands (Figure 4.3) indicate a high of some 5,600 kcal/hr, which decreases asymptotically as one travels farther from the site. In comparison, the highest return rate for squirrel is only 640 kcal/hr and decreases at a much slower rate. The difference between the two is primarily related to their associated processing costs, namely the effort needed to capture enough squirrels to comprise a 30-kg load. The decline in the graph for deer is due primarily to travel costs; handling costs are relatively low in comparison. By simply comparing the heights of the two graphs, it is readily observable that a hunter is more likely to pursue deer than squirrel at any distance from the site: a 30-kg load of deer yields

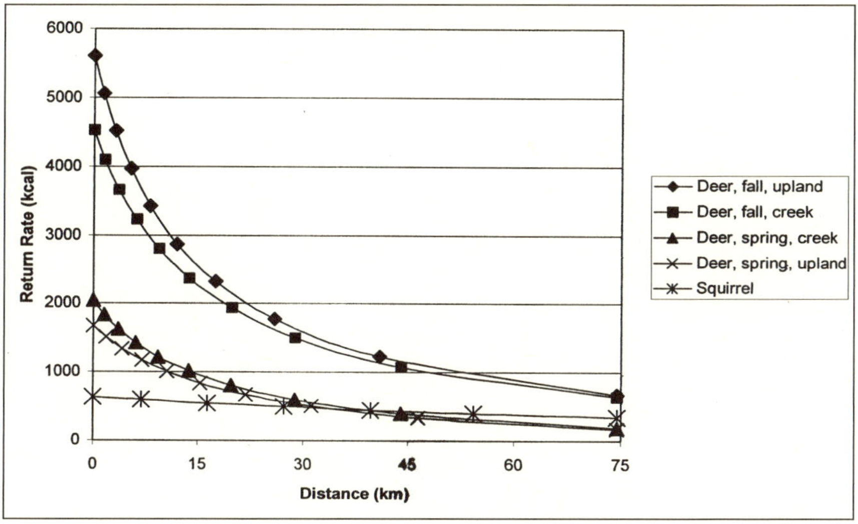

Figure 4.3. Comparison of return rates to distance for deer and squirrels.

over 1,500 kcal/hr at a distance of 15 km, while 30 kg of squirrel provides only 550 kcal/hr.

Fluctuations in prey in both time and space must be considered. Game animals are mobile, traveling primarily between food and water sources. In the spring, we might expect deer populations to be denser in areas where high-quality forage is readily available. In the project area, deer might be most frequently encountered in the creek bottoms in spring, where herbaceous plants are likely most abundant and a wide variety of trees and shrubs are present. In contrast, the largest population of deer in autumn should be found in the slopes and uplands, where nut mast is more plentiful. These population shifts change the encounter rate for hunters and therefore affect the handling time associated with hunting in particular settings. Thus the return rate for hunting deer in the spring should be highest in the creek bottoms, and even higher in the slopes and uplands in autumn, if the above assumptions are correct.

In addition, one must take into account seasonal variability in the quality of game meat. Animals are much leaner at the close of winter and the start of spring, prior to the availability of high-quality forage, namely spring leaves and shoots. As a result, the caloric content of meat is lower in spring than in autumn, when animals store fat for the coming winter. The affect of these seasonal differences on both the caloric value of game and the movement of populations is illustrated by deer in Figure 4.3. The return rate of deer in fall is much higher than that in spring; the return rate is also higher in settings in which deer populations are higher. Squirrels are also leaner in spring than autumn but do not travel far from wooded areas in any season.

Deer may also "yard" in winter, or aggregate in large groups in areas where forage is relatively easily obtained. This behavior is only observed in areas where snow stays on the ground throughout winter (Snyder 1991). This certainly does not apply to present-day Alabama, or perhaps to the region during the Early Holocene. Given the presence of spruce in the region during the Late Pleistocene, however, snow likely did remain on the ground through winter, as it does in boreal forests today. As such, deer likely did yard, forming dense congregations that Late Paleoindian hunters could track and exploit during winter. The lower encounter rates would be offset to some degree by lower caloric values.

These same considerations—the influence of handling time, seasonal availability, and seasonal fat content—apply to wild turkey and waterfowl (Figure 4.4). Because the time needed to acquire and clean 30 kg of turkey is estimated at roughly half that of waterfowl, the return rate of hunting wild turkey is twice that of waterfowl. Accordingly, foragers are more likely to hunt turkey at a considerable distance from a campsite than waterfowl. Both turkeys and waterfowl are also very seasonal in their availability. Waterfowl were presumably available in significant quantities only during several weeks in the spring and fall, as these migratory birds passed through the project area (Walker 1998). The seasonal availability of wild turkey is somewhat less restricted, but return rates would have been significantly higher in the fall, when these birds form flocks. The flocks disperse in early spring for breeding, and as a result these wily birds are much more difficult to hunt. Reidhead (1981:154) assumes that the time required to hunt wild turkeys in the spring and summer may be double that of the fall. Turkeys and waterfowl are also limited in their spatial distribution. Waterfowl are found only along waterways and in the vicinity of ponds and lakes. Turkeys are more likely found in the slopes and uplands in autumn to feast on nuts, and in creek bottoms in the spring to take advantage of spring foliage.

Among the most spatially limited animals are fish, which may supply calories at a surprisingly high rate. Reidhead (1981:135–136) provides several estimates of fishing costs. The first, which included experimental use of logs to trap fish in a slough and subsequently catch them by hand, gave a handling rate of 6.25 kg of fish per hour. Such a high rate may have been feasibly reached in the spring, when spawning fishes were likely available in

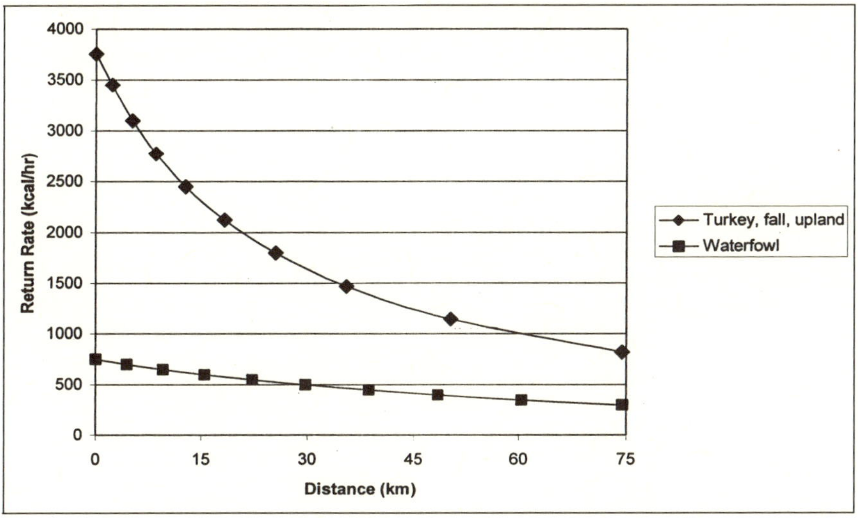

Figure 4.4. Comparison of return rates to distance for turkey and waterfowl.

large numbers in shallow creeks and backwaters (Walker 1998). This handling time yields an extraordinary return rate of over 6,000 kcal/hr; fishers can travel up to 7.5 km and still obtain fish at a rate of 3,000 kcal/hr (Figure 4.5). Reidhead (1981:136) also provides several other estimates of handling rates for fish. A more moderate estimation of 3.8 kg/hr for obtaining spawning fish with use of bow and arrow yields a return rate of 3,000 kcal/hr within 2.8 km of camp. A still lower estimate of 1.85 kg/hr for fishing in a sizeable creek, presumably with a hook, gives a return rate of over 1,400 kcal/hr within 3 km of the site. This last figure is more comparable to other smaller animal resources. Fish are available in spring, summer, and fall, but as noted above, several spawning species, including suckers, are present in significantly greater numbers in shallow streams and creeks during spring.

Also limited to aquatic settings but available year-round are mussels, which present several interesting choices to would-be collectors. Bettinger and colleagues (1997:896) note that while mussels may be collected either by plucking individuals or by detaching large sections of colonies (termed "stripping"), the latter method is much less efficient because many small individuals are collected as well. They also observe that depleted beds provide higher return rates than pristine ones, suggesting that plucking sizeable mussels from depleted beds is easier because they are not as strongly attached due

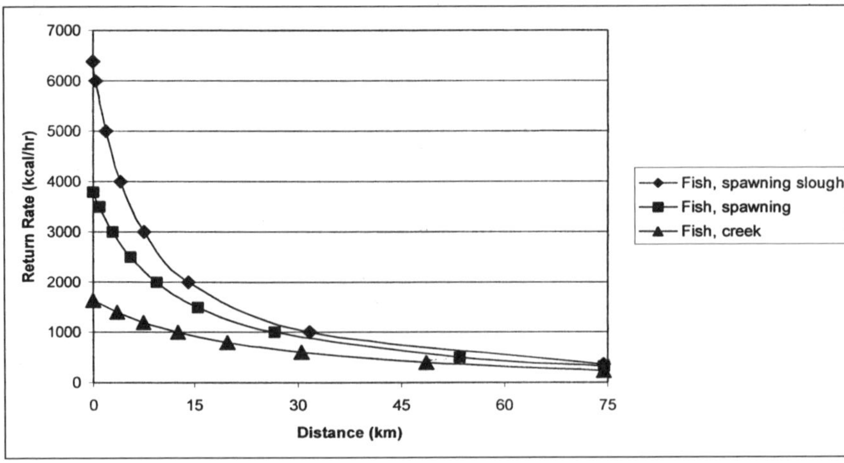

Figure 4.5. Comparison of return rates to distance for various fishing techniques.

to their rapid growth (Bettinger et al. 1997:896). I therefore assume that early shellfish collectors used the plucking method, and compare the return rates for both depleted and pristine colonies. It is possible that early foragers significantly impacted mussel beds both in the Muscle Shoals area and along creeks. Using these values, it is not surprising that depleted colonies yield significantly higher return rates than do pristine colonies (Figure 4.6). Perhaps more surprising is the fact that collectors might transport a 30-kg load of whole mussels, shells and all, from depleted beds at a distance of 8 km and still gain 900 kcal/hr.

Mussels also present collectors with a decision about whether to process the shellfish in the field. The majority of the weight of mussels is comprised of shell; collectors might be well served to spend more of their time processing a large quantity of mussels at the procurement site and transport just the meat back to camp (Bettinger et al. 1997). In the example here, collectors would profit from field processing if they traveled more than 70 m from the base camp to procure mussels.

The mussels also readily illustrate the differences in return rate between carrying a 15-kg and a 30-kg load. Comparing the return rate maps for the two load sizes of mussels collected from pristine beds without field processing, we see that the maximum return rates are not significantly different for the two. Handling times and costs both increase as the load increases, but the transport costs are slightly lower per kilogram for the larger-sized load. As such, this portion of the return rate equation increases at a slower rate, in

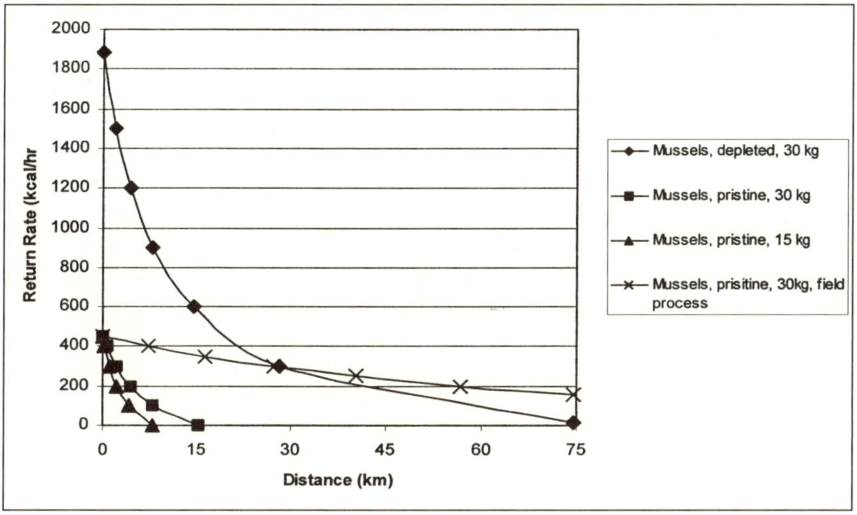

Figure 4.6. Comparison of return rates to distance for exploiting mussel beds.

turn increasing the distance at which it is still profitable to obtain and transport a load back to camp.

In sum, the animal data suggest that larger prey, such as deer and turkeys, are more likely to be exploited at farther distances from a campsite than smaller prey like squirrels and waterfowl. Foragers are also likely to use fish at a significant distance from their camp, as well as mussels, particularly if they process the shellfish in the field. Although limited to bodies of water, mussels are the only foodstuff that does not vary in time or space, however unpleasant it may be to collect them during winter. Fish are available in greater quantities during spring spawning runs; waterfowl are present only during spring and fall migrations; turkeys and deer frequent slopes and uplands in the fall and creek bottom communities in the spring. Squirrels, turkeys, and deer also vary seasonally in the calories that they provide. These variables of population density and caloric value duly affect return rates.

Plant Resources

Similar to the animal resources, the plant foods considered here generally fall into two categories: items with low caloric values and low handling costs, and high-calorie items with high handling costs. Fruits and greens comprise the first group, and nuts and seeds make up the latter. Plant foods also vary in their spatial and temporal distribution, although their lack of mobility makes their presence and abundance in a particular area considerably more predict-

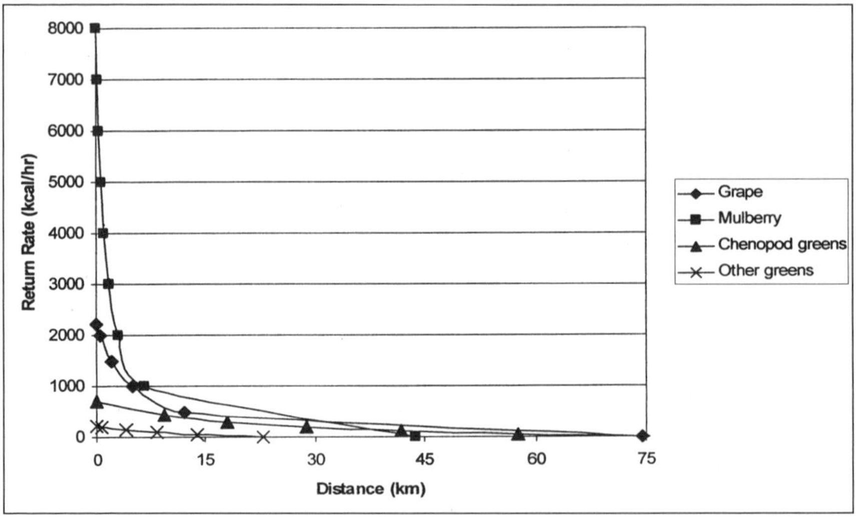

Figure 4.7. Comparison of return rates to distance for mulberry, grape, and leafy greens.

able. As such, search costs are minimal for plant resources, especially if foragers monitor their progress during the growing season to identify which groves, stands, or shrubs are likely to yield the greatest harvest. Monitoring would also aid in determining when plant resources are ripe enough to harvest, as humans face stiff competition from animals for many resources, particularly nuts and fruits.

Fruits examined here include grapes and mulberries (Figure 4.7). The high return rates of these items are notable. Grapes provide a maximum of just over 2,000 kcal/hr for a 15-kg load, while mulberries supply a staggering return rate of nearly 8,000 kcal/hr. These high values are related primarily to their low costs. They are easily gathered; ripe mulberries might have been knocked from trees using a long stick and then collected from the ground (Reidhead 1981). Although they may have been dried for future use, these fruits do not demand processing, making them particularly suited to children's foraging efforts (Hawkes et al. 1995).

It is also immediately apparent from the graphs that the return rates of these items decrease rapidly as one travels farther to obtain them. For these low-cost foods, the travel component dominates the equation.

A similarly rapid decline is apparent for greens, including higher-calorie chenopod leaves and other greens (Figure 4.7). Because these items are lower in calories than fruits, they have significantly lower return rates and are even more dramatically affected by travel costs. For example, a gatherer could not profitably gain from harvesting greens other than chenopod leaves by traveling farther than roughly 23 km.

These return rates are seasonally defined, corresponding with the availability of fruits in the summer and leafy greens in the spring. Because of their remarkable return rate, mulberries might well have been the focus of gatherers' efforts as they ripened in early summer. Gatherers would have had to monitor their maturation closely, as competition from birds and mammals for both mulberries and grapes is fierce (Burns and Honkala 1990; Carey 1994; Schopmeyer 1974:544–545; Sullivan 1993). The early spring availability of leafy greens certainly made them more valuable to foragers' diets than their low return rates suggest: they would have provided important vitamins and minerals at the end of a lean winter diet (USDA NDL 2004).

The return rates also assume that gatherers can collect the entire 15-kg load in a single patch. This may be possible at the height of seasonal availability and within settings where the fruits and greens thrive. Mulberries and spring greens likely occur in greatest quantities in creek bottom communities, while grapes may be found in various wooded, ecotone, and lowland habitats (Kurz 1997; Peterson 1977; Radford et al. 1964; Schopmeyer 1974). Outside of preferred areas, additional handling time and costs must be added for travel between patches in order to obtain a full load, which lowers the overall return rate of the resources.

Seeds and nuts present a different picture due to their high caloric value as well as the significant processing costs they require. Both chenopod and amaranth seeds are high in caloric content, but chenopod seeds apparently have slightly higher handling costs than amaranth. These costs are derived from experimental studies with more or less control over measurements of handling time (Peterson and Munson 1984; Seeman and Wilson 1984). Although the return rates may not be entirely accurate, they do estimate the relative ranking of the two and the impact of travel costs on their use.

Both sets of experiments compared the return rate of two collection methods. The first is cutting, in which seed heads are cut from mature (often dried) plants and taken back to the campsite to be threshed, winnowed, and to remove the papery perianth that encloses the seeds. The second method is stripping, in which the seeds are stripped from the seed head and collected in a container. While this method is relatively time consuming in the field, it negates the need for threshing. Stripping basically constitutes "field processing" (Bettinger et al. 1997; Jones and Madsen 1989; Metcalfe and Barlow 1992), in which the low-utility plant stems are left in the field and a larger load of high-utility seeds is transported back to the site.

The graphs of the two seeds and two methods (Figure 4.8) illustrate that

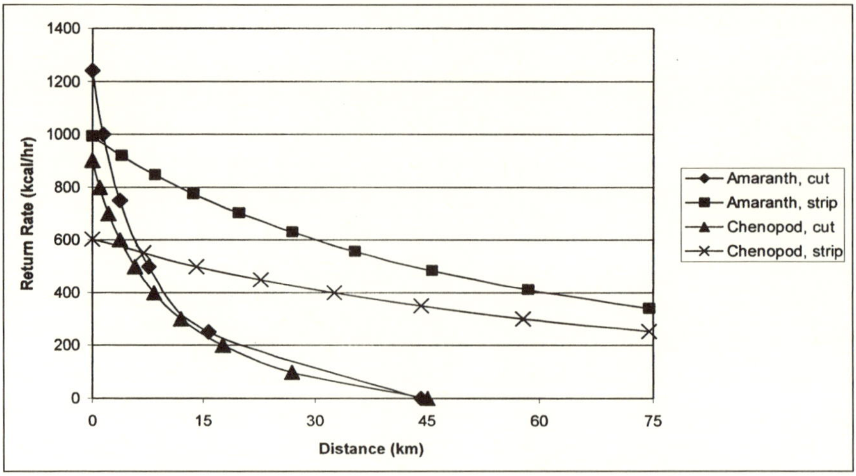

Figure 4.8. Comparison of return rates to distance for harvesting edible seeds.

while the cutting method yields a higher return rate at close distances, the stripping method is profitable at significantly greater distances. This can be demonstrated further by subtracting[3] the map of stripping return rates from the cutting return rates. The resulting map (Figure 4.9) readily displays the distance at which stripping becomes more profitable than cutting for chenopod, namely just over 4 km for a 15-kg load.

The nut taxa are also processed using two different methods. The first is crushing and boiling: the nuts are crushed in a nutting stone or mortar, and then the resulting hodgepodge of meats and shell are thrown into a container of boiling water. The meats, which float to the top, are skimmed off, while the shells sink to the bottom. The nutmeats may also be melted into an oil during boiling (Fritz et al. 2001; Gardner 1997; Talalay et al. 1984). The second method is cracking and picking, in which the nutmeats are simply picked out from the shell.

The first method is especially efficient for processing hickory nuts. The nutmeats are tightly encased in the shell, so that one actually loses energy by trying to pick the meats from the shell. However, boiling is not appropriate for black walnuts or hazelnuts. Portions of the black walnut hull adhere between the ridges of the shell; if boiled, tannins in the hull would be released and spoil the nutmeats. Hazelnut meats, in contrast, do not float, thus negating the usefulness of this method for separating nutmeats and shell. Both black walnuts and hazelnuts thus must be cracked and the meats picked from the shells (Gardner 1997; Talalay et al. 1984). Hazelnuts have large meats

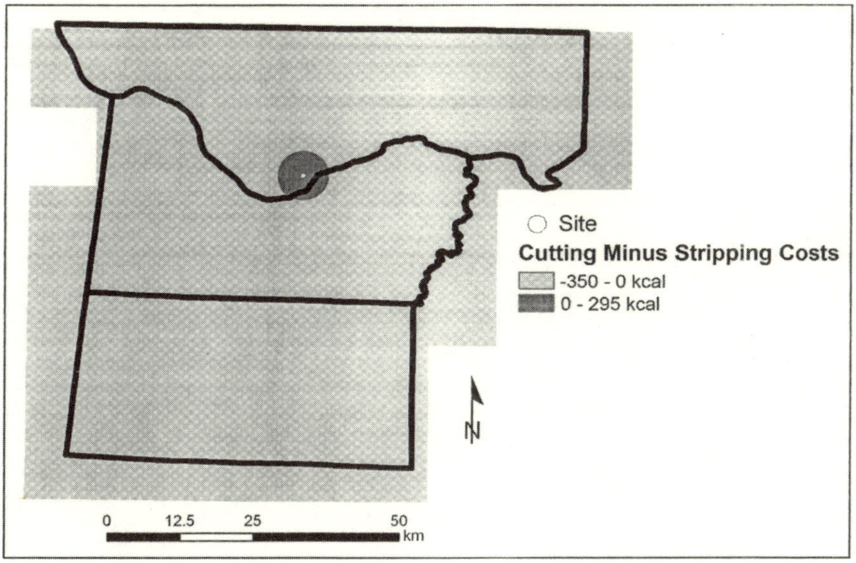

Figure 4.9. Distance at which stripping is more profitable than cutting a 15-kg load of chenopod seeds.

encased in thin shells that are easily cracked, making this method relatively effective. However, they must be picked from shrubs rather than collected from the forest floor, adding significantly to their handling time (Talalay et al. 1984).

Because the handling costs of black walnuts and hazelnuts are so high, the return rates of the two nuts are markedly low even though they are rich in calories (Figure 4.10). Chenopod greens actually yield higher return rates at short distances than do black walnuts and hazelnuts. These high handling costs also significantly influence the equation, so that the return rates of the two nuts slowly decrease with distance from the site; transport costs are small in comparison.

Hickory yields a notably high return rate (Figure 4.10). In fact, the return rate of a 30-kg load of hickory nuts is comparable to, if not greater than, the return rates for hunting any animals other than deer. Similar to the other nuts, the processing costs are high relative to travel costs, so that the return rate slowly diminishes with distance.

Although acorns are generally processed using the crack-and-pick method, they require a significant additional step: tannins must be leached from acorn meats before they are edible. This may be accomplished by parching, boiling

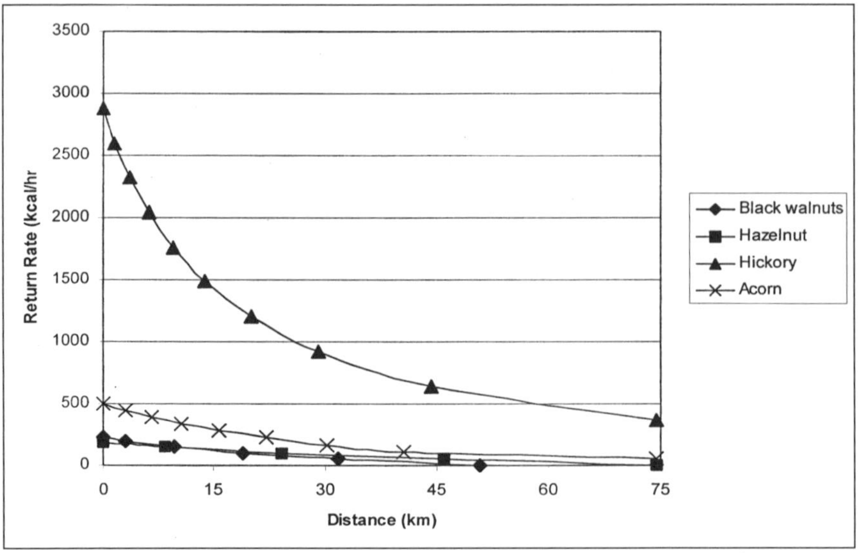

Figure 4.10. Comparison of return rates to distance for various nut taxa.

with several changes of water and often the addition of lye, or simply submerging the meats in running water (Bettinger et al. 1997; Gilmore 1932: 189; Kuhnlein and Turner 1991:200; Petruso and Wickens 1984; Yanovsky 1936:18–19). The leaching process gives acorn a relatively high handling cost, which, in combination with a lower caloric content, results in a lower return rate for acorn as compared to hickory (Figure 4.10). The return rates also decrease relatively slowly with distance.

Similar to leafy greens and fruits, seeds and nuts are limited in time and space. The weedy plants that produce edible seeds are found in quantity in creek bottoms, while nut taxa are more predominant in slopes and upland forests. Nuts ripen and fall in autumn, while seed heads mature and dry in late autumn and early winter (Kindscher 1987; Peterson 1977; Radford et al. 1964; Schopmeyer 1974). Stiff competition from wildlife, particularly for nuts, would have further narrowed their window of availability (Gardner 1997; Little 1995; Schopmeyer 1974; Smith 1990a, 1990b; USDA NRCS 2004; Walsh 1993). Outside of these areas and seasons, gatherers may incur additional costs in travel between patches in order to obtain a full load, or the plant foods may simply not be available.

In sum, the plant resources separate into two categories, based on their caloric value and handling costs. Fruits and greens generally conform to the standard notion that plant resources are not profitably acquired at long distances from a campsite. However, fruits in particular demonstrate significant return rates, comparable to or higher than animal resources at short distances. Seeds have lower return rates than fruits at short distances due to their higher processing costs, but also are profitable at much greater distances. Furthermore, they illustrate the utility of field processing at given distances from a site.

Among the nuts, hickory clearly yields the highest return rate, which is not surprising. What is perhaps surprising is that the return rate is comparable to or greater than hunting most animals. More intriguing is the very low return rate of black walnut and hazelnuts. Due to the high processing costs of the two, their maximum return rates are lower than any other resource except for "other greens." The fact that their nutshells, particularly hazel, are often poorly represented in archaeobotanical assemblages may thus be related more to their high processing costs than their local availability.

Plant versus Animal Resources

It is also useful to directly compare the return rates of various plant and animal resources on the same graph to highlight various topics discussed above. Figure 4.11 displays the return rates of various resources available in spring and summer. It is readily apparent that in spring, deer are not the resource with the highest return rate, but instead are significantly eclipsed by spawning fish. Even more marked is the extremely high return rate of mulberries as they ripen in summer. However, the decline in return rate with distance for both of these resources is much more rapid than for deer, waterfowl, or mussels.

It is also worth noting that the return rate of chenopod greens is predictably low, and also decreases significantly with distance. However, these tender spring greens provide invaluable vitamins and minerals, like vitamin C, that would have been sorely lacking in winter diets. Because of these dietary needs, early foragers would have utilized spring greens. And similar to other low-cost resources like fish and mulberries that quickly lose their return rate as travel increases, it would behoove foragers to procure them at short distances.

The picture displayed by fall resources is much more similar to common expectations (Figure 4.12). Deer and turkey top the chart, although interestingly, the lines for the two cross at approximately 25 km, at which point it becomes more beneficial to hunt turkey. This reflects the higher handling costs of procuring a 30-kg load of turkeys versus deer.

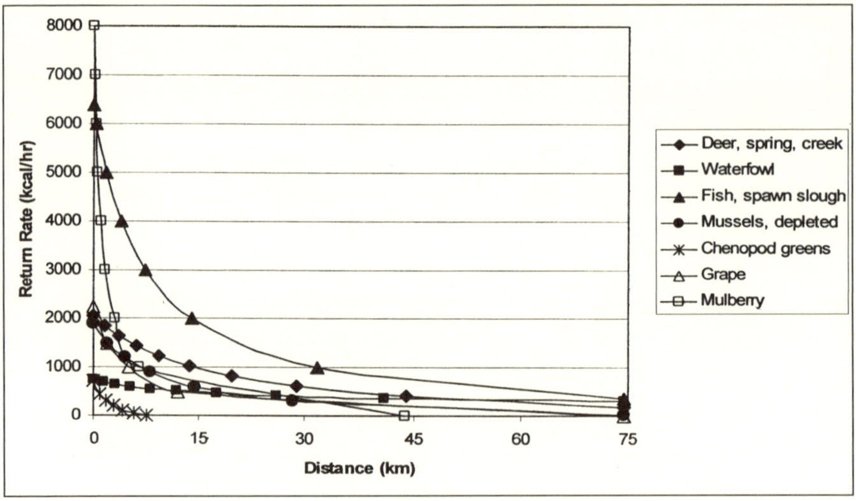

Figure 4.11. Comparison of return rates for resources available in spring and summer.

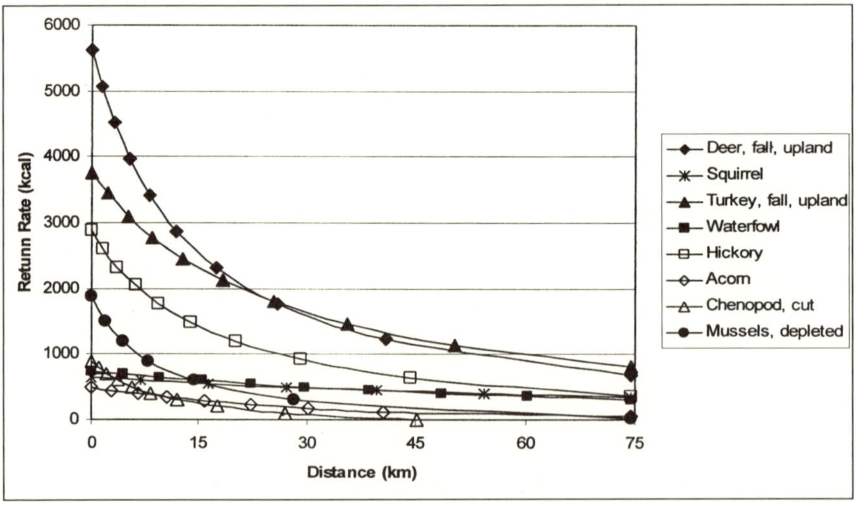

Figure 4.12. Comparison of return rates for resources available in fall.

Importantly, hickory nuts rank third among the resources displayed. But hickory nuts have the added advantage of being readily stored. As noted previously, these high-calorie nuts would have provided much needed fat in winter, when deer and other game are particularly lean. Hickory nuts were certainly an important fall resource to early foragers.

Task Groups

Evolutionary ecology assumes that individuals make foraging decisions. As such, the efforts of a single hunter or gatherer are calculated in the return rates discussed above. However, early foragers lived, traveled, and worked in groups. It is of interest, then, to consider the size of work groups assigned to different subsistence tasks, and the circumstances in which two or more people can yield a higher return rate than a single person who does twice the work.

There are several factors that might affect task group size. Perhaps the most important is prey package size. For large prey such as deer, which generally weigh over 60 kg, two people are required to carry back an entire animal. As such, two people can split several of the costs associated with hunting deer. Both incur travel costs, as well as the costs involved in searching for and pursuing prey. Butchering costs may be divided, but perhaps more importantly, two people can survey twice as much area, thus doubling the opportunity to encounter prey. The return rate is thus higher for two hunters by nearly 2,500 kcal/hr (Figure 4.13). However, hunting parties of more than two appear unlikely, as the third hunter would not carry a full load of venison back. An exception may be larger hunting drives, in which numerous group members surround and drive several animals toward waiting hunters. To the extent that this technique requires lower pursuit costs per person, and results in several prey being taken, it likely yields a higher return rate.

For smaller animals or plant foods, however, two people would simply have to capture or collect and process twice as many items to procure two loads. There do not appear to be energetic advantages to exploiting these resources in larger groups. However, there may well be safety in numbers, childcare opportunities, and a number of social reasons to travel in groups.

It may also be advantageous to focus group members' efforts on obtaining high-value food items that are available for relatively short periods of time, particularly if they can be dried and stored for future use. These resources might include migratory waterfowl, although the return rate for these birds is relatively low. More likely are spawning fishes, for which the return rate is significant. Autumn deer and turkeys, fattened for the winter and less skittish due to their mating efforts, might also have been seasonal targets of task groups.

Plant foods that might have been targeted include fruits, which have very high return rates due to their low processing costs, and hickory nuts, high in fats and readily processed in bulk. As noted above, gatherers also faced

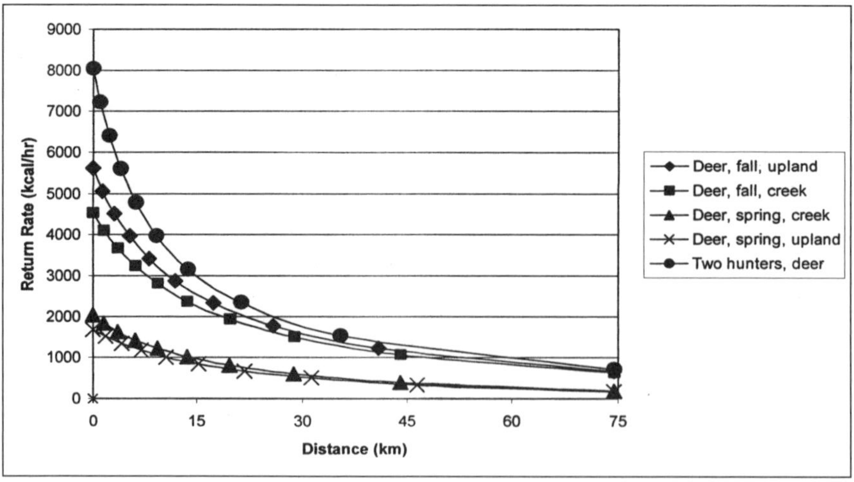

Figure 4.13. Comparison of return rate to distance for hunting deer, alone or with two hunters.

stiff competition from wildlife for fruits and nuts, which effectively shortens their period of availability. Ethnographic and ethnohistoric descriptions indicate that among groups for whom nuts served as a staple food item, all able-bodied men, women, and children participated in collecting nuts, primarily to harvest as many as possible before birds and animals did (Jackson 1991:303–304). Among the Cherokee of western North Carolina, entire towns headed into "the mountains gathering chesnuts [*sic*] upon which many of them depend principally for a subsistence" (Benjamin F. Curry to Elbert Herring, letter, National Archives 1831:11:7:1).

Task groups may also have been sent to obtain persisting edible seeds such as amaranth and chenopod in early winter, after the peak availability of higher-ranked foods such as hickory nuts. In contrast, individuals may have exploited items more generally available and/or associated with lower return rates, such as squirrels and leafy greens, in a more opportunistic fashion.

Stone Resource Procurement

The costs of procuring raw materials for making stone tools can also be evaluated using the portion of the equation that calculates transport costs. Figure 4.14 displays the round-trip costs of obtaining a 30-kg load of blue-gray Fort Payne chert from any given point in the project area. As should be expected, costs are mostly tied to the distance from outcrops of the chert. Differences in terrain appear to have relatively little effect on the costs, likely re-

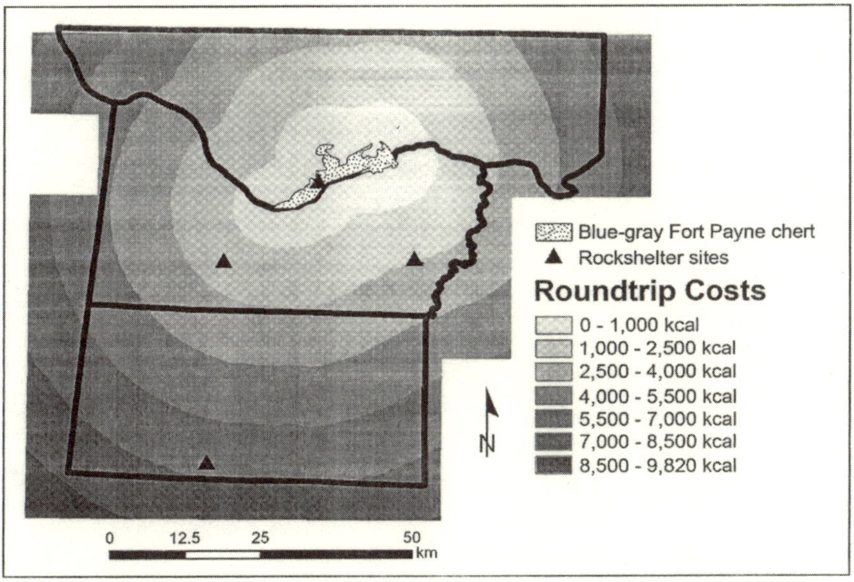

Figure 4.14. Costs of procuring blue-gray Fort Payne chert.

lated to the definition of costs associated with the given slopes. I assume that knappers fashioned early-stage preforms at the outcrops, a form of field processing (Metcalfe and Barlow 1992), in order to maximize the utility of the material they ultimately transported to subsequent camps.

Because there is no caloric return associated with obtaining chert, and because other chert sources were locally available throughout the region, it is likely that foragers obtained blue-gray Fort Payne chert during subsistence-related forays to the river. However, it is difficult to evaluate the advantage of using this high-quality chert over lesser-quality local cherts. If hunters could more efficiently kill or butcher game with certain styles of projectile points or knives, and if knappers could only make these tools on high-quality chert, then foraging groups might have scheduled more frequent forays to the river. Whether subsistence tasks or raw material needs drove these forays would then be debatable.

DISCUSSION AND SUMMARY

Several observations can be made about subsistence strategies in northwest Alabama from the perspective of central place foraging theory. The most important feature of a resource that affects its return rate on a given landscape is the handling cost associated with its use. High handling costs in effect mask the costs of transporting an item, dominating the return rate equation. As such, foragers can travel farther across the landscape to obtain these resources and still secure a positive return rate. These include most animal resources, as well as nuts and seeds. Items with lower processing costs are much more sensitive to travel costs; these include fish, mussels from pristine beds, fruits, and greens.

Two factors that increase the distance over which a forager can travel for a given food item are load size and field processing. The cost of transporting a 30-kg load is less per kilogram than the cost of a 15-kg load, reducing transport costs compared to handling costs. Field processing similarly minimizes transport costs relative to handling costs. In particular, field processing facilitates the exploitation of mussels and edible seeds over greater distances.

Temporal and spatial differences in availability must also be kept in mind. Among animal resources, larger populations may be found in particular environments, often at particular times of the year. For example, turkeys and deer likely frequented forests in uplands and along slopes in fall to take advantage of nut harvests, and in spring moved into creek bottoms where high-quality forage was likely available in greater quantities. Deer and turkey meat are also highest in calories in fall. Return rates for both of these animals thus vary with season and by habitat. Aquatic resources such as fish, mussels, and waterfowl are obviously spatially restricted, but spawning fish and migratory waterfowl are also temporally limited. Plant foods are similarly restricted seasonally, and to some degree spatially. Foragers therefore must have traveled to particular habitats in certain seasons to exploit these resources.

Using this information, I suggest the following seasonal rounds for early foraging groups living in northwest Alabama, and argue that stone procurement would have been embedded within these subsistence-focused rounds. In spring, groups likely would have resided in creek bottom areas, where they could exploit spawning fish and waterfowl passing through the area on their flight north, as well as denser populations of wild turkey and deer. By situating camps in creek bottom settings, gatherers could readily exploit spring greens without traveling far from camp. Hunters might have set off in pairs to pursue deer, while larger group efforts might have concentrated on exploiting fish.

Foraging groups also might have spent a significant portion of their summers in creek bottoms to take advantage of ripening fruits that have high return rates, such as mulberries. In bottom settings, foragers could also obtain aquatic resources such as mussels, turtles, and fish. Groups likely often traveled along slopes and into the uplands as well, to gather grapes and other fruits found in a variety of settings. Because animals also prize these fruits, gatherers presumably monitored their ripening in order to collect them before animals did, and likely sent sizeable work groups to collect as many berries as possible. While monitoring and collecting other plants, gatherers likely took note of nut-bearing trees, particularly which groves or individuals would produce bumper crops during a given year, as well as the status of ripening nuts. Not only are nuts soon eaten by competing wildlife or attacked by molds on the ground, but oaks, hickories, and walnuts produce substantial yields only once every two to five years (Schopmeyer 1974).

In autumn, foraging groups likely spent considerable time in the forests that occupied the slopes and uplands of the project area. Fattened deer and turkeys also frequented these forests to eat nuts. These animals would have provided high return rates to hunters, who may have pursued them in groups of two or more. Gatherers likely organized sizeable work groups to collect hickory nuts in particular, and to a lesser degree acorns, before other animals significantly reduced harvests. They probably also gathered hazelnuts and black walnuts as they encountered them, but most likely did not set out with the sole purpose to collect either nut.

Foraging peoples may have returned to creek bottoms in late autumn and early winter to gather edible seeds in quantity. Deer, turkeys, and other game may also have been drawn to this setting to take advantage of persisting seeds and fruits, giving hunters as well as gatherers reason to return to the floodplains.

Further into winter, as stores gave out, gatherers likely gleaned what remaining seeds and fruits they could, perhaps opportunistically, as the return rates would have been much lower than ideal. In the Late Paleoindian period, when winters may have brought significant snows to the area, hunters likely took advantage of yarding deer, perhaps in larger hunting groups. Foraging groups might then have moved into the uplands and slopes, particularly of the Tennessee Valley, where the conifers of the spruce woodlands might have provided shelter and food, serving as a winter yarding area for deer.

These models, both of central place foraging and of seasonal movements in northwest Alabama, can be modified and adapted to various situations. Many of the terms of the return rate equation can be further refined. Caloric content of various foodstuffs may be relatively constant, although different cooking methods affect the nutritive value of some foods. Perhaps more importantly, the value of nonfood by-products of animal and plant resources, as well as other resources such as stone, is not considered by the equation. Bone and shell may be used to make tools as well as ornaments and other material goods; nutshell may serve as a fuel; skins and hides are made into clothing, blankets, containers, and shelters; stems are woven into mats and baskets. As such, the utility of these various plant and animal resources is underestimated by considering nutritive value alone.

Moreover, estimates of handling costs in particular may be replaced by detailed ethnographic observations or experimental results. The handling costs might also be expanded to included efforts associated with cooking, drying, smoking, and/or storing various foodstuffs. Handling times also change with the density of resources, as noted above. Densities may change due to human predation and modification of landscape, as well as climate change. This is particularly seen in the example of mussels, for which the return rates increase markedly as humans deplete mussel colonies. Humans may also use fire to several ends: to clear underbrush to make travel easier and improve visibility; to promote the growth of favored plants; and to attract desirable game (Fowler 1996; Hammett 1997). All of the above would decrease handling costs and/or time.

Changes in technology also affect handling costs. As noted above, hickory nuts are efficiently processed only with use of boiling technology. Several researchers (Munson 1986; Stafford 1991) have suggested that early foraging groups did not employ stone boiling technology until the Middle Archaic period, when large features with significant quantities of carbonized hickory nutshell appear at archaeological sites throughout the Eastern Woodlands. However, there is nothing to indicate that earlier peoples were not familiar with this technique. As we will see in Chapter 6, the dominance of hickory above other nut taxa at all four rockshelter sites suggests that the early foragers in the region did employ an efficient manner of processing hickory nuts.

Travel costs might be adjusted to include consideration of ground cover, as well as travel by water. This would require a level of detail currently unavailable for the local environment in the project area. Finer-scale paleoenvironmental reconstructions would also enhance estimations of the availability of various plant resources, as well as rankings of the population density of animals, in the different physiographic regions and topographic zones considered here. These would improve approximations of handling costs as well.

Whether the above modifications are applied or not, this central place foraging model is highly useful, in that it highlights those resources that direct camp placement. The model of seasonal rounds developed above, at both the local and regional perspectives, places resources with relatively low handling costs and/or those that are reliable and predictable in time and space at the center of groups' decisions to move across the landscape. These are resources that are targeted by women and children, who require steady nutrition for their survival and success. It is the needs, the activities, and the decisions of women, the elderly, and children, then, that lie at the center of early foragers' mobility patterns.

NOTES

1. The term within the brackets is also multiplied by (pi/180) to transform the value into radians.

2. For aspect of slope, north corresponds to 0 and south to 180 degrees. However, direction to site is defined in the opposite manner, as a person walking north toward a site is actually south of the site.

3. A value for each 30-by-30-m grid square is calculated for each plant using each strategy, and then one is "subtracted" from the other.

5
Paleoethnobotanical Analysis—Data and Methods

In order to assess the viability of the model I developed in Chapter 4 for early foraging groups in northwest Alabama, detailed subsistence data are needed. Although organic remains are not frequently recovered from Paleoindian and Early Archaic sites in the southeastern United States, rockshelter sites are an important exception. Because they are sheltered from rain, which is inherently acidic, deposits in rockshelters provide excellent conditions for preservation of organic remains. Preservation is further enhanced in limestone shelters: as groundwater seeps down through the limestone it becomes less acidic, supplying an almost constant drip of a nearly neutral solution from the ceiling of the shelter onto the deposits beneath (Sherwood 2001). These sheltered deposits thus present us with an opportunity to study plant and animal remains, the spoils of both gathering and hunting, within the same context.

In this chapter, I detail my analysis of plant remains from the four rockshelter sites included in this project. After considering the nature of archaeological plant assemblages, their inherent biases, and the potential they hold for yielding valuable information about subsistence, I discuss the sample sets derived from each site. I also review the excavation and previous analyses performed at each site, which provide a context for understanding the use of plants at each site, and then I describe the nature of the samples and the methods used to collect them. Finally, I specify the methods I used to identify and quantify the plant remains in the samples, as well as my approaches to analyzing the resulting data.

THE DATASET

The data included in my paleoethnobotanical analysis consist of carbonized plant remains. Elemental carbon, or charcoal, is not consumed by any organism, and therefore is resistant to decay (Dimbleby 1967:100). Uncarbonized plant remains may be preserved in the dry confines of some rockshelters.

However, uncarbonized materials are not equally likely at the four sites considered here, for natural and recovery reasons. Despite its name, the deposits at Dust Cave are not dry, but instead are affected by dripping from the ceiling as well as percolation from the floor, thus preventing the preservation of uncarbonized plant remains. Furthermore, uncarbonized materials were not retained from all four sites. For example, uncarbonized plants had already been removed from the LaGrange samples, a by-product of the use of carbon tetrachloride to further isolate the light fraction (see below).

It is also possible that any uncarbonized plant remains are intrusive materials, brought into the sites by animals, wind, or gravity, either in the past or present. This includes uncarbonized hackberry seeds. The pits of these drupes have high mineral contents, primarily calcium carbonate, and therefore have excellent preservation potential (Wang et al. 1997). In addition to other uncarbonized plants, I exclude uncarbonized hackberry seeds from my analysis because it is difficult to distinguish older seeds from modern hackberry seeds that may have been introduced by other creatures that have more recently inhabited the shelters.

Potential for Preservation

Because I focus on carbonized remains, the greatest factor affecting the nature of the plant assemblages is how these materials become carbonized in the first place. They may be introduced to fire in two ways: by accident or on purpose (Yarnell 1982). Items that are purposefully burned include fuel materials, such as wood, and the by-products of food processing (Lopinot 1984; Welch and Scarry 1995:407). The latter include discarded nutshells and hulls, processed debris that site occupants dispose of by burning. We should therefore expect by-products and fuel materials to be well represented in the samples. In contrast, food items, such as nutmeats, fruits, and edible seeds, are eaten rather than discarded; these items are therefore likely to be burned only by accident (Scarry 1986; Yarnell 1982). We should expect fewer of these accidentally carbonized edible remains in the samples than fuel and by-product materials

Another factor influencing introduction to fire is how often foods are used near fire: those used more frequently near fires are more likely to be carbonized. These include foodstuffs that are toasted, cooked, or otherwise prepared using fire, as well as those that are more frequently eaten in general (Yarnell 1982). Just as dishes that are more frequently used are more likely to be broken, foods that are eaten more often are more likely to be accidentally spilled and carbonized (Hubbard 1980:51).

Potential for carbonization is also affected by the nature of the food item itself. Materials that are denser and more robust, such as hickory nutshell, are much more likely to be carbonized and recovered than more fragile items, like the papery shell of chestnuts or small seeds, which are more likely to be completely consumed by fire and turned to ash or crushed during recovery. This also includes items that are relatively high in water content, such as leafy greens and flowers. In addition, some items cannot be readily recognized once carbonized, such as tubers and other materials high in starch. These too are likely to be underrepresented (Yarnell 1982).

These biases must be kept in mind, but should not significantly hamper archaeobotanical analyses. Human behavior is habitual and patterned; people repeatedly use the same foods and prepare them in similar manners (Mintz 1985). Items that are commonly used are likely to be accidentally spilled or purposefully burned and therefore are likely to appear in a carbonized assemblage, while those that are infrequently used are less likely to be recovered (Scarry 1986:180; Yarnell 1982). Thus, with an adequate sample size, we can recognize important resources and measure changes in their use across different contexts and over time.

The Rockshelter Sites, Samples and Recovery Techniques

The four rockshelter sites comprising the assemblage were investigated over a span of forty years, from 1960 through 2002. As a result, the techniques used to excavate them and to obtain botanical samples vary from site to site. Carbonized plant remains are best recovered from archaeological deposits using floatation. With this technique, a sample of a deposit is placed in a container of water; the plant remains, being less dense than water, float to the surface and are collected, dried, and analyzed. Developed and advocated in the United States by Stuart Streuver (1968) in the early 1960s, floatation was not widely implemented at archaeological sites until the latter part of that decade (Chapman and Watson 1993; Pearsall 2000; Watson 1976). The technique and floatation apparatuses have been further refined over the past thirty-odd years, for example, as use of heavy chemicals to further enhance the difference in density between carbonized plants and the solution fell out of favor (Pearsall 2000).

Below I discuss the excavations conducted at each of the four sites, noting the recovery methods used and the samples included here. I also review previous findings developed from analyses of artifactual, faunal, and feature assemblages at the sites. These provide a context of site use and subsistence strategies in which the plant assemblages can be interpreted.

Stanfield-Worley Bluff Shelter

In search of early occupation in Alabama, David DeJarnette began an excavation program targeting the deep deposits of the numerous rockshelters located in the northern hills of the state. The first site to provide such evidence was Stanfield-Worley Bluff Shelter (1CT125), excavated between 1960 and 1963 (Futato 1996). Located approximately seven miles south of the Tennessee River, the shelter is situated in one of the many coves carved out of the Hartselle sandstone formation that caps the Little Mountain region. Eroded from the 100-ft-high bluff that lines the cove, Stanfield-Worley Shelter measures roughly 200 ft in length and between 20 and 60 ft in depth (DeJarnette et al. 1962).

During three field seasons in the summers of 1960, 1961, and 1963, DeJarnette and his crew, comprised of University of Alabama students and volunteers from local chapters of the Alabama Archaeological Society, dug the majority of the deposits in the shelter. Test trenches in the right half of the shelter, excavated in 1960, demonstrated that the deposits contained the evidence for early occupation that DeJarnette was looking for: Dalton points, as well as Side-Notched forms. Both were found in Zone D, also known as the "Dalton zone," which was described as a "dark-brown, midden stratum" (DeJarnette et al. 1962:2), only a few inches to 18 inches thick and flecked with charcoal. Radiocarbon samples from this zone provided uncalibrated dates between roughly 9,000 and 10,000 years before present (DeJarnette et al. 1962; Goldman-Finn 1997:Table 3). A recent accelerator mass spectrometry (AMS) date from Zone D provided a date of 10,010 ± 50 (11,250–11,670 cal. B.P.) (Hollenbach 2005:Table 4.2). The Dalton zone was sealed off from later Middle Archaic deposits (Zone B) by Zone C, a sterile sandy layer (DeJarnette et al. 1962:2).

The site was excavated using 5-x-5-ft units. In 1960, the crew excavated arbitrary 4-inch levels; in 1961, levels were dug using natural stratigraphy as well. Special care was given to the Dalton zone, which was dug in 1-inch arbitrary levels. All deposits were screened through 1/4-inch mesh.

The crew spent one final season at the site in 1963, mainly concentrating their efforts on the left half of the shelter. While they were able to discern several zones, they had difficulty matching these with the four zones described in the previous seasons, including the Dalton zone. Perhaps because of these difficulties, the report for the 1963 season was never completed (Graham and Pearson 1964).

Today the site remains much as it had since the close of the 1963 season.

The excavations were not backfilled, although dirt was added to the profiles to create a slope so that the cattle that subsequently occupied the shelter would not be harmed (Bobby Stanfield, personal communication 2001). The bedrock of the shelter is exposed in a number of places. This includes a large, flat boulder into which numerous small, circular depressions had been ground. The similarities between these golf-ball-size cups and nutting stones are striking, so much that I would confidently describe it as the latter. Three "hominy holes" are also located in the bedrock around the perimeter of the shelter. Unfortunately, the site has been significantly impacted by looters; they have dug a number of pits along the back wall of the shelter, where local legends suggest Native American burials are likely to be located. These areas are also strewn with milk crates, gloves, and other refuse.

In the hopes of finding intact deposits from which floatation samples could be taken, Asa Randall (University of Florida) and I excavated two test pits, measuring 1 x 2 m, in the unexcavated area in the right half of the shelter during the summer of 2001 (Hollenbach 2005; Randall and Detwiler 2002). We fortunately clipped part of the 1963 excavations with one of our test pits. While we dug through zones similar to DeJarnette and colleagues' (1962) descriptions of Zones A, B, and C, we did not encounter Zone D, nor any diagnostic artifacts. In our test pits, Zone C appeared to grade into DeJarnette's underlying sterile zone of sand and gravel (Randall and Detwiler 2002). The Dalton zone seems to have been located primarily in the central area of the site, pinching out toward the sides of the shelter. This corresponds to field drawings of profiles made by DeJarnette's crews, as well as Goldman-Finn's (1997) analysis of vertical distributions of artifacts at the site, which both illustrate a thinning of Zone D toward the edge of the shelter. We returned to the shelter in the summer of 2002 and similarly dug two test pits in the talus slope in front of the shelter with the assistance of students from Middle Tennessee State University (Hollenbach 2005). Unfortunately, we found more backfill, gravel, and poison ivy than anything else.

Artifacts. The original analysis of artifacts from Stanfield-Worley concentrated primarily on descriptions and tabulations of various stone and bone tools and ceramic sherds. Diagnostic points recovered from the Dalton zone include Beaver Lake, several variations of Dalton, and Big Sandy or Early Side-Notched points. Depth distributions of these diagnostic tools suggested that they were coeval (DeJarnette et al. 1962), but in the original analysis, all levels greater than 36 inches in depth were lumped together. Goldman-Finn (1997) reanalyzed the vertical distribution of diagnostic points by unit along several of the gridlines, demonstrating that in some areas Side-Notched and

Dalton tools can be separated by depth below datum. However, mixing of components was evident in other areas, not only by Dalton and Side-Notched points but also the inclusion of at least one Late Archaic form (Goldman-Finn 1997:8, 10).

Goldman-Finn (1997) analyzed an additional sample of the stone tools by artifact type, raw material, and use-wear. Artifact types include bifaces, unifacial blades, scrapers, and flake tools, as well as bone awls and at least one hammerstone and pecked sandstone slab (DeJarnette et al. 1962:83–85; Goldman-Finn 1997). Microwear analysis of several of the bifaces, scrapers, and flake tools suggests occupants worked hide and wood at the site (Goldman-Finn 1997:29). In contrast, biface production seems to be limited. Few early-stage preforms are present, and many of the hafted bifaces show evidence of resharpening and/or have been reworked into drills, scrapers, awls, and chisels (Goldman-Finn 1997:15). In addition, the majority of tools are made from blue-gray Fort Payne chert, which outcrops along the Tennessee River, rather than materials available near the site. This differs from later occupations of the site, when local raw materials were used more extensively (Goldman-Finn 1997:15).

Randall (2002:100) also notes the preferred use of blue-gray Fort Payne chert for Early Side-Notched hafted bifaces at Stanfield-Worley, as well as the significant quantity of late-stage bifaces (2002:103). He contrasts this high degree of "tool consumption" with the much more expedient toolkits used during the Early Side-Notched occupations at Dust Cave and the Hester site (1FR311; Randall 2002:105). Randall (2002:103–104) suggests that the occupants of Stanfield-Worley were not replacing their worn-out tools while they were residing at the shelter because it was not convenient for them to do so; instead, they were busy with other activities, such as hunting deer and collecting and processing nuts.

Faunal Analysis. Faunal remains were collected from the 1/4-inch mesh used to screen the deposits. Paul Parmalee (1962) analyzed specimens from the 1960 and 1961 excavations, including materials from the Dalton zone. Of the latter, some 94 percent could not be identified due to its fragmentary nature. Parmalee (1962:112) suggests that the occupants purposefully broke many of these, particularly the nearly 5,000 large mammal bones that appear to be primarily deer, to extract the marrow. Of the 297 specimens identified to species, 162 are white-tailed deer, further indicating its importance to the diets of the site's occupants (Parmalee 1962:112, Table 32). However, Parmalee (1962:112) suggests that squirrel might have been selectively hunted as well, given the 57 identified squirrel remains and numerous unidentified small mammal elements that are likely squirrel. Similarly, turkey ($n = 7$, plus unidentified bird remains that are likely turkey) and turtles ($n = 31$) might have been relatively important (Parmalee 1962:112–113, Table 32).

Features. Few Dalton features were noted during the 1960–1961 excavations. DeJarnette and colleagues (1962:Figure 17) assigned eight features to Zone D, two of which were described as animal burrows. The remaining six are termed "midden-filled depressions," interpreted as "midden accumulation in natural depressions" (DeJarnette et al. 1962:25). In her analysis of rockshelter features, Homsey (2004:269) suggests that these features may be thought of as refuse deposits.

Homsey (2004:269–270, Figure 8.7) further examined features excavated during the unreported 1963 excavation, based on field forms. These include at least two additional midden-filled depressions, eight circular refuse pits, two centrally located hearths, two patches of "fire-hardened clay," and three instances of bedrock mortars. The latter two feature types bear special mention. Fire-hardened clay masses at sites such as Dust Cave have been termed "prepared surfaces" by Sherwood (2001; Sherwood and Chapman 2005). These surfaces were intentionally constructed, through transport, smoothing, and firing of clay, and appear to have been multipurpose in function, whether providing a surface for activities, cooking, or heating (Homsey 2004:145–146; Sherwood 2001; Sherwood and Chapman 2005). At Stanfield-Worley, these prepared surfaces are located near bedrock mortars in Zone D (Homsey 2004:269). These mortars likely served as nutting stones; they include numerous small, circular depressions pecked into the large exposed sandstone boulders or bedrock encountered at the base of excavations and associated with Zone D.

Previous Site Interpretations. Using these various datasets, researchers have developed several interpretations regarding the early occupation of Stanfield-Worley. DeJarnette and colleagues (1962:85–88) concluded that, based on the recovery of tools associated with hunting and hide preparation, the high proportion of deer remains and lack of implements for processing plant foods, the occupants who deposited Zone D relied heavily on hunting for their subsistence, at least during their time at the shelter. Goldman-Finn (1997:28) observes that the artifacts at the site are relatively dispersed through space, suggesting that the site was used sporadically for short stays. Occupation of the site may have become more intense by the Early Archaic period, as Early Side-Notched points are more prevalent than Dalton forms. While hunting and hide-working are among the activities performed by site occupants, woodworking is also evident from use-wear analyses (Goldman-Finn

1997:29). Based on the heavy use of blue-gray Fort Payne chert, Goldman-Finn (1997:29) postulates that groups headed toward Stanfield-Worley and the uplands after visiting the Tennessee River in their seasonal rounds.

Randall (2002:103–105) reaches similar conclusions based on the large number of late-stage bifaces, noting that the Early Archaic occupants of Stanfield-Worley prepared their toolkits elsewhere, when it was more convenient. While at the site, likely during autumn, they focused their activities on food procurement and processing, notably hunting deer and gathering various nuts. These resources do present time constraints. Deer rut during the fall and as such are more active and less nocturnal, and therefore easier to hunt, than other times of the year. In addition, they carry extra fat. Nuts begin to drop from trees in autumn, and are only available for several weeks before they are eaten or spoiled by squirrels, mold, and other competitors. Randall (2002:103–104) suggests that the occupants of Stanfield-Worley had little time to make tools, busy as they were with hunting, preparing hides, and collecting and processing nuts. He cautions, however, that increases in Early Side-Notched bifaces are not necessarily equated with increases in population or intensity of site use (Randall 2002:106). He demonstrates that these bifaces have shorter use-lives than highly curated Dalton forms, and links their inexpensiveness to the fact that Early Side-Notched bifaces are more likely to be made with local materials than Dalton bifaces. The higher quantity of Early Side-Notched versus Dalton points at Stanfield-Worley should be viewed in light of this.

Botanical Samples. Because the site was excavated prior to the widespread use of floatation, plant materials from Stanfield-Worley were either recovered from the 1/4-inch mesh used to screen all excavated deposits or collected apparently as "pinch samples." These are small samples of sediment that excavators collect from spatially limited concentrations of carbonized materials. At Stanfield-Worley, these samples vary roughly between a handful and a quart of sediment in size.

The two sets of samples yield different data. The 1/4-inch screen samples are skewed toward items that are relatively large and dense, such as nutmeats and hickory and walnut shell. Smaller and more fragile items that would pass through the mesh openings, such as seeds and acorn shell, should be underrepresented in these samples. The pinch samples likely provide a better indication of use of more fragile foodstuffs at the site. The two datasets are not directly comparable, and therefore the screen samples are not included in quantitative analyses.

In spite of their limitations, the samples from Stanfield-Worley are important because they provide some indication of the gathering activities that occurred at the site. As discussed above, interpretations of the shelter's deposits lean heavily toward a focus on hunting (DeJarnette et al. 1962). However, I found several large bags of carbonized acorn meats among the collections from the site, housed at the DeJarnette Laboratory at the University of Alabama Museums in Moundville, Alabama. In addition, the nutting stones ground into bedrock at the base of the Dalton zone, which can be observed at the site today, indicate that Stanfield-Worley's early occupants were certainly engaged in more than hunting. Because of the preeminent position that the site holds within Alabama prehistory, I feel it is important to incorporate these data, although perhaps skewed, in my discussion of early lifeways in the region.

Because of the degree of stratigraphic mixing at the site, only those samples that are referred to directly as "Dalton" and are more than 45 inches below the surface are included in this analysis. These samples include six 1/4-inch screen samples and 20 pinch samples (Table 5.1). All derive from general contexts, usually from particular excavation units or "squares." The 1/4-inch screen samples were collected from the 1960 exploratory trenches, while the pinch samples, collected during the 1961 season, are from the three excavation blocks.

No samples from 1963 are included because of the difficulties encountered by the field crew in identifying the various zones, including the Dalton zone. Although Goldmann-Finn (1997) has demonstrated that the Early Archaic and Dalton components can be teased apart to some degree using the vertical position of diagnostic points, I do not distinguish between the two here because of the vagaries of sample collection. Because detailed notes of the locations from which the samples were collected do not exist, such an exercise would be more speculative than productive.

Rollins Bluff Shelter

Rollins Bluff Shelter (1FR323) is another of the shelter sites excavated by DeJarnette, a crew of University of Alabama field school students, and volunteers from the Alabama Archaeological Society. Noel Read Stowe served as field supervisor and compiled the site report (Stowe 1970) for the 1968 season as part of his master's thesis. A second field season was apparently conducted at the site in 1969 but never reported (Futato 1983:6). The neighboring Sheeps Bluff Shelter (1FR324) was excavated concurrently but did not contain evidence of a Dalton occupation (Hollingsworth 1989).

Similar to Stanfield-Worley, Rollins Bluff Shelter eroded from the Potts-

Table 5.1. Paleoethnobotanical Samples from Stanfield-Worley Bluff Shelter.

Sample Type: Catalog Number	Block	Unit	Level	Depth Below V Surface (in)	Zone	Sample Weight (g)
Screen samples–1960 Excavations:						
22*		125R1	9	45		5.95
30*		130R2	9	45		.36
29*		130R2	11	55		.37
27*		130R3	12	60		4.85
10		130R3/4			Dalton	8.00
36*		145R2	12	60		77.18
Pinch samples–1961 Excavations:						
2261	Block 1	110R6	4		Dalton	10.11
2258	Block 1	110R8			Dalton	4.86
2260	Block 1	110R8	1		Dalton	5.25
2276	Block 2		3		Dalton	106.36
2277	Block 2		5		Dalton	74.50
2278	Block 2		6		Dalton	40.06
2280	Block 2		8		Dalton	59.77
2281	Block 2	120R3	11		Dalton	.37
2270	Block 2	120R6	2		Dalton	11.45
2266	Block 2	125R3	9		Dalton	22.40
2267	Block 2	125R3	11		Dalton	9.88
2268	Block 2	125R3	12		Dalton	6.93

Continued on the next page

Table 5.1. *Continued*

2282	Block 2	125R3	13	Dalton	9.94
2272	Block 2	125R3	14	Dalton	3.54
2269	Block 2	125R4	11	Dalton	.87
2283	Block 3	135-140	1	Dalton	11.85
2285	Block 3		2	Dalton	11.15
2286	Block 3		3	Dalton	28.49
2287	Block 3		4	Dalton	9.74
2284	Block 3		10	Dalton	24.68

*Samples tentatively assigned to Dalton zone.

ville sandstone formation, creating a semicircular shelter some 85 ft wide and 30 ft deep (Stowe 1970:81). It had been used in the recent past as a sheep barn and to house a liquor still operation (Stowe 1970:83). At present, a small, intermittent stream flows over the roof in the northern half of the shelter, making this area damp and relatively unsuitable for habitation. Excavations were thus concentrated in the southern half of the shelter and talus slope (Stowe 1970:81–82, Plate 11).

The crew excavated a 5-x-25-ft trench in 4-inch arbitrary levels through the shelter and down the talus slope to obtain an extensive profile of the deposits. From these, the crew delineated seven zones of stratigraphy, the upper five of which contained diagnostic cultural materials spanning from the Dalton through Woodland periods. These cultural deposits thinned toward the rear of the shelter, as well as on the northern side, and indicated significant disturbance in these areas (Stowe 1970:84). Early Archaic deposits include the lower levels of Zone C. Hickory nutshell from Level 5 of Zone C gave an AMS date of 8160–8360 cal B.P. (Hollenbach 2005:Table 4.3).

Zone D also appears to represent an Early Archaic occupation. Stowe (1970:101) notes that some "Transitional Paleoindian" materials were recovered from the lower levels of Zone D, but he also includes Big Sandy or Early Side-Notched bifaces in this Transitional Paleoindian category.[1] An AMS date of 9890–10,200 cal B.P. was obtained from hickory nutshell in Level 2 of Zone D (Hollenbach 2005:Table 4.3). Dalton artifacts were recovered from Zone E, although only in units near the front of the shelter, even though it extended across the site. Zone F produced few artifacts other than a few small chert flakes (Stowe 1970:87–90). Hickory nutshell from Level 3 of Zone E gave an AMS date of 11,250–11,650 cal B.P. (Hollenbach 2005:Table 4.3).

Excavation of the remaining units proceeded in arbitrary 4-inch levels, with the exception of a central control block, which was dug by natural stratigraphy in .2-ft levels (Stowe 1970:84). All deposits from these units were screened through 1/4-inch mesh. Sediment from the control block, features, and lower levels of several units were processed in the field using floatation to collect plant remains, after previously being screened through 1/4-inch mesh to remove larger artifacts. Water from the stream flowing over the shelter roof was diverted into a coal scuttle using a gutter fitted with a screen to remove contaminants. Floating materials were collected from the scuttle using a "fine-mesh screen," dried, and stored (Stowe 1970:85).

Artifacts. Analysis of stone tools recovered from the site consists primarily of identification and tabulation of various types by level. In addition to hafted bifaces, Dalton toolkits included a variety of unifacial and bifacial scrapers—end, side, ovate, core, and blade scrapers—as well as blades, utilized flakes, cores, pebble tools, and ground stone implements (Stowe 1970: Tables 14–16). Pebble tools include ovate and side scrapers, "split side and end" tools, and spokeshaves, and are fashioned from locally available yellow jasper, or Tuscaloosa gravel, in keeping with other pebble tools in the region (Futato 1996:301; Walthall 1980:23–25). Among the pecked and ground tools are hammerstones made from quartz, sandstone mortars, and nutting stones. Mortars include stones with large circular depressions, while nutting stones claim one or more small circular depressions (Stowe 1970:119). Dalton artifacts cluster spatially in the area near the drip line (Stowe 1970:101). The reason for this is unclear, although fluvial activities may be to blame. Wet conditions may have made habitation of other areas of the shelter unpleasant. Alternatively, fluvial agents might have swept evidence of occupation from these other areas.

Early Archaic toolkits are broadly similar to Dalton artifacts, including unifacial and bifacial scrapers and knives, mortars, mullers, anvil stones, nutting stones, utilized flakes, and cores. Two differences stand out between the Dalton and Early Archaic deposits. The first is an increase in the number of artifacts recovered from Early Archaic levels (Stowe 1970:Tables 14–16). This trend is reflected as well by a substantial increase in the quantity of waste flakes greater than 1/4 inch in size (Stowe 1970:Table 17), suggesting increasing intensity of site use or significant changes in the activities conducted at the site.

The second difference between the two components is the prevalence of raw materials used for tool manufacture. While locally available materials occur in significant quantities, Dalton points made from blue-gray Fort Payne chert slightly outnumber those manufactured from red jasper, or heat-treated Tuscaloosa gravel. During the Early Archaic, red jasper bifaces slightly outnumber blue-gray Fort Payne chert forms (Stowe 1970:109). Patterns among waste flakes greater than 1/4 inch are strikingly different, however. Red jasper flakes significantly outnumber blue-gray Fort Payne chert flakes during both periods of occupation (Stowe 1970:Table 17). In fact, the ratio of Fort Payne to red jasper flakes is roughly similar for the two components, with a value of .10 for the Dalton and .12 for the Early Archaic (Table 5.2). This pattern suggests that blue-gray Fort Payne hafted bifaces were manufactured elsewhere, while occupants of the site made and maintained red jasper bifaces during their stay. Indeed, the cores recovered from these levels are of red and yellow jasper. The only other tool types consistently made from blue-gray

Table 5.2. Comparison of Waste Flakes of Red Jasper and Blue-Gray Fort Payne Chert from Rollins Bluff Shelter by Time Period (Stowe 1970: Table 17).

Period	Level	Red Jasper* (count)	Blue-Gray Fort Payne (count)	Ratio of Blue-Gray Fort Payne to Red Jasper (count/count)
Early Archaic	7	414	47	.11
	8	297	23	.08
	9	420	41	.10
	10	348	53	.15
	11	298	49	.16
	12	403	35	.09
	13	391	59	.15
E. Archaic Total		2571	307	.12
Dalton	14	175	28	.16
	15	261	36	.14
	16	195	1	.01
	17	20	4	.20
	18	32	2	.06
	19	34	1	.03
	20	3	0	.00
	21	6	2	.33
Dalton Total		726	74	.10

*Heat-treated Tuscaloosa gravel.

Fort Payne chert are unifacial tools and utilized flakes (Stowe 1970:Tables 14–16).

Faunal Analysis. Animal remains were scarce at Rollins Bluff Shelter. Stowe (1970:124) postulates that conditions for bone preservation at the site are poor for two reasons. First, the presence of a stream flowing over the roof of the shelter, as well as moisture dripping from the ceiling onto the deposits, likely subjected the deposits to wet and dry periods not conducive to preservation. In addition, the deposits are acidic, which leads to decomposition of organic materials. Of the small amount of bone present, Stowe (1970:124) states that many appear to be white-tailed deer.

Features. Few features were recorded from the early deposits at Rollins. None are associated with the Dalton period. Among the Early Archaic features are five pits and a "sandstone arrangement" 2 ft across that Stowe (1970: 127, Tables 9 and 10) interprets as a hearth. Stowe does not postulate about the function of the pits, but simply describes their contents, which consist primarily of waste flakes, chipped stone tools, and in some instances charcoal and ash (Stowe 1970:Table 9).

Previous Site Interpretation. Because little analysis was available other than that of the stone tools, Stowe (1970) relied heavily on this artifact class for his interpretations regarding the occupation of Rollins Bluff Shelter. He highlighted the presence of ground stone tools in the Dalton component of the site, including mortars, mullers, and nutting stones, and noted the contrast these presented with contemporary views of early groups as primarily relying on hunting. Based on these, as well as the burned nutshell that had been cursorily examined from the floatation samples, Stowe (1970:126) argued that Dalton occupants were likely gathering seeds and nuts on a seasonal basis as well as hunting. The recovery of similar artifacts from the Early Archaic levels at the site suggests that the site's occupants continued to both gather and hunt various resources (Stowe 1970:127–128). Stowe also (1970:127) notes that blue-gray Fort Payne chert, or at least tools manufactured from it, was imported to the site from the Tennessee Valley. Early Archaic peoples living at Rollins might have used less of this higher quality chert, but they evidently continued to travel to or trade with peoples in the floodplain to some degree.

Botanical Samples. Collected during the 1968 excavation of the site, the samples from Rollins Bluff Shelter were processed using floatation. As noted above, the samples were first screened through 1/4-inch mesh (Stowe 1970), presumably to remove large artifacts. This screening exposed the plant remains to mechanical stress, likely breaking fragile items into smaller pieces. Thus we might expect the materials from these samples to be smaller in size, and biased toward more robust taxa. Once screened, the samples were floated using water (Stowe 1970).

I analyzed 29 samples, all deriving from general (or nonfeature) contexts (Table 5.3). Of these, 24 were collected from the control block isolated at the center of the excavation; the remaining five are from Square 95L5. Although Zone D may contain some Dalton deposits in some areas (Stowe 1970), there is not enough information available from the site report to determine which levels and which samples from Zone D may be assigned to Dalton. Therefore I consider the 16 samples from the lower levels of Zone C and all of Zone D to be Early Archaic. Dalton samples include the seven from Zone E as well

Table 5.3. Paleoethnobotanical Samples from Rollins Bluff Shelter.

Component: Catalog Number	Unit	Cut	Level	Depth within Zone (ft)	Zone	Sample Weight (g)
Early Archaic:						
127/132	Control Block 1	1	1	0	D	18.40
136/137	Control Block 1	1	1	0	D	14.18
114	Control Block 1	1	3	.4	D	5.82
154/155	Control Block 1	1	3	.4	D	14.47
157	Control Block 1	1	3	.4	D	143.08
133/138	Control Block 1	1	4	.6	D	30.62
146	Control Block 1	1	4	.6	D	9.68
121/126	Control Block 1	2	1	0	D	15.51
145/150	Control Block 1	2	2	.2	D	19.15
158/159	Control Block 1	2	1	0	D	21.00
160	Control Block 1	2	1	0	D	81.17
142/143	Control Block 1	3	5	.8	C	17.02
148/149	Control Block 1	3	2	.2	D	9.54
130/131	Control Block 2		6	1	C	12.72
151/156	Control Block 2		1	0	D	16.87
147	Control Block 2		3	.4	D	7.14
Dalton:						
124/125	Control Block 1	1	1	0	E	2.81
153	Control Block 1	1	1	0	E	13.95
128/129	Control Block 1	1	2	.2	E	18.27
122/123	Control Block 1	2	1	0	E	2.42
139/140	Control Block 1	2	2	.2	E	7.38
115/120	Control Block 1	3	1	0	E	12.65
118/141	Control Block 1	3	3	.4	E	4.46
134/135	Control Block 2		5	.8	L	21.43
119	Square 95L5		16	60"*		11.57
112/113	Square 95L5		16	60"*		32.62
152	Square 95L5		16	60"*		9.46
116/117	Square 95L5		17	64"*		17.17
144	Square 95L5		18	68"*		12.87

*Depth for Square 95L5 is given as inches below surface.

as the five samples from Square 95L5, whose depth below datum puts them well within the Dalton component at the site, given the vertical distribution of diagnostic points (Stowe 1970:Table 14).

LaGrange Bluff Shelter

LaGrange was the last of the bluff shelters excavated by DeJarnette and his crew from the University of Alabama (Futato 1996:299). LaGrange was created through the erosion of Hartselle sandstone, similar to the other two rockshelters, but it is located on the escarpment between the upland hills and the floodplain of the Tennessee River. Situated at the base of LaGrange Mountain, the shelter measures roughly 15 ft deep by 40 ft long (DeJarnette and Knight 1976:3).

Charles Hubbert of Florence State University (now known as the University of North Alabama) and a crew of volunteers conducted initial testing at the site in 1972, revealing evidence of a Dalton and a likely pre-Dalton occupation at the site. DeJarnette and his crew returned to the shelter in the summer of 1975 to excavate two 5-x-5-ft units that Hubbert had left as a control block, as well as two 1-x-5-ft units (DeJarnette and Knight 1976:4–5). With three profiles exposed, the crew delineated six strata at the site.

Early Archaic materials were recovered from zones B and C (DeJarnette and Knight 1976:7–9). However, hickory nutshell from Level 15 in Zone C yielded an AMS date of 8340–8410 cal B.P., placing it at the start of the Middle Archaic (Hollenbach 2005:Table 4.5). Zone D contained materials from the "Transitional Paleoindian" or Dalton period, but these materials include Big Sandy, or Early Side-Notched, and St. Albans points (DeJarnette and Knight 1976:38), suggesting that the upper levels of Zone D should be classed as Early Archaic. Zone E contained few artifacts other than chert flakes, but its position beneath Zone D suggests that it is associated with a Dalton occupation. This is corroborated by an AMS date of 11,200–11,340 cal B.P. obtained from hickory nutshell in Level 19 of Zone E (Hollenbach 2005:Table 4.5). DeJarnette and Knight (1976:9) presume that materials recovered from Zone F, a sandy layer of decomposed sandstone bedrock, migrated down through the deposits from the overlying zones D and E.

Excavation of the control block proceeded in 3-in arbitrary levels and all deposits were screened through 1/4-inch mesh. Soil samples, weighing roughly 40 lbs, were also collected from each zone and processed through a three-column water screen. Plant materials, as well as small animal bones and chert flakes, were recovered from the smallest screen, with .59 mm openings. The plant remains were further removed through floatation using carbon tetrachloride (DeJarnette and Knight 1976:5).

Artifacts. Analysis of artifacts consisted primarily of tabulations and descriptions of various chipped stone tools by level. Dalton toolkits, in addition to hafted bifaces, included cores, bifacial blades and backed knives, and a variety of unifacial tools, such as knives, end scrapers, and utilized flakes (DeJarnette and Knight 1976:45–47, Tables 5 and 6). Five small fragments of abraded red ocher were also recovered from Dalton levels. DeJarnette and Knight (1976:47) speculate that these may have had ritual uses. The majority of the flakes from these lower levels are less than 10 mm in size, suggesting that site occupants regularly retouched the edges of their tools (DeJarnette and Knight 1976:48–49, Table 10). However, the five Dalton points recovered from the site showed no evidence of significant resharpening, nor were preforms found. This suggests that while points may not have been regularly manufactured at the site, at least within the area of excavation, Dalton bifaces were relatively disposable. This may be related to the availability of blue-gray Fort Payne chert in the nearby Tennessee River floodplain.

The upper levels of Zone D, which are associated with the Early Archaic period, yielded Big Sandy and St. Albans points, as well as numerous cores, a backed bifacial knife, retouched flakes, abraded red and yellow ocher, and a bone awl (DeJarnette and Knight 1975:Table 5). In addition, a large, tabular fragment of sandstone with a single "nutting depression" was recovered from one of the upper levels, and was associated with burned hickory nutshell (DeJarnette and Knight 1975:47).

Zone C, associated with the Early Archaic period, contained few artifacts. Several corner-notched points were recovered, as well as a bifacial knife and three flake tools. In addition, a concentration of flakes was encountered toward the rear of the shelter, accompanied by nine cores (DeJarnette and Knight 1976:32). These cores are likely of blue-gray Fort Payne chert, which dominated the lithic assemblage at the site (DeJarnette and Knight 1976:49).

Similar artifacts were recovered from the lower levels of Zone B. These include Big Sandy, Decatur, and Kirk Corner-Notched points, bifacial blades, cores, and abraded red and yellow ocher (DeJarnette and Knight 1976:Table 3). In addition, specialized unifacial tools clustered in the lower levels of this zone, including a knife and side and end scrapers, which DeJarnette and Knight (1976:29) associate with wood-, bone-, and hide-working.

Chert flakes recovered from the water screen were sorted by size and grouped according to zone. The greatest quantities of flakes were recovered from zones D and B, and the vast majority of flakes—at least 65 percent from each zone—are less than 10 mm in size. DeJarnette and Knight (1976:49) conclude that occupants retouched tool edges while using the site.

Although no quantitative data are given, the researchers remark that blue-gray Fort Payne chert dominates the lithic assemblage, practically to the exclusion of other chert types. They note the presence of Tuscaloosa gravel, but the relatively local availability of high-quality Fort Payne chert apparently precluded significant use of other cherts by site occupants (DeJarnette and Knight 1976:49).

Faunal Analysis. Faunal remains were recovered in relatively low quantities from the site, and include no fish or bird species and very few mollusks or snails (Curren 1976:56). Species recovered from the Dalton levels include deer, snake (Crotalidae), opossum, raccoon, and turtle. Skunk, rabbit, deer, snake, and ground squirrel (*Citellus columbianus*) were identified among the upper, presumably Early Archaic levels of Zone D. All bone fragments recovered from Zone C were unidentifiable, and the only species evident among the lower levels of Zone B was fox (Curren 1976:Table 3).

Features. Few early features were encountered within the excavation block. One small, shallow, basin-shaped pit was excavated in Zone D. The fill of the pit, which intruded into Zone E, was similar to the matrix of Zone D but contained no artifacts. In addition, excavators noted an "occupational floor" in Zone D, described as "a large, irregular area showing signs of fire, with gray to black consolidated clayey soil" that covered the front half of the control block. The nutting stone and a Big Sandy point, as well as charcoal and animal bone, are associated with the floor (DeJarnette and Knight 1976:48, Figure 4).

The most significant feature excavated was a secondary burial located toward the rear of the shelter in Zone C. DeJarnette and Knight (1976:32) are confident of its association with Zone C rather than B because of the stark difference in color between the lighter sand of Zone C and the darker, more consolidated Zone B. The burial, a middle-aged adult of indeterminate sex, was covered by four sandstone boulders and interred with four flakes, one core, and one limestone fragment. A similar secondary burial, capped by sandstone, was encountered during the 1972 excavation of LaGrange, apparently near the base of Zone B. This individual was also a middle-aged adult of indeterminate sex, buried with a large, thick biface (DeJarnette and Knight 1976:32–34).

While several pits and hearths were encountered during excavation of

Zone B, it is difficult to determine whether they are associated with the Early Archaic or subsequent Archaic occupations at the site. One small, circular pit containing charcoal and chert flakes was excavated near the base of Zone B, which DeJarnette and Knight (1976:31) suggest might have been used briefly as a fire basin.

Previous Site Interpretation. DeJarnette and Knight (1976:49–50) made few interpretations about the nature of the various occupations at LaGrange. They highlight the presence of plant processing tools, namely nutting stones, in the early levels of this site. Noting that similar artifacts were recovered at sites like Rollins Bluff Shelter, they suggest that previous understandings of Dalton peoples as relying heavily upon hunting should be reexamined. DeJarnette and Knight (1976:50) also postulate that the variety of diagnostic points recovered from the site is the result of many visits at the site by many different groups. In other words, the six point styles found in the Dalton level (Big Sandy, St. Albans, Dalton, Hardaway, Browns Valley–like, and Beaver Lake) were deposited by six different social groups. They further relate this to relatively flexible territorial boundaries that shift frequently so as to accommodate these various groups within a single site over a relatively short period of time. Today, archaeologists might agree that these point styles were used by different social groups, but consider few of them to be strictly contemporaneous (Anderson et al. 1996).

Botanical Samples. Excavated in 1972 and 1975, the samples from LaGrange represent a mix of collection strategies. The sediment was first screened with water through a set of graduated sieves, the smallest of which had .59 mm openings. To extract plant remains, the screened sediment was then floated in a laboratory using carbon tetrachloride (DeJarnette and Knight 1976:5). I analyzed all 11 available floatation samples (Table 5.4). Six derive from Early Archaic contexts as determined by the distribution of diagnostic points. These contexts include the lower levels (12 through 15) of Zone B, Zone C, and the upper levels (14 and 15) of Zone D, as well as Burial 1, located in Zone C (DeJarnette and Knight 1976:Tables 3 and 5). The remaining five samples are designated as Dalton, again based on the distribution of diagnostic points, and include the lower levels of Zone D (16 through 18), Zone E, and Zone F (Dejarnette and Knight 1976).

In addition to the floatation samples, I analyzed 24 samples collected from the 1/4-inch mesh at LaGrange (Table 5.4). Of these, 13 derive from Early Archaic and 10 from Dalton zones, as determined above. The final sample was from Zone D but did not indicate the level from which it was collected, and therefore I did not assign a time period to it. The screen samples were in-

Table 5.4. Paleoethnobotanical Samples from LaGrange Bluff Shelter.

Context: Catalog Number	Unit	Level	Zone	Period	Sample Weight (g)
Screen Samples:					
71	S5E11	12		Early Archaic	2.20
70.5	S5E11	13		Early Archaic	.08
49	S5E11	15	D	Early Archaic	.29
47/74	S10E5	13	C	Early Archaic	.45
88/89	S10E5	14	D	Early Archaic	.44
78/79	S10E5	15	D	Early Archaic	.52
41	S10E9	15	D	Early Archaic	5.36
77/84	S10E10	12	B	Early Archaic	.83
61	S10E10	13	B	Early Archaic	2.66
46	S10E10	10	C	Early Archaic	1.75
75	S10E10	13	C	Early Archaic	.49
48	S10E10	14	C	Early Archaic	.83
76	S10E11	12	C	Early Archaic	.31
42/80/81	S10E5	16	D	Dalton	4.43
54/82	S10E5	17	D	Dalton	6.60
43/83	S10E5	18	D	Dalton	.78
44	S10E5	16	E	Dalton	1.95
51	S10E5	17	E	Dalton	1.08
52/53	S10E10	16	D	Dalton	2.63
55	S10E10	17	D	Dalton	.76
96	S10E10	15	E	Dalton	.12
50	S10E10	19	E	Dalton	.56
40	S10E10	20	F	Dalton	.56
87	S10E11		D		.21
Floatation Samples:					
106	S10E10	14	B	Early Archaic	1.55
107	S10E10	14	B	Early Archaic	2.38
105	S10E10	15	C	Early Archaic	4.92
104	S10E5	14	D	Early Archaic	3.59
103	S10E5	15	D	Early Archaic	2.41
108	S10E10	Burial 1	C	Early Archaic	4.87
101	S10E5	16	D	Dalton	4.33
102	S10E5	16	D	Dalton	5.62
99	S10E10	19	E	Dalton	.86
100	S10E10	19	E	Dalton	.82
98	S10E10	22	F	Dalton	.33

cluded in order to supplement the limited number of floatation samples, to provide a better indication of the range of plant foods used by occupants of the site. However, I do not include these samples in quantitative comparisons between sites.

Dust Cave

Dust Cave was originally recorded in 1984 by Richard Cobb, a local spelunker, and slated for testing as part of the investigation of caves along the Tennessee River funded by TVA and directed by Boyce Driskell (Cobb 1987; Cobb et al. 1995; Goldman-Finn and Driskell 1994). The present-day entrance of the cave was only about 50 cm high and 2 m across, leading to an entrance chamber measuring roughly 40 m^2 in size. Passageways adjoin this chamber and extend another 20 m or so into the bluff before becoming too tight for exploration (Goldman-Finn and Driskell 1994:1–4). The cave opens to the southeast and overlooks Coffee Slough, a slow-moving backwater of the Tennessee River. Prior to damming of the river by the TVA, the slough would have been a stream fed by a permanent spring roughly 100 m up the bluff line from Dust Cave.

In the summer of 1989, a small crew of University of Alabama field school students and volunteers dug five 30-x-30-cm test units at the site, two in the entrance chamber and three in the back passages of the site. The crew had decided to abandon the test pits and the site, as no artifacts had been recovered and the bottom of the pits were at arm's length, when excavators found several chert flakes and noticed a change in sediment color in Test Units A and D. Test Unit A was expanded to 2-x-2 m in size and excavated to a depth of 160 cm, revealing Benton (Middle Archaic) artifacts, a human burial and a dog burial, and complex stratigraphy (Goldman-Finn and Driskell 1994:5–6).

Driskell returned with field school students in 1990 through 1994 and expanded test efforts. Students increased the size of existing test units, opened new ones, and excavated all except Test Unit G to bedrock. This included a 2-x-12-m trench through the talus and entrance chamber of the site. This trench provided an extensive profile of the site, revealing almost 5 m of cultural deposits, represented by over 200 zones (Goldman-Finn and Driskell 1994:6–7; Sherwood 2001; Sherwood et al. 2004). Forty-three radiocarbon samples from the site provide dates that span from the Late Paleoindian (Quad) through late Middle Archaic (Benton) periods (Sherwood et al. 2004).

Zone P is associated with Kirk Stemmed and Serrated points, placing it at the transition between the Early and Middle Archaic periods. Two Kanawha bifurcate points were also recovered from this zone, which yielded dates between 10,200 and 7800 cal B.P., although bifurcates usually date between 9800 and 8600 cal B.P. and Kirk Stemmed bifaces between 8900 and 8300 cal B.P. in the Middle Tennessee Valley (Sherwood et al. 2004:548).

Zone Q represents several significant erosional events and slope washes, which seem to have mixed Early Side-Notched materials from underlying Zone R with limited human occupation (Sherwood 2001). These occupations are associated with several Kirk Corner-Notched and Kirk Stemmed points among other stone tool artifacts, organic remains, and features. Kirk Corner-Notched points (n = 10) are relatively rare at Dust Cave, leading Sherwood and colleagues (2004:548) to speculate that deposits associated with a Kirk Corner-Notched occupation may have been largely removed by the erosional events associated with Zone Q. A radiocarbon sample from the top of Zone Q yielded a date of 9570 cal B.P. (Sherwood et al. 2004:548).

Zone R represents intensive occupations of the entrance chamber between 11,200 and 10,500 cal B.P. In addition to Early Side-Notched points, several Kirk Corner-Notched points were also recovered from the upper levels of this zone (Sherwood 2001; Sherwood et al. 2004:546). Zones T and U are associated with Quad and Beaver Lake points. Zone T also appears to include a Dalton component, suggested by four Dalton and Hardaway Side-Notched points. These deposits date between 12,650 and 11,200 cal B.P. (Sherwood et al. 2004:544). The underlying Zone Y is culturally sterile, although faunal remains of extinct Pleistocene fauna including giant beaver (*Castoroides ohioensis*) and dire wolf (*Canis dirus*) were recovered (Sherwood 2001; Sherwood et al. 2004:540–542; Walker 2007).

With this stratigraphic and chronological information derived from the entrance trench, Driskell returned to Dust Cave with field schools in the summers of 1996 through 2000 and 2002 to excavate another 2 m on either side of the entrance trench. These efforts aimed to gain more information about the use of the cave not only for the sake of research itself, but also because the site is threatened by the seasonal flooding of the Tennessee River each spring, when the water level in Pickwick Reservoir is raised and lowered by TVA. Subsequently, up to a meter of the lower deposits are saturated and then dried each year. During particularly wet seasons (such as the summer of 1997), up to 2 m of deposits have been affected by standing water. This wet-dry cycle has serious implications for the future preservation of organic remains at the site, as well as the complex microstratigraphy (Driskell 1996). Although major excavation at the site has concluded, a final season is planned to collect an additional set of micromorphological samples, stabilize the remaining deposits, and re-inter burials that had been excavated during previous seasons (Boyce N. Driskell, personal communication 2008; Sherwood et al. 2004).

Methods of excavation shifted over the 11 seasons spent at Dust Cave. The entrance trench was originally excavated in 2-x-2-m units, but the crew quickly shifted to 1-x-1-m units for more horizontal control. Similarly, the units were originally dug in arbitrary 10-cm levels, but as different zones were recognized and the need for finer vertical control became evident, levels were dug by zone in 5-cm increments. In 1992, the crew began excavating a 50-x-50-cm floatation column from every 2-x-2-m unit in the entrance trench, and then from just over half of the 1-x-1-m units excavated from 1996 through 2002. All features were floated in their entirety; remaining deposits were water screened through 1/4-inch mesh.

From the outset, Driskell engaged a variety of specialists at the site in order to better understand the various aspects of the cave's complex archaeological record (Driskell 1996:317). These include geoarchaeologists (Collins et al. 1994; Goldberg and Sherwood 1994; Gose 2000; Homsey 2003a, 2003b, 2003c, 2004; Homsey and Capo 2006; Sherwood 2001; Sherwood and Chapman 2005), lithic specialists (Johnson and Meeks 1994; Meeks 1994, 1998; Randall 2001, 2002, 2003), zooarchaeologists (Goldman-Finn and Walker 1994; Grover 1994; Morey 1994; Parmalee 1994; Walker 1998, 2001, 2003, 2007; Walker and Parmalee 2004; Walker and Richardson 1999; Walker et al. 2005), archaeobotanists (Detwiler 2001; Detwiler-Hollenbach 2003; Gardner 1994; Hollenbach 2005, 2007; Pike 2003), bioarchaeologists (Hogue 1994, 2003), and a researcher interested in fabric impressions (Freeman 2003). The close work of many of these specialists has led to the integration of various avenues of research (e.g., McMillan et al. 2007; Pike et al. 2005; Sherwood et al. 2004; Walker et al. 2001; Walker et al. 2007). Below I briefly discuss what is currently known about the Late Paleoindian and Early Archaic occupations at the site.

Artifacts. Stone tools and the debris (debitage) associated with making and using them comprise the majority of artifacts recovered from Dust Cave. The most striking characteristic of this artifact assemblage is that the overwhelming majority of the stone tools are made from blue-gray Fort Payne chert. This high-quality stone resource, which outcrops in the immediate surroundings of the site, accounts for some 97 percent of all analyzed debitage and tools (Meeks 1994; Randall 2001).

The local availability of high-quality stone significantly shapes the lithic assemblage at Dust Cave. First, occupants of the site appear to have made new tools and maintained their old ones. This is evidenced by the presence of middle- and late-stage bifacial preforms in all components, further suggesting that initial shaping of preforms occurred elsewhere (Meeks 1994:93, 96). In addition, the majority of the debitage falls into smaller size grades, also indicative of final shaping of tools and resharpening (Meeks 1994; Randall 2001, 2002:102). However, resharpening appears to be related to maintenance of tools and not conservation of materials, as suggested by the number of discarded used tools at the cave (Randall 2002:101–102). Randall (2001) notes that more than 30 percent of Late Paleoindian points at the site were discarded due to breakage during use, and a significant number of the blades associated with the Late Paleoindian are highly fractured or have been retouched. In addition, Early Side-Notched points appear to have been discarded prior to being significantly reworked (Randall 2002).

Based on this evidence, Randall (2001, 2002) suggests that the site's occupants did not feel a need to heavily conserve their stone tools in light of the ready availability of a high-quality local resource: the tools could be easily replaced. Occupants did not necessarily manufacture these tools for use at the cave, however, but more likely for subsequent use beyond the site. Similarly, all of the discarded tools were not necessarily used at the site, but might have been tossed out of toolkits as people retooled and geared up for future forays (Randall 2001, 2002; Walker et al. 2001:189).

In addition to making and maintaining tools, people were actively using them. Nondiagnostic tools present at the site include end and side scrapers, gravers, and drills, as well as expedient flakes (Meeks 1994; Randall 2001, 2003). Formal unifacial tools, including blades, scrapers, and gravers, are associated with the early occupations at the site; over 70 percent of these tools derive from the Late Paleoindian component (Meeks 1994:88; Randall 2001). Meeks (in Walker et al. 2001) performed a microwear analysis of a sample of 33 Late Paleoindian bifacial and unifacial tools, which indicated that most were used in tasks associated with butchering and hide-working. These include cutting meat and bone, scraping hide and bone, and perforating hides. Woodworking, such as adzing and whittling, was also evidenced by polish on several tools, as was the production of bone tools (Walker et al. 2001:184–187).

While the stone tool assemblage demonstrates a considerable degree of continuity through time, there may be a trend toward increasing use of high-quality Fort Payne chert for making points, although the sample size is relatively small (Table 5.5). Twelve of 14 (83 percent) Late Paleoindian points are made from blue-gray Fort Payne chert (Randall 2001, personal communication 2005), in contrast to 38 of 40 (95 percent) Early Side-Notched points (Randall 2002), and 100 percent of 21 Kirk Stemmed points (Randall 2003). This trend may suggest a decrease in mobility or in range of settlement patterns through time (Randall 2001), or more frequent returns to areas in which blue-gray Fort Payne is readily available. This possible increase in use of blue-gray Fort Payne chert is interesting because archaeologists usually associate the more technically demanding Late Paleoindian points with high-quality chert. Raw material choice might also have had as much of a social as a techno-functional component (Meeks 1998; Randall 2003).

Comparing points and nonhafted bifaces, it is interesting that greater percentages of nonhafted bifaces were made from other cherts. This likely does reflect a preference for high-quality blue-gray Fort Payne for points. Occupants of Dust Cave seem more willing to use other cherts to make scrapers and other bifacial tools, and more willing to dispose of them at the site, perhaps as they retooled their kits.

As mentioned above, formal unifacial technology is highly associated with the Late Paleoindian component. This holds true not only at Dust Cave but also at other Late Paleoindian (including Dalton) sites throughout the Southeast (Meeks 1994:88). No blade cores have been recovered from Dust Cave, although several have been found at other sites in Coffee Slough near Dust Cave (Meeks 1994:101). Notably, all but one of the 156 unifaces studied by Randall (2001) were made from blue-gray Fort Payne chert.

Cores for producing expedient flakes are present at the site, all but one of which are blue-gray Fort Payne (Randall 2001, 2003). Of the 31 cores examined by Randall (2001), there are three times as many from the Early Side-Notched component as from the Late Paleoindian. Similarly, lithic debitage is notably higher in the Early Side-Notched than any other component at Dust Cave (Meeks 1994:91; Randall 2001). A boxplot of the density of lithic material (debitage weight divided by volume of sample) from the floatation samples I have analyzed with this project further demonstrates this trend (Figure 5.1). This may indicate more intensive use of the cave, a different focus of activities by the people who occupied the site (Meeks 1994:91; Randall 2001), and/or different technological constraints (Randall 2002:104).

In addition to chipped stone tools, ground stone and bone tools have been recovered from Dust Cave. Only five nutting stones have been recovered from the early components at the site, all from the Kirk Stemmed component

Table 5.5. Comparison of Raw Material Use for Manufacturing Bifaces by Component at Dust Cave.

	Points			Bifaces		
Raw Material Type	Late Paleoindian	Early Side-Notched	Kirk Stemmed	Late Paleoindian	Early Side-Notched	Kirk Stemmed
Bangor	0	0	0	1	3	4
Blue-gray Fort Payne	13	30	21	29	87	78
Camden	0	1	0	0	1	0
Fossiliferous Bangor	0	0	0	0	2	1
Fossiliferous Fort Payne	0	0	0	0	5	0
Other Fort Payne	2	0	0	3	0	6
Pickwick	1	0	0	2	0	0
Tuscaloosa gravel	0	0	0	0	0	1
Total	16	31	21	35	98	90

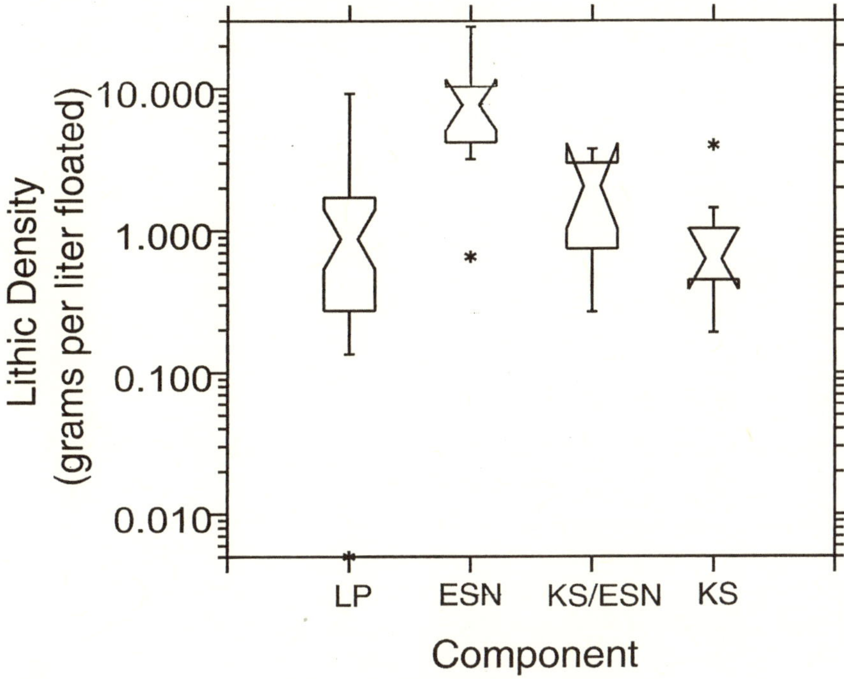

Figure 5.1. Boxplot comparing density of lithic debitage in floatation samples by component at Dust Cave.

(Randall 2003). This is not to say, however, that processing of nuts and use of nutting stones did not occur prior to this time at Dust Cave. The lack of nutting stones from earlier components is more likely related to the fact that excavators had difficulty recognizing nutting stones as such. Fashioned from limestone, the nutting stones initially appear to be spall from the ceiling of the cave; only when viewed from a different perspective are the depressions evident. Having narrowly rescued one from being tossed by a student, I wonder how many nutting stones have gone unrecognized and now lie in the slough beneath the water screen.

Bone tools are more numerous, however. Awls, a perforated raccoon tooth, and a worked bone object were recovered from the Late Paleoindian component. Early Side-Notched bone tools include awls, one bead or tube, needles, a bone point, and an antler tine. In addition to awls and needles, the Kirk Stemmed bone tool assemblage includes fishhooks, a perforated raccoon tooth, fragments of polished turtle shell, and a worked object (Goldman-Finn and Walker 1994:110; Walker 1998:163). Most of the bone awls were

Table 5.6. Distribution of Animal Classes by Component at Dust Cave (Walker 1998).

Class	Late Paleoindian (%)	Early Side-Notched (%)	Kirk Stemmed (%)
Mammals	19	24	35
Birds	69	38	33
Amphibians	1	0.1	0
Reptiles	3	5	5
Fish	8	33	27

made from the long bones of mammals, but several were fashioned from bird bones (Goldman-Finn and Walker 1994:110). Also of interest is a cache of 23 paired goose humeri excavated from the Late Paleoindian component at the cave, 13 of which had cut marks. Walker and Parmalee (2004:30) suggest that these humeri might have been cached for the purpose of making tools and/or decorative objects, and note that caches of bird bones are extremely rare for such early deposits.

Faunal Analysis. Walker (1998, 2007; Walker et al. 2001) analyzed faunal remains from randomly sampled proveniences within the entrance trench. Her samples include 46 floatation samples and 161 1/4-inch water-screen samples. These samples yielded over 2,400 specimens from Late Paleoindian contexts, over 3,900 from the Early Side-Notched, and nearly 1,500 from the Kirk Stemmed component (Walker 1998). Of these, a smaller subset could be identified to class, family, genus, or species (Table 5.6).

Before comparing the faunal assemblages of the various components, it is important to note that bone preservation at the site is remarkable for all components. Comparisons of ratios of more durable fish vertebrae to more delicate fish ribs through time actually suggest that bone preservation is better in the Late Paleoindian and Early Side-Notched deposits than any of the subsequent components (Walker 2007; Walker and Richardson 1999). Indeed, I frequently found fish scales in the floatation samples from these lower zones. It is possible that bone preservation appears better in the earlier occupations because of the intensive nature of subsequent occupations: increases in the intensity of daily activities, including trampling, sweeping, and cleaning, might have had negative consequences for the preservation and later recovery of fragile bone. Regardless, preservation of bone is remarkable throughout the cave, and as such does not introduce significant bias to the recovery of particular animal classes.

Walker's (1998, 2007; Walker et al. 2001; Table 5.6) results suggest several significant changes through time. Birds, particularly waterfowl, represent nearly 70 percent of the identifiable specimens in the Late Paleoindian faunal assemblage. Prairie chicken (*Tympanuchus cupido*), bobwhite, and passenger pigeon (*Ectopistes migratorius*) are also present, as well as one specimen identified as turkey. Mammals constitute less than 20 percent of the sample and are better represented by moles (Talpidae), shrews, mice, rats, and voles than larger mammals. Other mammals include raccoon, squirrels, eastern cottontail, swamp rabbit, gray fox, opossum, mink (*Mustela vison*), and muskrat (*Ondatra zibethica*). Only seven white-tailed deer specimens were identified. Fish, primarily suckers (Catostomidae), redhorse (*Moxostoma* spp.), catfish (Ictaluridae), and drum (*Aplodinotus grunniens*), comprise 8 percent of the Late Paleoindian assemblage. Reptiles and amphibians are present in low numbers, which changes little through time. Amphibians are represented primarily by frogs (*Rana* sp.), and reptiles by eastern box turtles and nonvenomous snakes (Colubridae) (Walker 1998). Walker's (2007) research also indicates that the Late Paleoindian assemblage is more diverse and evenly distributed among species than the other components.

By the Early Side-Notched, birds drop significantly to only 38 percent of the assemblage, but are still heavily represented by waterfowl. Mammals increase to 24 percent, bolstered by an increase in gray squirrel and white-tailed deer (number of identified specimens [NISP] = 35). Shrews and moles are notably absent from this and later components, and voles decrease significantly. Also of note is the significant increase in fish to 33 percent of the assemblage, most of which are suckers, bass/sunfish (Centrarchidae), and drum (Walker 1998).

The Kirk Stemmed assemblage was the smallest analyzed, with only 43 percent of the 1,479 specimens identifiable. Of these, mammals comprised 35 percent, a considerable increase over earlier deposits. The mammals are represented primarily by gray squirrel, as well as opossum, raccoon, rabbits, and white-tailed deer. Birds decrease further to 33 percent, and are more evenly represented by terrestrial birds such as turkey, bobwhite, prairie chicken, and owls in addition to waterfowl. Fish, dominated by suckers, drop slightly to 27 percent (Walker 1998).

Walker (1998) also examined use of various habitats by the site's occupants through time. Not surprisingly, due to its close proximity to both a

Table 5.7. Distribution of Species Assignable to Habitat by Component (Walker 1998).

Habitat	Late Paleoindian	Early Side-Notched	Kirk Stemmed
Open	7 (35%)	6 (20%)	1 (7%)
Ecotone	5 (25%)	8 (27%)	3 (20%)
Closed	8 (40%)	16 (53%)	11 (73%)
Total	20	30	15

stream and the Tennessee River and its backwaters, aquatic species (waterfowl, muskrat, swamp rabbit, pond turtles) significantly outnumber terrestrial species (white-tailed deer, turkey, squirrels, box turtle) in all three components (Walker 1998:139). Greater differences through time are apparent when the fauna are divided among open, ecotone, and closed habitats. Species representative of open habitats significantly decrease from the Late Paleoindian and Early Side-Notched to the Kirk Stemmed component. Closed habitat species comprise increasingly greater proportions of the assemblage through time, increasing from 40 percent in the Late Paleoindian to over 50 percent in the Early Side-Notched and 70 percent in the Kirk Stemmed component. Species suggestive of ecotone habitats remain fairly stable, between 20 and 25 percent of the faunal remains (Walker 1998:141, Figure 7.3; Table 5.7).

The faunal assemblage can be used to assess seasonal use of the site. The presence of migratory birds, such as the passenger pigeon, ducks, and geese, suggest late spring and early fall occupations (Walker 1998:148–150; Walker et al. 2001:183). A large fragment of deer antler still attached to the skull was recovered from the Early Side-Notched component, implying that this deer was taken during the fall to early winter (Walker 1998:150). Also supportive of a cooler season occupation is the low recovery of cold-blooded reptiles and amphibians (Walker 1998:153; Walker et al. 2001:183). A spring occupation may be suggested, however, by the presence of suckers, which leave larger rivers to spawn in shallow streams in the spring. The inhabitants of Dust Cave might have exploited these spawning runs in the small streams of the area, such as the one that likely ran in front of the site (Walker 1998:152).

In addition to the animal remains analyzed by Walker, Parmalee (1994) identified some 358 freshwater mussel valves from the entrance trench, although only 36 derive from the components considered here (Table 5.8). Notably few were recovered from the Late Paleoindian and Early Side-Notched

Table 5.8. Mussels Recovered from the Late Paleoindian and Early Archaic Components at Dust Cave (Parmalee 1994:Table 2).

Taxon	Late Paleoindian	Early Side-Notched	Kirk Stemmed
Actinonaias ligamentina	1		1
Cyclonaias tuberculata	3	1	1
Dromus dromas			2
Elliptio dilatata	1	3	1
Fusconaia barnesiana			1
Lampsilis ovata		1	4
Lexingtonia dolabelloides	1		3
Medionidus conradicus			1
Potamilus alatus			1
Toxolasma lividus			1
Villosa cf. *iris*			1
Villosa taeniata	1		5
Villosa sp.			2
Total	7	5	24

components; the numbers increase significantly for the Kirk Stemmed component. Regardless of the low numbers, the mussel shells indicate that the occupants of Dust Cave occasionally supplemented their diet with this resource, which would have been available nearly year-round (Parmalee 1994:159). The species recovered suggest that the occupants collected mussels not only from the Tennessee River but also smaller streams, creeks, and shallow backwaters (Parmalee 1994). Parmalee (1994:159) also notes that aquatic gastropod shells are abundant in the site's deposits. These would have provided a considerable quantity of meat as well, and also would have been available throughout the year.

Also of interest is a *Canis* burial, excavated from the lower levels of the Early Side-Notched component in Test Unit F. Morey (1994:168–169) identified the five specimens, which include the right femur, two fragments of the left maxilla, and one of the left mandible, as well as a fragment of a tooth, and estimated the age at nearly two years. Morey (1994:169) considers the individual too small to be a gray wolf, but the femur is also too long and slender to be a dog. Coyote (*Canis latrans*) is more likely, although the Early Holocene range of coyotes may be considerably west of Alabama (Morey 1994:169).

Botanical Analysis. Paul Gardner (1994) analyzed a set of floatation samples from Test Unit A. The Late Paleoindian and Early Side-Notched components were not well defined in this unit, and therefore Gardner discusses the samples from the lower levels as the Early Side-Notched component. Hickory nutshell, at around 2,000 fragments, dominates the recovered plant remains, although acorn shell is relatively well represented by nearly 500 fragments. In contrast, only three black walnut fragments were recovered (Gardner 1994:192). Seeds were only found in the earliest component, and include one grape seed and three chenopod seeds. Gardner (1994:193) notes that the chenopod seeds indicate that the relationship between humans and this eventual cultigen extends back at least to the beginning of the Holocene.

Gardner (1994) discusses several trends through time. The density of wood recovered from the samples increases significantly between the Early Side-Notched and Kirk Stemmed components, as does hickory nutshell (Gardner 1994:193, 198). Acorn patterns differently, with a huge peak in occurrence associated with the uppermost Early Side-Notched level. Otherwise, acorn is recovered in relatively low amounts (Gardner 1994:193). Gardner (1994:206) also notes an increase in the ratio of nutshell to debitage between the Early Side-Notched and Kirk Stemmed components and suggests that it may indicate an increase in importance of nut gathering relative to hunting. This trend may in part be related to the higher quantities of debitage recovered from the Early Side-Notched component (Meeks 1994; Randall 2001), and although it may be more indicative of differences in tool manufacture and maintenance than in hunting per se, the trend does suggest different use of the site between the two components.

Features. Homsey (2003b, 2004) has elaborated upon a typology of Dust Cave features begun by Sherwood (2001) by combining geochemical and micromorphological analyses of feature matrix. Comparing these with field descriptions and feature morphology, Homsey (2004) divides the features into two major categories: those associated with burning deposits and those associated with unburned deposits (Table 5.9). The latter include burials, possible storage/refuse pits, and rock clusters; of these, only rock clusters are found in the deposits considered in this project. Rock clusters may represent cooking stones kept near hearths for ready use (Homsey 2004:187).

Features related to burning activities are further divided into in situ fireplaces, fireplace rake-out, and mixed burning deposits. In situ fireplaces include prepared surfaces and a variety of hearths. Prepared surfaces are lenses of clay fashioned by the site's occupants, upon which they built fires, perhaps

Table 5.9. Distribution of Feature Types by Component (Homsey 2004: Table 7.1).

Feature Type	Late Paleoindian	Early Side-Notched	Kirk Stemmed
Surface hearth	1		3
Pit hearth		1	5
Expedient hearth			7
Charcoal pit	9	14	12
Ash pit	2	1	6
Charcoal concentration	4	8	4
Ash concentration	1	1	
Charcoal/ash stringer	11	2	4
Rock pit	2	2	1
Unknown	3	3	8
Total	33	32	50

to grill fish, toast nuts, and/or simply warm the cave (Homsey 2004:144, 146). Hearths include surface, expedient, and pit hearths, and often contain rocks. These hearths might have been used not only to broil or smoke fish and other meats, for processing nuts, or for heating stones for use in boiling, but also as sources of light and warmth for people performing other activities, such as tool maintenance (Homsey 2004).

Fireplace rake-out features are associated with burned materials cleaned from hearths or prepared surfaces. These include small accessory pits with rocks located adjacent to larger features, and thin charcoal lenses (Homsey 2004:169–170, 174–176). Charcoal rings and charcoal/ash stringers appear to be ash and charcoal deposits that were altered after deposition by fluvial activity (Homsey 2004:176–177, 185–186).

Thirty-three features are associated with the Late Paleoindian component (Table 5.9), and include mostly charcoal stains, charcoal/ash concentrations, and rock clusters, which were likely affected by fluvial activities such as slope wash and flooding. A number of charcoal pits, one surface hearth, and portions of prepared surfaces appear to have been little affected by these post-depositional processes (Homsey 2004:204–205).

Thirty-two features are associated with the Early Side-Notched component (Table 5.9). Most of these are charcoal pits, which often contained large amounts of fish bone. Additional features include charcoal concentrations and stringers, two rock pits, and a pit hearth (Homsey 2004:205). The features are associated with significant areas of prepared surfaces (Homsey 2004:223).

The number of features recognized in the Kirk Stemmed component increases significantly to 50 (Table 5.9). These include charcoal and ash pits; expedient, pit, and surface hearths; and a rock pit that may have been an earth oven (Homsey 2004:205–206). Similar to the other components, hearths are coincident with prepared surfaces (Homsey 2004:228).

In general, Homsey (2004:210–214) notes that features from the Late Paleoindian and Early Side-Notched components might have been significantly affected by postdepositional processes, particularly fluvial activity. Features from these deposits tend to be smaller in size than those from later deposits, perhaps due to the dissolution of ash and/or compaction of sediments. Charcoal/ash stains and stringers, which appear to have been formed by water, are more common in the lower levels. The Late Paleoindian and Early Side-Notched components also had the lowest diversity of feature types, which Homsey (2004:214–215) suggests is related to postdepositional processes.

Previous Site Interpretations. Interpretations of the use of Dust Cave have been refined and redefined as research of the site's extraordinary assemblage continues. Noting the relatively low density of artifacts, Goldman-Finn (1994:215–216) suggests that occupation of the site was short term and intermittent. She further hypothesizes that, given the low recovery of white-tailed deer, Dust Cave might have been occupied primarily during the cold season, when deer were lean or low in number, forcing occupants to rely on plants and animals from a variety of ecological zones.

Walker and colleagues (2001:191) view the wide variety of resources locally available to the Late Paleoindian inhabitants of Dust Cave as a positive draw, providing ample opportunity for hunting, gathering, and collecting. They suggest groups visited the cave during the autumn and early winter as part of their seasonal rounds. Highlighting the increase in bifaces, expedient flakes, and scrapers in the Early Side-Notched component, Randall (2001) suggests that occupants might have stayed for longer periods than did preceding Late Paleoindian groups. Expanding on this, he postulates that during their visits, occupants were discarding their exhausted tools and adding new ones, perhaps gearing up for extended forays into the uplands. While at Dust Cave, they also took advantage of the waterfowl, mussels, and ripening nuts and seeds that were locally abundant (Randall 2002:105).

From the perspective of the feature assemblage, Homsey (2004:289) suggests that use of Dust Cave does not change so much in terms of the types of activities performed there as in the intensity of these activities. She hypothesizes that groups, whose base camps were likely situated in the lowlands along the river, logistically used Dust Cave as a specialized extraction site (Homsey 2004:290). Based on the chemical signatures of features that closely mirror the signatures of hickory nuts, as well as visual identification of hickory nuts in thin sections of features, she suggests that this specialized extraction might have targeted hickory nuts. As climatic conditions warmed by roughly 10,000 cal B.P., and hickory stands subsequently improved, use of the site to process hickory nuts might have intensified (Homsey 2004:292–293).

Botanical Samples. The Dust Cave samples are the most extensive and best documented of the four rockshelter sites. All features from the site were floated in their entirety, and samples were collected from 50-x-50-cm columns in nearly half of the 1-x-1-m units excavated at the site. These columns were excavated in 5-cm arbitrary levels, as well as by zone. The majority of the samples were processed in the field using a modified SMAP machine (Watson 1976), which was fitted with a bubbler in the 1998 season to further enhance the floatation of plant remains. The samples were processed using either a 1-mm mesh or window screen (1/16-inch) to capture the heavy fraction, while .03-mm mesh was used for the light fraction. For each sample, the crew recorded the volume of sediment floated, the size of mesh, and whether the bubbler was used (Dust Cave Floatation Logs, 1990–2002). Several samples were not floated in the field due to time constraints. These were processed in the laboratory by the University of Alabama's Office of Archaeological Research, using a modified SMAP machine fitted with window screen to capture the heavy fraction and .03 mm mesh to collect the light fraction.

I selected three floatation columns for analysis: N62W64 (or Test Unit F) in the center of the entrance chamber, N62W62 on the east side of the chamber, and N60W65 in the west half of the chamber. I chose these columns because they are located within the heart of activity at the site (Homsey 2004), but also provide some spatial differentiation. The columns include 65 samples: 35 from the Late Paleoindian component (Zones U and T); 12 Early Side-Notched samples (Zone R); 10 samples from Zone Q, a mix of Early Side-Notched and Kirk Stemmed materials; and eight Kirk Stemmed samples from the lower levels of Zone P (Table 5.10).

In addition, I analyzed 41 samples from features. These include 14 from Late Paleoindian contexts, 11 from the Early Side-Notched component, six from Early Side-Notched/Kirk Stemmed samples, and 10 samples from the

Table 5.10. Paleoethnobotanical Samples from Dust Cave Flotation Columns.

Bag Number	Unit	Level	Depth Below Datum (cm)	Zone	Period	Volume (L)	Sample Weight (g)
5176	N60W65	40	315–320	P2	Kirk Stemmed	4.5	283.57
5230	N60W65	42	325–330	P3e	Kirk Stemmed	8	350.56
5319	N60W65	44	335–340	P3e	Kirk Stemmed	6	549.16
5340	N60W65	46	345–350	P2	Kirk Stemmed	4	387.00
5512	N60W65	48	355–360	P14	Kirk Stemmed	1	29.77
5647	N60W65	50	365–370	Q4	ESN/Kirk Stemmed	7	333.31
6131	N60W65	54	385–390	R3	Early Side–Notched	0.5	147.60
6152	N60W65	54	385–390	R3e	Early Side–Notched	4.7	153.16
6159	N60W65	55	390–395	R3e	Early Side–Notched	5.5	799.54
6192	N60W65	56	395–400	R3f	Early Side–Notched	6	548.06
6212	N60W65	57	400–405	R3f	Early Side–Notched	7.5	932.70
6296	N60W65	58	405–410	R3f	Early Side–Notched	7	686.61
6343	N60W65	59	410–415	R3f	Early Side–Notched	8	1235.01
6360	N60W65	60	415–420	R3f	Early Side–Notched	6	768.85
6378	N60W65	61	420–425	R3f	Early Side–Notched	8.3	525.66
6379	N60W65	61	420–425	T5	Late Paleoindian	7.5	706.19
6401	N60W65	62	425–430	T5	Late Paleoindian	4	536.22
6402	N60W65	62	425–430	U3	Late Paleoindian	8	272.74
6431	N60W65	63	430–435	U3	Late Paleoindian	12	668.04
6465	N60W65	64	435–440	U3	Late Paleoindian	11	289.08
6502	N60W65	65	440–445	U8	Late Paleoindian	13	175.50

6531	N60W65	66	445–450	U8	Late Paleoindian	9	286.41
6551	N60W65	66	445–450	U6	Late Paleoindian	7	211.58
6554	N60W65	67	450–455	U6	Late Paleoindian	5	196.79
6557	N60W65	68	455–bedrock	U6	Late Paleoindian	6.5	206.25
6565	N62W62	50	320–325	P18	Kirk Stemmed	6	122.89
6583	N62W62	51	325–330	P18	Kirk Stemmed	6	1657.84
6592	N62W62	52	330–335	P18	Kirk Stemmed	7	1519.44
6606	N62W62	53	335–360	Q5	ESN/Kirk Stemmed	8	1010.66
6647	N62W62	54	340–345	Q5	ESN/Kirk Stemmed	7	1129.55
6690	N62W62	55	345–350	Q5	ESN/Kirk Stemmed	7	778.71
6695	N62W62	56	350–355	Q5	ESN/Kirk Stemmed	9	845.54
6716	N62W62	57	355–360	Q5	ESN/Kirk Stemmed	8.5	888.60
6735	N62W62	58	360–365	Q5	ESN/Kirk Stemmed	8.5	1266.18
6749	N62W62	59	365–370	R1	Early Side–Notched	9	703.29
6825	N62W62	60	370–375	R1	Early Side–Notched	9	1071.66
6854	N62W62	61	375–380	R1	Early Side–Notched	1.5	1993.16
6870	N62W62	62	380–385	Q5	ESN/Kirk Stemmed	6	457.93
6886	N62W62	63	385–390	Q5a	ESN/Kirk Stemmed	6	773.68
6983	N62W62	64	390–395	Q5a	ESN/Kirk Stemmed	6	689.15
7135	N62W62	67	405–410	T10	Late Paleoindian	9	1092.80
7172	N62W62	68	410–415	T2g	Late Paleoindian	4	3447.99
7189	N62W62	69	415–420	T10b	Late Paleoindian	7.5	1323.30
7250	N62W62	70	420–425	T10b	Late Paleoindian	10	2661.76
7288	N62W62	71	425–430	U1	Late Paleoindian	10	2609.81
7314	N62W62	72	430–435	U1	Late Paleoindian	9	4269.68

Continued on the next page

Table 5.10. *Continued*

Bag Number	Unit	Level	Depth Below Datum (cm)	Zone	Period	Volume (L)	Sample Weight (g)
7356	N62W62	73	435–440	U2a	Late Paleoindian	10	3166.22
7396	N62W62	74	440–445	U2	Late Paleoindian	3	448.35
7426	N62W62	75	445–450	U2a	Late Paleoindian	7	1695.61
7429	N62W62	75	445–450	U2	Late Paleoindian	0.8	151.27
7443	N62W62	76	450–455	U2a	Late Paleoindian	5.5	1494.68
7484	N62W62	76	455–460	U2a	Late Paleoindian	10	1849.79
7496	N62W62	78	460–bedrock	U2c	Late Paleoindian	2	353.00
944	N62W64	32	430–435	T1	Late Paleoindian	10	637.91
965	N62W64	33	435–440	T1a	Late Paleoindian	6	610.30
980	N62W64	34	440–445	T1a	Late Paleoindian	6	700.78
981	N62W64	34	440–445	T1	Late Paleoindian	13	641.50
989	N62W64	35	445–450	T1	Late Paleoindian	14	748.86
999	N62W64	36	450–455	T1	Late Paleoindian	14	492.20
1012	N62W64	37	455–460	T1	Late Paleoindian	9	432.00
1022	N62W64	38	460–465	U	Late Paleoindian	10	1717.43
1036	N62W64	39	465–470	U2	Late Paleoindian	8	875.75
1049	N62W64	40	470–475	U2	Late Paleoindian	13	1266.16
1049.1	N62W64	40	475–bedrock	U2	Late Paleoindian	12	119.29

Kirk component (Table 5.11). I chose the feature samples for analysis as follows. First, I analyzed all available samples included in Homsey's (2004) geochemical and micromorphological analyses of Dust Cave features to allow for comparison between the two datasets. Second, I included a range of feature types, from small charcoal and ash pits to larger "hearths." Finally, I chose features from various locations within the cave. By selecting a variety of feature types, as well as samples from different areas of the site, I have attempted to obtain a set of samples more representative of the range of activities associated with features at the site than a random sampling of the features would afford.

METHODS

Laboratory Methods

Although the four sample sets each represent distinct collection and processing techniques, I analyzed each sample, to the extent possible, using the same standard ethnobotanical methods (Hastorf and Popper 1988; Pearsall 2000).[2] After weighing, I partitioned each sample by size using geologic sieves. All materials greater than 2.00 mm in size were sorted into categories, including bone, lithic material, shell, and contaminants, as well as various plant taxa. The items in these categories were then weighed; all plant taxa were both counted and weighed. All materials less than 2.00 mm in size were scanned for seeds, as well as taxa not represented in the portion greater than 2.00 mm. In other words, if hazelnut was not recovered in the portion greater than 2.00 mm in size, I removed it from the next size grade (1.40 mm). I also counted and weighed these plant taxa.

There are two exceptions, however. Acorn shell and acorn meat counts include fragments from both the 2.00 mm and 1.40 mm size grades. This is done to mitigate the biases against their recovery, particularly in comparison to hickory and black walnut shell. For example, the more fragile acorn shells tend to break into smaller fragments than the denser shells of hickory and walnut (Lopinot 1984). I did not include 1.40 mm acorn shell from the 1/4-inch screen samples, however, as these more likely represent fragments that broke after the samples were collected and would artificially inflate the number of acorn shells recovered.

Identifications of plant specimens were made with reference to seed identification manuals (e.g., Martin and Barkley 1961), as well as the compara-

Table 5.11. Paleoethnobotanical Samples from Dust Cave Features.

Component: Bag Number	Unit	Level	Depth Below Datum (cm)	Feature	Volume (L)	Sample Weight (g)
Kirk Stemmed:						
1702	N63W64	38	355	114	14	991.09
5209	N61W65	48	355	350	6	795.47
5444	N63W66	45	340	358	3	386.73
5630	N60W66	44	335	368	4.5	619.84
5700	N60W66	45	340	375	4.5	556.36
5967	N63W66	47	350	389	2	755.55
6572	N62W62	50	320	444	1.5	306.46
6600	N62W62	52	330	448	1	109.15
6622	N62W62	53	335	450	8	1795.49
6652	N60W62	49	315	451	8	1183.33
Early Side-Notched/Kirk Stemmed:						
4395	N60W68	53	380	330	3.5	273.31
5469	N62W65	52	375	360	1	346.54
5649	N60W65	50	365	363a	3.5	468.38
6082	N60W66	52	375	397	4	9.19
6875	N60W62	59	365	459	13.5	2323.02
6943	N62W62	64	390	462	4	697.21
Early Side-Notched:						
1509	N60W64	42	375	111	16	2384.26
1751	N59W64	51	420	115	3.5	328.30
5706	N63W65	56	385	377	NA	557.95
5732	N63W65	57	395	380	2	170.61
6099	N60W65	53	380	402	1	407.49
6111	N60W66	53	380	405	1.5	408.43
6118	N60W65	53	380	406	3	480.88
6129	N60W65	53	380	410	1.5	454.20
6144	N60W66	55	390	413	5.8	787.31
6874	N61W62	53	375	458	NA	393.82
6972	N60W62	65	395	467	1	167.84
Late Paleoindian:						
293	N62W64	32	425	37	0.8	159.88
1001	N62W64	37	455	99	1	280.40
1761	N60W64	50	415	116	1	111.95
1900	N60W64	58	455	118	2	137.37
5747	N62W65	56	390	382	5	866.77
5790	N62W66	57	395	384	1	403.81
5826	N62W65	61	415	387	3	404.46

Component: Bag Number	Unit	Level	Depth Below Datum (cm)	Feature	Volume (L)	Sample Weight (g)
6283	N60W66	58	405	420	2.5	279.17
6308	N60W66	59	410	423	10	1309.87
6326	N60W65	59	410	117	8	1242.91
6493	N60W66	66	445	438	4	49.04
7068	N62W62	66	400	473	8	1232.65
7076	N62W62	66	400	474	4	628.75
7438	N61W62	66	445	486	2	585.41

tive collection housed in the Ethnobotany Laboratory at the Research Laboratories of Archaeology, University of North Carolina, Chapel Hill.

Analytical Approach

Once the samples were sorted and the materials identified, I organized the resulting data in a database. With raw counts and weights compiled, I approached the data with several questions in mind. These included the following: Which plant species did early foragers living in northwest Alabama use? Are there differences in the use of plants between the Late Paleoindian and Early Archaic periods within each site? Are there differences in the use of plants between the different sites during a single time period? These questions can be answered on both qualitative and quantitative levels.

Qualitative analysis of the samples relies simply on the presence or absence of plant remains within the samples. The first question, regarding which plant species were used by early foragers, is answered succinctly with a list of the plant taxa recovered from the four rockshelter sites. Similarly, differences between time periods within sites and differences among sites within time periods can be addressed at some level using presence/absence data. Qualitative comparisons become particularly important among samples that were collected and/or processed using different techniques. Comparisons made with the 1/4-inch mesh samples from Stanfield-Worley and LaGrange will be restricted to presence/absence data.

Quantitative analyses are used to further address questions regarding differences by cultural periods and differences between sites. I employ several standard measures such as ubiquity, density, and relative density to quantitatively compare data. *Ubiquity* is calculated as the number of samples in which a particular taxon is found divided by the total number of samples. It is expressed as a percent, and measures the frequency with which a taxon was recovered. Ubiquity is calculated using only those samples that include taxa other than wood. The higher the ubiquity of a taxon, the greater its use (Hubbard 1980; Popper 1988:60–61).

The use of ubiquity relies on two assumptions, however. First, it assumes that preservation is similar between all samples; otherwise a lower ubiquity may simply be related to poorer preservation (Kadane 1988). This assumption is generally safe to make for these sheltered sites. The possible exception may be the lower levels of Dust Cave, which is threatened by the fluctuation of the water table due to the raising and lowering of the Pickwick Reservoir (Driskell 1996). However, small and fragile seeds are recovered from all sites, including the lower levels, suggesting that preservation is not drastically different among the sites. Differences due to the use of varying recovery methods must be considered, however.

The second assumption is that the samples consist of comparable volumes of sediment (Kadane 1988). In general, larger samples yield a wider range of taxa (Jones et al. 1983). Volumes not only should be comparable in size, but also in the time span they represent. Depending on the sedimentation rate, a 50-x-50-x-5-cm sample can contain plant remains used over the span of five years or over 500. The volumes of the samples I analyzed appear to be roughly similar within sites, although the only site for which volumes are available is Dust Cave. Volumes seem to differ significantly between sites, however; those from the sandstone rockshelters might have been particularly small. Perhaps more significant are differences in sedimentation rate, both within and among sites. I therefore use ubiquity only tentatively to compare plant use among sites.

Density is calculated as the count or weight of a particular taxon or artifact category in a sample divided by the volume of sediment floated for that sample. By standardizing the count of each taxon by the volume floated, changes in the deposition and/or preservation of each taxon through time at a single site can be demonstrated (Miller 1988:73). As with ubiquity, possible changes in sedimentation rates must also be taken into account, as one liter of sediment may represent different time spans for different zones. One should also be aware of possible differences in preservation, as these directly affect the recovery of taxa and therefore the numerator of the ratio (Kadane 1988:212). Density ratios can only be calculated for the Dust Cave samples, as volumes were not recorded for samples from the other sites.

Relative density, which measures the importance of a particular plant taxon relative to other plants, is calculated as the count of a taxon in a sample divided by the total weight of all plant materials recovered from that sample (Scarry 1986:206). This ratio is useful in that it does not hinge directly on the volume of the sample. While infrequent taxa may not be present in smaller samples, relative density does take into account size differences in that the denominator will be greater for large samples and smaller for small samples. Similarly, sedimentation rates do not affect the measure. The influence of possible differences in preservation between taxa (such as wood compared to hickory) is lessened by including all taxa in the denominator. However, differences in preservation among sites or among components within a site would impact both the numerator and the denominator, making the ratio unsuitable for comparing the assemblages. As mentioned above, significant differences in preservation are not likely for these sheltered sites, but the possibility should be explored.

Along a similar vein, density relative to another plant taxon can also be measured. For example, acorn shell density relative to hickory nutshell can be calculated as the count of acorn shell divided by the count of hickory nutshell. Relative density is useful to detect changes in the use of taxa relative to other plant materials through time within sites.

I approach the quantitative data from the perspective of exploratory data analysis (Scarry 1986; Velleman and Hoaglin 1981). This framework is useful for two reasons. First, it advocates the use of robust descriptions of data, such as medians and quartiles, which are less influenced by outliers than descriptors such as means and standard deviations. This is important because archaeobotanical data often include such outliers (e.g., one sample may contain an extraordinary number of a particular taxon) and cannot be assumed to follow a normal distribution. Second, exploratory data analysis emphasizes the use of graphs to facilitate the detection of patterns within the data. These graphs succinctly summarize datasets, enabling researchers to see the larger picture as well as identify outliers. Both can be important for understanding the range of activities performed by the occupants of a site.

To explore the quantitative data from my samples, I use boxplots to demonstrate change through time. Boxplots succinctly present and compare summary data for a set of samples, either by site or by time component (Figure 5.2). The range of the data is depicted in the form of a notched box, the "waist" of which is the median; the ends of the box mark the 25th and 75th percentiles of the data. The notch itself denotes the 95 percent confidence interval around the median. If the notches of two boxes do not overlap, then their differences are statistically significant at the 95 percent confidence level.

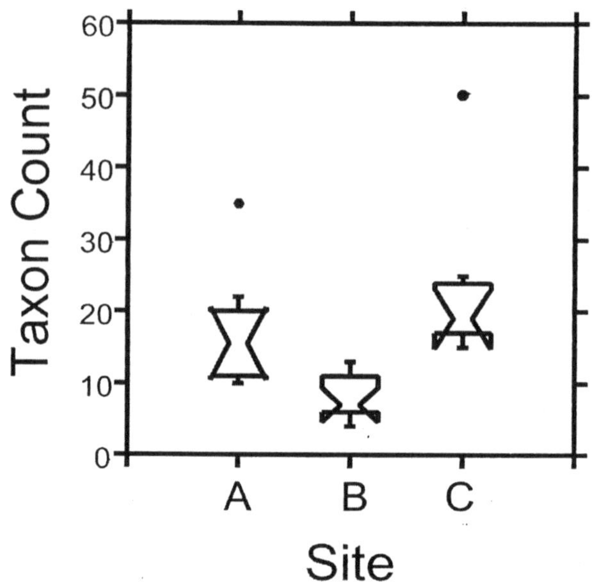

Figure 5.2. Boxplot comparing summary data for assemblages from sites A, B, and C.

"Whiskers" extend from the ends of the boxes to the lowest values within 1.5 times the hinge spread, where the hinge spread is the distance between the 25th and 75th percentiles. Outliers are shown as asterisks, and defined as values beyond 1.5 times the hinge spread. Extreme outliers, defined as values beyond three times the hinge spread, are displayed as open circles (Wilkinson et al. 1992).

In Figure 5.2, the assemblage from Site A is significantly different from Site B, because their notches do not overlap. Note that the notches, or 95 percent confidence intervals, extend beyond the horizontal bars marking the 25th and 75th percentiles, particularly for sites B and C. However, the differences between the assemblages from sites A and C are not statistically significant. Furthermore, the data from Site A includes one outlier, while Site C includes an extreme outlier.

I further compare the data, particularly among sites, using correspondence analysis. This technique essentially reduces the variation of a data matrix (rows and columns) into two (or more) dimensions, and then displays the data along these dimensions, or x and y axes, in a graph (Baxter 1994). Correspondence analysis can be viewed as a particular form of principal component analysis, in which the data have been transformed into chi-square residuals.

Table 5.12. Hypothetical Data Matrix Used in Correspondence Analysis (adapted from Baxter 1994; Bush 2004:Table 6.1).

Site	Taxon 1	Taxon 2	Taxon 3	Taxon 4	Row total
A	27 ($x_{1,1}$)	16 ($x_{1,2}$)	7 ($x_{1,3}$)	18 ($x_{1,4}$)	68 ($\sum x_{1,j}$)
B	13 ($x_{2,1}$)	32 ($x_{2,2}$)	11 ($x_{2,3}$)	41 ($x_{2,4}$)	97 ($\sum x_{2,j}$)
C	5 ($x_{3,1}$)	12 ($x_{3,2}$)	3 ($x_{3,3}$)	8 ($x_{3,4}$)	28 ($\sum x_{3,j}$)
					Overall total
Column total	45 ($\sum x_{i,1}$)	60 ($\sum x_{i,2}$)	21 ($\sum x_{i,3}$)	67 ($\sum x_{i,4}$)	193 ($\sum x_{i,j}$)

In short, correspondence analysis "is an attempt to 'explain' as much of this [chi-squared] statistic as possible in a low number of dimensions" (Baxter 1994:114). Of the two, correspondence analysis is considered more appropriate for discrete data, such as the counts of taxa I use in my analysis, while principal component analysis is more appropriately used with continuous data (Baxter 1994:100). Wymer (1987) and Bush (2004) have employed correspondence analysis in their investigations of archaeobotanical assemblages. VanDerwarker and Scarry (VanDerwarker et al. 2005) have also successfully applied principal component analysis to archaeobotanical materials.

Correspondence analysis is based on a chi-squared analysis of the data matrix. The chi-squared statistic tests the null hypothesis that there is not an association between the rows and columns of the matrix (Baxter 1994:112). For example, using the data in Table 5.12, the null hypothesis is that the four taxa are distributed equally among the three sites. The formula for the chi-squared statistic is $X^2 = \sum (O - E^2) / E$, where O is the observed value and E is the expected value if no association is present. Applying this to the data matrix, the expected values are defined as E = (row total x column total) / overall total. The importance of each cell's contribution to the X^2 is termed the cell's residual, and is defined as $r_{i,j} = (O_{i,j} - E_{i,j}) / (E_{i,j})^{1/2}$. So for Site A in Table 5.12, Taxon 1 has an expected value of (68 x 45) / 193 = 15.85. Its observed value is 27, however, and greater than would be expected if there were no association between taxon and site. This cell's residual can be calculated as $r = (27 - 15.85) / (15.85)^{1/2} = 2.80$.

The residual can then be plotted on a graph as $y_{i,j} = r_{i,j} / (\sum x_{i,j})^{1/2}$ (Baxter 1994:112–113). The origin of the graph is the expected value, and the axes are drawn in the direction of the greatest spread of points (Baxter 1994:114; Bush 2004:106). Row values are thus plotted with respect to how they differ from the expected value. Those that differ most will be plotted farthest from the origin, and those that differ in similar ways will be plotted near each other. Similarly, column values are plotted along the same axes. The variables (columns, or taxa) that cause the rows (site assemblages) to differ from the expected profile are those that plot near the rows (Baxter 1994:114).

I used SYSTAT 9 (SPSS 1999) to perform the correspondence analyses. This program generates correspondence plots and also computes the inertia, or total variation, in the data. Additional statistics produced by the program include the proportion of the inertia explained by each axis (or factor), as well as the mass, quality, and inertia of each column and row (or variable). The *mass* is the row total or column total divided by the overall total, and denotes the influence of each variable on the correspondence analysis. *Quality* describes how well each variable is represented in the plot. The *inertia* of each variable indicates the proportion of the total variation in the data for which that variable accounts.

Correspondence analysis is useful to this study for several reasons. First, it reduces the various taxa, recovered at the sites in varying quantities, to two factors and then plots these, facilitating the identification of similarities and differences among the samples. Second, it handles samples of different sizes, enabling me to compare assemblages from the four sites even though some are relatively small, both in number and size. Although these smaller samples may or may not adequately represent the use of plants at the sites, their use within correspondence analysis is mathematically justified (Bush 2004:107).

SUMMARY

My data include carbonized plant remains from four rockshelter sites in the Middle Tennessee River Valley. These shelters provide excellent conditions for preservation of organic materials, and also contain deeply stratified deposits that include Late Paleoindian and Early Archaic occupations. The faunal, artifact, and feature assemblages from the site provide a context of use in which the plant remains can be interpreted.

While similar in terms of preservation, the assemblages from the sites differ in size, collection technique, and processing method. I analyzed the samples from the sites using standard paleoethnobotanical techniques. While I use ubiquity and various ratios to describe the resulting data, I approach the data from the framework of exploratory data analysis, using graphical displays such as boxplots and correspondence analysis to facilitate the detection of patterning within the data. With these analytical devices and an exploratory approach in mind, I turn to the results and interpretation of the paleoethnobotanical analysis in the next chapter.

NOTES

1. Based on Stowe's (1970) tabulation of artifacts by level rather than by zone, it is difficult to determine the association between levels, zones, and artifacts. While such analysis is beyond the scope of the present study, these tabulations should be revisited in future studies to clarify these associations, similar to Goldman-Finn's (1997) reassessment of the Stanfield-Worley artifacts.

2. A number of the Dust Cave samples were analyzed with the assistance of four students from the University of North Carolina–Chapel Hill, hired with funds from National Science Foundation Dissertation Improvement Grant #0332275.

6
Paleoethnobotanical Analysis—Results

The analysis of plant remains from the four rockshelter sites provides important information about the use of plants by early gatherers. These data complement previous analyses of animal remains, stone tools, and features at the sites, which contribute comparable data about hunting, fishing, collecting, and site use.

The plant materials recovered from the four rockshelter sites can be placed in five categories. These include wood, nuts, fruits, edible seeds, and weedy seeds (Table 6.1). These seeds are likely commensal taxa, brought into the sites accidentally or by natural agents. Also recovered from the samples are miscellaneous taxa, including cane, possible pine nut, and possible squash rind, which likely were not used for food.

Below I detail the results of paleoethnobotanical analyses for each site, discussing trends through time where appropriate. I then compare the four assemblages to gain a larger picture of gathering practices in the region. While the use of plants appears to change relatively little through time, spatial differences are suggested by quantitative analyses.

STANFIELD-WORLEY BLUFF SHELTER

The plant remains recovered from the Stanfield-Worley samples are listed in Table 6.2.[1] Among the 1/4-inch screen samples, wood is the primary plant material recovered, with one exception. Sample 36, from Square 145R2, toward the back of the shelter, contained large amounts of acorn meats. No acorn shell was recovered, although it is likely to have fallen through the screen during recovery and might be underrepresented. This sample in particular may represent a cache of cleaned acorn meats that was accidentally burned, perhaps during toasting. However, this sample is only tentatively assigned to the "Dalton" zone and must be viewed cautiously. In general, among

Table 6.1. Plant Taxa Recovered from the Four Rockshelter Sites.

Category: Common Name	Scientific Name
Nuts:	
Acorn	*Quercus* spp.
Beech family	Fagaceae
Black walnut	*Juglans nigra*
Hazel	*Corylus* sp.
Hickory	*Carya* spp.
Walnut family	Juglandaceae
Fruits:	
Black gum cf.	*Nyssa sylvatica* cf.
Grape	*Vitis* spp.
Hackberry	*Celtis* sp.
Honey locust cf.	*Gleditsia triacanthos* cf.
Maypop cf.	*Passiflora incarnata* cf.
Mulberry	*Morus* sp.
Persimmon	*Diospyros virginiana*
Sumac	*Rhus* sp.
Edible seeds:	
Bean cf. (intrusive)	*Phaseolus vulgaris* cf.
Chenopod	*Chenopodium* sp.
Chenopod-amaranth	*Chenopodium/Amaranthus* sp.
Grass family	Poaceae
Purslane	*Portulaca* sp.
Smartweed	*Polygonum* sp.
Wild bean cf.	*Strophostyles* sp. cf.
Wild legume	Fabaceae
Weedy seeds:	
Bedstraw	*Galium* sp.
Composite family cf.	Asteraceae cf.
Morning glory cf.	*Ipomoea* sp. cf.
Mustard family cf.	Brassicaceae cf.
Nightshade cf.	*Solanum* sp. cf.
Poke	*Phytolacca americana*
Miscellaneous:	
Cane	*Arundinaria gigantea*
Pine nut cf.	*Pinus* sp. cf.
Squash rind cf.	*Cucurbita* sp. cf.
Yellow stargrass	*Hypoxis hirsuta*

Table 6.2. Plant Materials Recovered from the Stanfield-Worley Bluff Shelter Samples.

Type Catalog Number	Unit	Level	Depth	Zone	Plant Weight (g)	Wood Weight (g)	Acorn Count, Weight (g)	Acorn Meat Count, Weight (g)	Black Walnut Count, Weight (g)	Hickory Count, Weight (g)	Walnut Family Count, Weight (g)	Persimmon Count, Weight (g)	Other
Screen samples													
22*	125R1	9	45″		1.14	1.14							
30*	130R2	9	45″		.36	—							2 cane, .36 g
29	130R2	11	55″		.37	37							
27	130R3	12	60″		4.85	4.85							
10	130R3/4			Dalton	7.99	6.46		3, .62		7, .28		1	4 hickory hull, .63 g
7	140R1	10	50″		.69	.17		1, .52					
39	145R2	10	50″		673.97	5.85	30, .86	5386, 665.67	4, .29	4, .59	5, .09		8 acorn meat cf., .08 g; 8 pine cone, .10 g; 2 unidentifiable, 0.44 g
36	145R2	12	60”		69.19	3.09		240, 65.75	1, .15	1, .10			7 pine cone, .06 g; 5 unidentifiable, 0.04 g
Pinch samples													
2261	110R6	4		Dalton	.80	.30		2, .04	8, .18	10, .22	4, .05		1 unidentifiable, .01 g
2258	110R8			Dalton	.10	.01			1, .04	2, .03	1, .01		1 unidentifiable, .01 g

2260	110R8	1	Dalton	.09	.04				3, .05			
2276	Block2	3	Dalton	12.83	8.19	5, .02	11, .07	59, 2.90	84, 1.34	11, .13	8, .05	1 hazel; 20 unidentifiable, .13 g
2277	Block2	5	Dalton	7.10	4.00			73, 1.69	79, 1.00	31, .31	3, .01	1 acorn cf.; 17 unidentifiable, .09 g
2278	Block2	6	Dalton	4.16	1.89	4, .03	3, .02	43, 1.19	56, .70	16, .19	4, .11	1 pitch, .01g; 2 sumac cf.; 4 unidentifiable, .02 g
2280	Block2	8	Dalton	5.35	2.32		7, .29	36, 1.03	110, 1.36	36, .29	3, .03	1 hazel; 2 grape; 7 unidentifiable, .03 g
2281	120R3	11	Dalton	.03	—			1, .01	1, .01	2, .01		
2270	120R6	2	Dalton	.92	.59	1		1, .02	21, .31			1 unidentifiable
2266	125R3	9	Dalton	3.19	1.96		3, .02	13, .44	47, .69	4, .03	5, .04	2 unidentifiable, .01 g
2267	125R3	11	Dalton	4.23	4.07	1	7, .03	1, .05	2, .02			2 bark, .05 g; 1 unidentifiable, .01 g
2268	125R3	12	Dalton	2.39	1.95	1, .01	2, .02	12, .29	2, .04	6, .05		4 bark, .02 g; 1 unidentifiable, .01 g
2282	125R3	13	Dalton	2.28	2.03		2, .01		9, .23		1, .01	1 acorn cf.; 1 unidentifiable
2272	125R3	14	Dalton	.97	.67	2	3, .02	3, .09	11, .14	1, .01		4 bark, .04 g; 1 unidentifiable
2269	125R4	11	Dalton	.15	.14					1, .01		

Continued on the next page

Table 6.2. *Continued*

Type Catalog Number	Unit	Level	Depth	Zone	Plant Weight (g)	Wood Weight (g)	Acorn Count, Weight (g)	Acorn Meat Count, Weight (g)	Black Walnut Count, Weight (g)	Hickory Count, Weight (g)	Walnut Family Count, Weight (g)	Persimmon Count, Weight (g)	Other
2283	135-140	1		Dalton	.41	.05	2, .02		5, .18	9, .14	1, .01		3 honey locust cf., .01 g; 1 unidentifiable, 2 unidentifiable,.01 g
2285	Block3	2		Dalton	2.20	.27	2	1	56, 1.23	34, .53	12, .12	6, .04	2 unidentifiable, .01 g
2286	Block3	3		Dalton	1.56	.95	5, .01	10, .12	5, .06	25, .35	2, .01	4, .02	2 bark, .02 g; 3 hazel, .01 g; 1 pitch; 4 unidentifiable, .01 g
2287	Block3	4		Dalton	1.00	.27		1	7, .18	32, .52	2, .02	1, .01	1 unidentifiable
2284	Block3	10		Dalton	1.43	.94			1, .06	32, .41	1, .01		5 sumac; 1 unidentifiable, .01 g

*Samples tentatively assigned to Dalton zone.

the screen samples acorn shell is poorly represented and hickory and black walnut are also sparse.

This contrasts with the materials found in the pinch samples, where black walnut and hickory represent the majority of nonwood plant taxa recovered. Acorn meats are regularly recovered, although in much lower quantities than the screen samples. A wider range of plant taxa is also present in the pinch samples. This includes persimmon, which appears regularly. Several fragments of hazelnut shell were also recovered, along with two grape seeds, one definite and one possible sumac seed, and three possible honey locust seed fragments.

In general, the plant remains recovered from the Dalton and Early Side-Notched zone at Stanfield-Worley indicate that the site's occupants extensively used nuts and supplemented their diets with fruits, particularly persimmon. Edible and weedy seeds are notably absent from the samples, although this may well be due to sampling error rather than lack of use by site occupants, as none of the samples were processed using floatation. Two grape seeds and one possible sumac seed were recovered from the pinch samples, indicating that recovery of smaller seeds from the samples is not entirely impossible, but the small size of these samples lowers the possibility of recovering rare taxa like weedy seeds. Cane was also identified in the samples, and likely served utilitarian purposes.

ROLLINS BLUFF SHELTER

The plant materials recovered from Rollins Bluff Shelter are listed in Table 6.3. The samples are dominated by hickory nutshell, which is ubiquitous (Table 6.4). Additional nut taxa include acorn shell, which occurs in nearly all samples, and black walnut, recovered in low numbers in roughly one-third of the samples. Acorn meats were identified in several samples.

Fruit taxa are represented by six fragments of persimmon seed, 11 grape seeds, one possible grape seed, and two sumac seeds. In addition, one wild legume, one possible squash rind fragment, and one possible common bean were recovered. The latter is intrusive, as bean is not recovered from Eastern Woodland sites until approximately 800 B.P., shortly after the advent of maize agriculture (Hart et al. 2002). It is not implausible, however, for the possible squash rind to be an early, weedy variety, which might have been used as a container or net float rather than a foodstuff (Fritz 2000:227; Prentice 1986; but see Cowan 1997:70–72).

Comparisons between the Dalton and Early Archaic period occupations

Table 6.3. Plant Materials Recovered from the Rollins Bluff Shelter Samples.

Context Catalog Number	Cut	Level	Depth (ft)	Zone	Period*	Plant Weight (g)	Wood Weight (g)	Acorn Count, Weight (g)	Acorn Meat Count, Weight (g)	Black Walnut Count, Weight (g)	Hickory Count, Weight (g)	Persimmon Count, Weight (g)	Other
Control Block 1													
127/132	1	1	0	D	E.A.	4.58	.38	2, .01			324, 4.12		1 grape; 3 pitch, .06 g; 1 wild legume; 3 unidentifiable, .01 g
136/137	1	1	0	D	E.A.	3.69	.33	2			280, 3.33		1 pitch, .01 g; 4 unidentifiable, .02 g
114	1	3	.4	D	E.A.	5.05	.93	15, .07			158, 3.89		1 black walnut cf., .01 g; 12 pitch, .09 g; 2 unidentifiable, .06 g
154/155	1	3	.4	D	E.A.	1.89	.13				119, 1.74		1 pitch, .01 g; 1 unidentifiable, .01 g
157	1	3	.4	D	E.A.	16.82	7.88	57, .14 g			572, 6.40	1	1 black walnut cf., .01 g; 1 bud; 1 pine cone; 230 pitch, 2.13 g; 36 unidentifiable, .26 g
133/138	1	4	.6	D	E.A.	4.55	.15	1		1, .01	375, 4.32		2 black walnut cf., .03 g; 1 grape; 3 pitch, .03 g; 1 unidentifiable, .01 g
146	1	4	.6	D	E.A.	1.42	.09	1			103, 1.27		1 black walnut cf., .03 g; 1 pitch, .01 g; 3 unidentifiable, .02 g

124/125	1	1	0	E	Dalton	.89	.08	2		1, .01	70, .79		1 grape cf. ; 1 pitch; 1 unidentifiable, .01 g; 2 unidentifiable seed
153	1	1	0	E	Dalton	2.02	.07	1		4, .05	203, 1.86		1 Walnut family, .01 g; 1 pitch, .02 g; 2 unidentifiable, .01 g; 1 unidentifiable seed
128/129	1	2	.2	E	Dalton	1.51	.05	3	3, .02	1, .01	149, 1.41		4 grape, .01 g; 1 pitch, .01 g; 1 unidentifiable; 4 unidentifiable seed
121/126	2	1	0	D	E.A.	3.59	.30	2, .01			229, 3.20		5 pitch, .06 g; 2 unidentifiable, .02 g
145/150	2	2	.2	D	E.A.	3.00	.13	1		1, .01	248, 2.79		2 pitch, .03 g; 6 unidentifiable, .04 g; 2 unidentifiable seed
158/159	2	1	0	D	E.A.	5.30	2.82	8, .03	1		156, 2.17		1 common bean cf., 0.01g; 1 pine cone; 25 pitch, .22 g; 4 unidentifiable, .05 g; 2 unidentifiable seed
160	2	1	0	D	E.A.	10.07	7.13	21, .05	8, .03		204, 1.81	3, .02	1 pine cone, .01 g; 82 pitch, .92 g; 16 unidentifiable, .10 g
122/123	2	1	0	E	Dalton	.44	.03		1, .01		40, .38	1	5 grape; 1 pitch, .01 g; 1 unidentifiable, .01 g; 2 unidentifiable seed
139/140	2	2	.2	E	Dalton	.36	.06	1			31, .28	1	1 pitch, .02 g; 1 unidentifiable
142/143	3	5	.8	C	E.A.	3.24	.86	3, .01		1, .01	178, 2.09		20 pitch, .22 g; 9 unidentifiable, .05 g

Continued on the next page

Table 6.3. *Continued*

Context Catalog Number	Cut	Level	Depth (ft)	Zone	Period*	Plant Weight (g)	Wood Weight (g)	Acorn Count, Weight (g)	Acorn Meat Count, Weight (g)	Black Walnut Count, Weight (g)	Hickory Count, Weight (g)	Persimmon Count, Weight (g)	Other
148/149	3	2	.2	D	E.A.	1.29	.28	4, .01			97, .97		20 pitch, .22 g; 9 unidentifable, .05 g
115/120	3	1	0	E	Dalton	1.35	.13				127, 1.18		2 pitch, .02 g; 2 unidentifiable, .02 g
118/141	3	3	.4	E	Dalton	.19	.01				19, .17		1 black walnut cf., .01 g; 1 unidentifiable
Control Block 2													
130/131		6	1	C	E.A.	4.02	.57	1		1, .01	248, 3.20		4 black walnut cf., .05 g; 9 pitch, .17 g; 5 unidentifiable, .02 g
151/156		1	0	D	E.A.	3.75	.41	3			270, 3.29		1 black walnut cf., .01 g; 6 unidentifiable, .04 g
Square 95L5													
119		16	60		Dalton	.73	.07				58, .64		1 pitch, .01 g; 1 unidentifiable, .01 g

112/113	16	60	Dalton	.44	.07	1		41, .35	1	2 pitch, .02 g; 1 unidentifiable; 1 unidentifiable seed
152	16	60	Dalton	1.31	.15		2, .06	103, 1.08		1 acorn cf.; 1 squash rind cf.; 3 unidentifiable, .02 g; 2 unidentified seed
116/117	17	64	Dalton	2.00	.09	1	5, .08	195, 1.73		1 black walnut cf.; 8 pitch, .09 g; 1 sumac; 1 unidentifiable, .01 g
144	18	68	Dalton	.87	.14		1, .01	57, .67		5 pitch, .05 g; 1 sumac; 1 unidentifiable

*E.A. stands for Early Archaic period.

Table 6.4. Ubiquity of Plant Remains in Samples from Rollins Bluff Shelter.

Taxon	Dalton Samples (N = 12)	Early Archaic Samples (N = 16)
Acorn shell	50%	94%
Acorn meat	17%	19%
Black walnut	50%	25%
Hickory	100%	100%
Grape	17%	13%
Persimmon	25%	13%
Squash rind cf.	8%	
Sumac	17%	
Wild legume		6%

at the site suggest several trends. While the density of wood relative to other plant materials does not change significantly between the two periods, as shown by the overlapping notches of the boxplots in Figure 6.1, Early Archaic samples do include higher values for the relative density of wood charcoal. This difference is not likely related to preservation issues; preservation of small and fragile taxa, such as seeds and acorn, seems to be similar for the two periods. An increased rate of plant deposition, related to an increase in the intensity of site use, may well be the case. Debitage increases significantly in the Early Archaic component (Stowe 1970), also suggesting more intensive use of the site.

In contrast, the relative density of hickory is significantly lower in Early Archaic samples, a shift overshadowed by the 100 percent ubiquity values. The boxplots for acorn shell show a slight decrease in use relative to other plants in the Early Archaic. The notches of the boxplots overlap slightly, however, so the trend is not statistically significant. The relative density of black walnut, which drops in Early Archaic samples, does coincide with its lower ubiquity for this period. Comparing the nut taxa among one another (Figure 6.2), it appears that acorn and hickory are used in similar quantities relative to each other in both periods; in other words, neither hickory nor acorn become more important than the other in the Early Archaic as compared to the Dalton period. In contrast, black walnut decreases in use relative to hickory in the Early Archaic.

Drawing on these patterns, it appears that the occupants' use of nut taxa, particularly hickory and black walnut, changed significantly from the Dalton

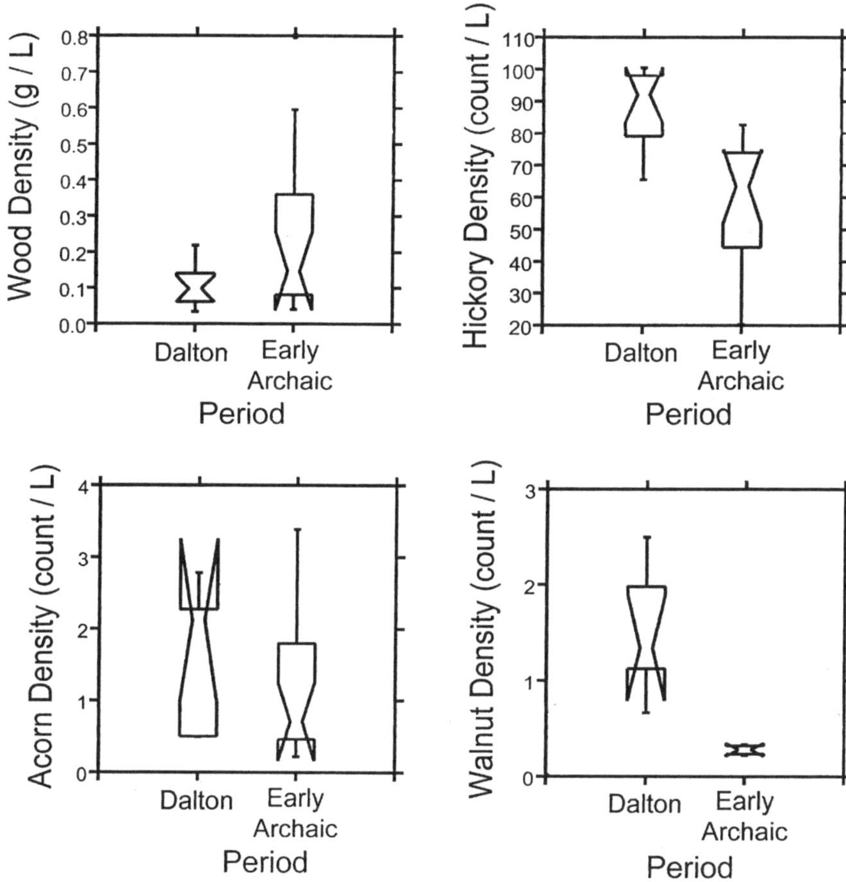

Figure 6.1. Boxplots comparing the relative densities of wood, hickory, acorn, and black walnut in floatation samples from Rollins Bluff Shelter.

to the Early Archaic period. This shift may be related to the nuts' consumption, processing and deposition, and/or use as a fuel source. Shifts in acorn use are not as clear. Acorn shell did not increase in use relative to other plants, but did have a higher ubiquity in the Early Archaic period. This suggests that the higher ubiquity may be related to changes in use of the site at this time. Increased use of the shelter, along with an increased deposition of plant materials in general, may account for an increase in ubiquity. If this is the case, the decrease in the ubiquity of black walnut is even more significant.

The relatively narrow range of taxa recovered from the Rollins Bluff Shelter is notable. While hickory, acorn, and black walnut appear in the Rol-

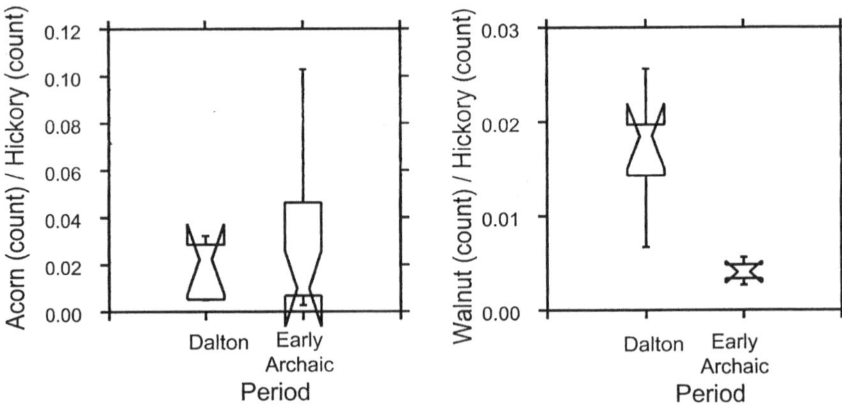

Figure 6.2. Boxplots comparing the relative quantities of acorn and hickory, and black walnut and hickory, in samples from Rollins Bluff Shelter.

lins samples, hazel nutshell was not recovered, unlike the Stanfield-Worley samples. Similarly, the major fruit taxa are present, namely persimmon, grape, and sumac, but the only other taxa recovered were a single wild legume and possible squash rind fragment. While smaller seeds may have been adversely affected by the screening of materials prior to floatation, it seems likely that if the site's occupants used them in significant quantities, they would have been recovered along with the grape, sumac, and wild legume. I suggest instead that the occupants of Rollins Bluff Shelter used a relatively limited range of nut, fruit, and edible seed taxa.

LAGRANGE BLUFF SHELTER

Plant remains recovered from LaGrange are listed in Table 6.5. Samples that derive from the 1/4-inch screen are best represented by wood, black walnut, and hickory nutshell. Four acorn meats and two persimmon seeds were also recovered, but small and fragile taxa, such as acorn shell and smaller seeds, are missing. This is highlighted by the regular, although low, recovery of acorn shell in the floatation samples, as well as by the significant number and range of smaller taxa in these samples. In addition to hazel nutshell, these include grape, mulberry, sumac, and possible maypop among fruits; chenopod, a seed from the Grass family, a possible cheno-am, possible wild bean, and other wild legumes representing edible seeds; and tentatively identified members of the Mustard and Composite families.

Although the number of samples, particularly floatation samples, is small,

Table 6.5. Plant Remains Recovered from the LaGrange Bluff Shelter Samples.

Type Catalog Number	Unit	Level	Period*	Zone	Plant Weight (g)	Wood Weight (g)	Acorn Count, Weight (g)	Acorn Meat Count, Weight (g)	Black Walnut Count, Weight (g)	Hickory Count, Weight (g)	Walnut Family Count, Weight (g)	Persimmon Count, Weight (g)	Other
Screen Samples													
71	S5E11	12	E. A.		1.00	.49				7, .51			
70.5	S5E11	13	E. A.		.04	.04							
49	S5E11	15	E. A.	D	.27	.27							
47/74	S10E5	13	E. A.	C	.08	—			1, .01	1, .07			
88/89	S10E5	14	E. A.	D	.43	.07			4, .27	1, .09			
78/79	S10E5	15	E. A.	D	.32	.06				2, .26			
42/80/81	S10E5	16	Dalton	D	.59	—			8, .19	11, .38	3, .02		
54/82	S10E5	17	Dalton	D	.85	.02		3, .10	14, .57	5, .15	1, .01		
43/83	S10E5	18	Dalton	D	.39	—			5, .39				
44	S10E5	16	Dalton	E	.35	—			8, .29	2, .03	5, .03		
51	S10E5	17	Dalton	E	.10	—			4, .05	7, .05			
41	S10E9	15	E. A.	D	.94	—			10, .56	15, .38			
77/84	S10E10	12	E. A.	B	.69	.07				16, .62			

Continued on the next page

Table 6.5. *Continued*

Type Catalog Number	Unit	Level	Period*	Zone	Plant Weight (g)	Wood Weight (g)	Acorn Count, Weight (g)	Acorn Meat Count, Weight (g)	Black Walnut Count, Weight (g)	Hickory Count, Weight (g)	Walnut Family Count, Weight (g)	Persimmon Count, Weight (g)	Other
61	S10E10	13	E.A.	B	.40	—			1, .18	5, .22			
46	S10E10	10	E. A.	C	1.00	1.00							
75	S10E10	13	E. A.	C	.48	—				8, .48			
48	S10E10	14	E. A.	C	.49	—			1;, .36	3, .13			
52/53	S10E10	16	Dalton	D	.95	—			4, .21	14, .73		1, .01	
55	S10E10	17	Dalton	D	.54	—			2, .04	15, .50			
96	S10E10	15	Dalton	E	.11	—				1, .11			
50	S10E10	19	Dalton	E	.07	—				1, .07			
40	S10E10	20	Dalton	F	.04	—				1, .03			1 pitch, .01 g
76	S10E11	12	E. A.	C	.30	—				1, .30			
87	S10E11			D	.21	—				2, .21			
Floatation Samples													
106	S10E10	14	E. A.	B	.32	.04	1			26, .26			1 wild legume; 6 unidentifiable, .02 g; 4 unidentifiable seed

107	S10E10	14	E. A.	B	.51	.03	1		2, .03	34, .37	7, .07		1 unidentifiable, .01 g
105	S10E10	15	E. A.	C	1.33	.19	3, .01			89, 1.10	1, .01		1 Composite family cf.; 1 mulberry; 2 unidentifiable, .02 g; 2 unidentifiable seed
111	S10E10	Burial 1	E. A.	C	1.21	.28	1			74, .86			1 acorn cf.; 1 bedstraw; 1 cheno-am cf.; 1 grape; 9 unidentifiable, .07 g; 2 unidentified seeds
104	S10E5	14	E. A.	D	1.45	.10	3	6, .13	34, .67	27, .28	10, .11	15, .14	1 chenopod; 3 chenopod cf.; 1 grape; 1 hazel; 1 wild bean cf.; 1 sumac; 7 wild legume; 7 unidentifiable, .02 g; 7 unidentifiable seed
103	S10E5	15	E. A.	D	.86	.04	4, .01		14, .27	47, .53	1		2 chenopod; 1 chenopod cf.; 1 grape; 1 maypop cf.; 5 wild legume; 2 unidentifiable, .01 g; 1 unidentifiable seed; 1 unidentified seed

Continued on the next page

Table 6.5. *Continued*

Type Catalog Number	Unit	Level	Period*	Zone	Plant Weight (g)	Wood Weight (g)	Acorn Count, Weight (g)	Acorn Meat Count, Weight (g)	Black Walnut Count, Weight (g)	Hickory Count, Weight (g)	Walnut Family Count, Weight (g)	Persimmon Count, Weight (g)	Other
101	S10E5	16	Dalton	D	1.67	.14	10, .02		30, .57	71, .84	6, .06		1 chenopod; 1 hazel; 3 wild legume; 16 unidentifiable, .04 g; 7 unidentifiable seed
102	S10E5	16	Dalton	D	1.85	.09	5, .01		29, .67	92, .92	6, .06	1	2 chenopod cf.; 2 grape; 1 Grass family; 1 hazel, .01 g; 1 sumac; 9 unidentifiable, .09 g; 6 unidentfiable seed
99	S10E10	19	Dalton	E	.36	.01	1		7, .13	11, .12	4, .07		1 hazel, .01 g; 1 Mustard family cf.; 2 pitch, .01 g; 1 sumac; 2 unidentifiable; 3 unidentifiable seed; 1 unidentified, .01 g
100	S10E10	19	Dalton	E	.13	.01	1		1, .01	12, .09	1, .01		1 pitch, .01 g; 5 unidentifiable seed
98	S10E10	22	Dalton	F	.01	negl.				1, .01			

*E.A. stands for Early Archaic period.

Table 6.6. Ubiquity of Plant Remains in Samples from LaGrange.

Taxon	Screen Samples: Dalton (N = 10)	Screen Samples: Early Archaic (N = 10)	Floatation Samples: Dalton (N = 5)	Floatation Samples: Early Archaic (N = 6)
Acorn shell			80%	100%
Acorn meat	10%			17%
Black walnut	70%	50%	80%	50%
Hazel			60%	17%
Hickory	90%	100%	100%	100%
Grape			20%	50%
Persimmon	10%		20%	17%
Sumac			40%	17%
Chenopod			20%	33%
Wild legume			20%	50%
Other seeds			60%	67%

some brief quantitative comparisons can be made. Not surprisingly, ubiquity values demonstrate that smaller and more fragile items, including most seeds, acorn shell, and hazel, are underrepresented in the 1/4-inch screen samples (Table 6.6). Hickory is nearly 100 percent ubiquitous at the site. Among floatation samples, acorn also has a high ubiquity, present in all but one sample. These high values likely reflect their importance to the site's occupants. Black walnut and hazelnut appear to decrease in use from the Dalton to Early Archaic occupation, but again the number of samples is small. Fruits and seed taxa do not seem to change significantly through time, although sumac may decrease somewhat, while grape and wild legumes may increase slightly. Preservation does not appear to be a factor in these ubiquity values, as small seeds are recovered in similar numbers from both Dalton and Early Archaic samples. Possible differences in rates of deposition, either of sediment or of plant materials, between the two components are unclear.

Boxplots of relative densities of taxa recovered from the floatation samples demonstrate greater similarities than differences between the Early Archaic and Dalton samples at LaGrange (Figure 6.3). The notches for wood, hickory, walnut, and acorn overlap significantly. Of course, this could be related to the low number of samples available. It is of note, however, that the possible drop in black walnut suggested by the ubiquity values of both screen and floatation samples is not borne out by the relative densities of the floatation samples.

In general, there seem to be more similarities between the Dalton and

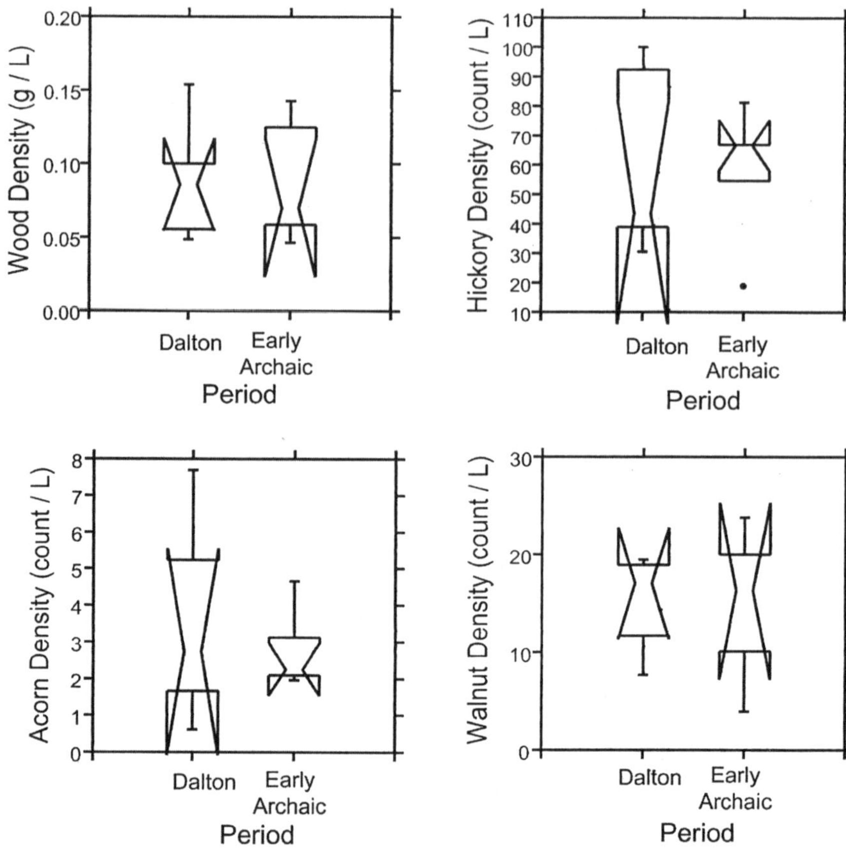

Figure 6.3. Boxplots comparing densities of wood, hickory, black walnut, and acorn in floatation samples from LaGrange.

Early Archaic samples than not, reflected by ubiquity and relative density measures. In addition to hickory, black walnut, acorn, and hazel, both Dalton and Early Archaic occupants of LaGrange apparently used a wide variety of fruits and wild seeds. These include persimmon, grape, and sumac, as well as chenopod and wild legumes. This variety of plant foods stands in contrast to the more narrow range of foods seen at Stanfield-Worley and Rollins Bluff shelters.

DUST CAVE

The samples from Dust Cave allow us to examine early foodways in much broader fashion than those from the previous sites. Not only are more samples available for analysis, the samples also come from various contexts, including features and floatation columns, and from several components within the site. In addition, more information is available for each sample: the volume of each sample was recorded, and detailed notes were taken for each feature. In addition, Homsey's (2004) geomorphological and geochemical analysis of features is available for comparison. The Dust Cave samples are thus amenable to a wider range of analyses.

I discuss the column samples separately from the feature samples. The latter represent activities that are relatively isolated in time and space. The features include, for example, plant remains from rock-lined hearths that may have been used on several occasions, or charcoal pits that were used and filled over a relatively short period of time. Column samples, however, represent general contexts, or an aggregate of plant remains that were swept up, trampled about, bioturbated out of features, and mixed into the matrix of anthropogenic sediments that comprise the cave's deposits. These aggregate deposits may be considered to provide an averaged account of plant use at the site, while the features reflect use of plants that is bounded both in time and space.

Column Samples

The plant remains recovered from the Dust Cave column samples are listed in Table 6.7. A cursory glance shows that hickory is the dominant taxon: not only is it found in all samples, it also often outnumbers other taxa within samples. Hackberry, however, is also frequently recovered, also in significant quantities. Additional nut taxa present include acorn, black walnut, and hazelnut. Interestingly, nutmeats from the Walnut family (hickory or black walnut) were recovered, as well as acorn meats. Twelve fragments of nutshell were also assigned to the Beech family; I could not determine whether these were acorn, chestnut, or beechnut. Fruits other than hackberry include the familiar grape, persimmon, and sumac, as well as tentatively identified black gum and nightshade. In addition, a range of smaller seed taxa are present in the samples, including chenopod, wild legumes, bedstraw, cheno-am, poke, purslane, smartweed, and stargrass.

Comparisons of ubiquity for the column samples demonstrate several trends through time (Table 6.8). Of note is the 100 percent ubiquity of hickory nutshell, which reflects its importance to the cave's occupants. Acorn shell shows a notable increase in ubiquity after the Late Paleoindian component, although this is not necessarily the case for acorn meats. Black walnut may decrease through time, although it is important to note that its absence from Early Side-Notched and Kirk Stemmed samples is not significant, as

Table 6.7. Plant Materials Recovered from Dust Cave Column Samples.

Unit: Bag Number	Level	Depth (cm)	Zone	Period*	Plant Weight (g)	Wood Weight (g)	Acorn Count, Weight (g)	Black Walnut Count, Weight (g)	Hickory Count, Weight (g)	Hackberry Count, Weight (g)	Hazel Count, Weight (g)	Chenopod Count, Weight (g)	Other
N60W65:													
5176	40	315	P2	KS	11.95	.74	16, .02		980, 11.01	19, .07		3	16 Walnut family nutmeat, .06 g; 1 poke cf.; 27 unidentifiable, .06 g
5230	42	325	P3e	KS	8.16	.73	12, .03		1021, 7.14	18, .16			4 persimmon, .03 g; 4 sumac; 12 unidentifiable, .07 g; 13 unidentifiable seed
5319	44	335	P3e	KS	6.03	1.70	9, .02		342, 4.19	7, .04			1 grape; 2 wild legume; 18 unidentifiable, .08 g; 1 unidentifiable seed
5340	46	345	P2	KS	4.64	.59	46, .10		285, 3.90	5, .04	1		1 persimmon seed coat; 2 sumac; 1 unidentifiable, .01 g; 3 unidentifiable seed; 2 unidentified seeds
5512	48	355	P14	KS	.86	.04	10, .01		70, .81	1			2 wild legume; 1 unidentifiable seed
5647	50	365	Q4	ESN/KS	1.83	.06	24, .05		121, 1.57	34, .14			1 acorn cf.; 2 unidentifiable, 0.01 g; 1 unidentifiable seed

6131	54	385	R3	ESN	.28	.10	1	16, .14	12, .04		8 unidentifiable
6152	54	385	R3e	ESN	.82	.25	8, .02	24, .23	66, .29	7	2 grape; 1 grape meat cf.; 50 unidentifiable, .03 g
6159	55	390	R3e	ESN	.97	.31	7, .02	24, .24	58, .35	5	43 unidentifiable, .05 g; 6 unidentifiable seed
6192	56	395	R3f	ESN	1.32	.53	7, .01	46, .42	61, .31	2	3 bedstraw; 3 chenopod cf.; 31 unidentifiable, .05 g; 1 unidentifiable seed
6212	57	400	R3f	ESN	1.11	.30		36, .28	57, .41	5	54 unidentifiable, .12 g
6296	58	405	R3f	ESN	.61	.16	1	14, .08	44, .27	7	6 chenopod cf.; 1 persimmon cf., .03 g; 1 sumac; 35 unidentifiable, .07 g
6343	59	410	R3f	ESN	.54	.26	5, .01	7, .02	51, .23	4	4 chenopod cf.; 13 unidentifiable, .02 g
6360	60	415	R3f	ESN	.53	.22	6, .01	2, .02	35, .25	4	4 chenopod cf.; 12 unidentifiable, .03 g
6378	61	420	R3f	ESN	.39	.22	2	5, .03	22, .11	5	4 chenopod cf.; 2 pine nut cf., .02 g; 4 unidentifiable, .01 g
6379	61	420	T5	LP	.42	.39		2, .01	5, .02	3	2 chenopod cf.; 3 poke cf.; 3 unidentifiable
6401	62	425	T5	LP	.13	.11	1	2, .01	2, .01	1	8 chenopod cf.; 1 stargrass; 2 unidentifiable; 1 unidentifiable seed

Continued on the next page

Table 6.7. *Continued*

Unit: Bag Number	Level	Depth (cm)	Zone	Period*	Plant Weight (g)	Wood Weight (g)	Acorn Count, Weight (g)	Black Walnut Count, Weight (g)	Hickory Count, Weight (g)	Hackberry Count, Weight (g)	Hazel Count, Weight (g)	Chenopod Count, Weight (g)	Other
6402	62	425	U3	LP	.33	.19		1, .01	8, .07	11, .05		2	5 chenopod cf.; 1 stargrass; 8 unidentifiable, .01 g
6431	63	430	U3	LP	.53	.17	4, .01	11, .16	23, .17	3, .01		3	3 chenopod cf.; 1 stargrass; 13 unidentifiable, .01 g
6465	64	435	U3	LP	.49	.30		2, .03	25, .14				3 unidentifiable, .02 g
6502	65	440	U8	LP	.77	.56			37, .20			2	5 unidentifiable, .01 g
6531	66	445	U8	LP	.30	.10		2, .02	26, .17			1	1 acorn cf.; 1 acorn meat, .01 g; 1 unidentifiable seed
6551	66	445	U6	LP	.14	.01	1		16, .13	1		1	1 chenopod cf.
6554	67	450	U6	LP	.09	.04	1		8, .05			1	2 chenopod cf.; 1 nightshade cf.; 1 poke cf.; 1 unidentifiable
6557	68	455	U6	LP	negl.	negl.			1				
N62W62:													
6565	50	320	P18	KS	2.40	.28	2		149, 1.93	21, .16			1 grape; 1 persimmon, .01 g; 1 pine cone, .01 g; 1 sumac; 1 wild legume; 7 unidentifiable, .01 g; 8 unidentified seed

6583	51	325	P18	KS	1.52	.15	10, .01		113, 1.20	20, .14	1		5 unidentifiable, .02 g; 1 unidentifiable seed
6592	52	330	P18	KS	.91	.06	1		70, .46	19, .15			3 acorn meat, .02 g; 1 Beech family shell (acorn or chestnut); 14 Walnut family nutmeat, .21 g; 3 unidentifiable, .01 g
6606	53	335	Q5	ESN/KS	.39	.04	1	3, .03	28, .18	12, .13			1 chenopod cf.; 1 persimmon; 1 pitch, .01 g; 3 wild legume; 2 unidentifiable; 1 unidentifiable seed
6647	54	340	Q5	ESN/KS	.85	.53	1		24, .21	17, .08			7 acorn meat, .01 g; 1 cheno-am; 2 unidentifiable, .02 g; 3 unidentifiable seed
6690	55	345	Q5	ESN/KS	.20	.10	1		7, .05	14, .05			1 unidentifiable
6695	56	350	Q5	ESN/KS	.52	.22	4, .01		8, .08	44, .19			4 acorn meat, .02 g; 5 grape; 8 unidentifiable seeds; 1 unidentified seed
6716	57	355	Q5	ESN/KS	1.56	.24	9, .01	10, .13	131, .76	63, .35		10	2 black walnut cf., .03 g; 4 cheno-am; 3 grape; 2 pitch; 29 unidentifiable, .04 g; 22 unidentifiable seed

Continued on the next page

Table 6.7. *Continued*

Unit: Bag Number	Level	Depth (cm)	Zone	Period*	Plant Weight (g)	Wood Weight (g)	Acorn Count, Weight (g)	Black Walnut Count, Weight (g)	Hickory Count, Weight (g)	Hackberry Count, Weight (g)	Hazel Count, Weight (g)	Chenopod Count, Weight (g)	Other
6735	58	360	Q5	ESN/KS	.45	.06	14, .01		24, .13	27, .11		1	1 acorn cf., 7 acorn meat, .06; 5 pitch,.02 g; 1 sumac cf.; 6 Walnut family nutmeat, .05 g; 30 unidentifiable, .01 g; 1 unidentifiable, seed
6749	59	365	R1	ESN	.58	.14	1, .01		5, .01	89, .42			2 acorn cf.; 2 chenopod cf.; 14 unidentifiable,; 11 unidentifiable, seed
6825	60	370	R1	ESN	.69	.06	1		12, .04	93, .49		3	5 acorn meat, .03 g; 2 chenopod cf.; 9 pitch, .07 g; 1 unidentifiable
6854	61	375	R1	ESN	.23	.12	1		1, .01	20, .10			1 chenopod cf.; 1 unidentifiable
6870	62	380	Q5	ESN/KS	.08	.05	4, .01		1	6, .02			1 acorn meat; 1 chenopod cf.; 1 unidentifiable; 10 unidentifiable seed

6886	63	385	Q5a	ESN/KS	.39	.19	6	1	47, .20			10 Beech family shell (acorn or chestnut); 1 pitch; 12 unidentifiable
6983	64	390	Q5a	ESN/KS	.38	.05	1	2	64, .31			4 chenopod cf.; 2 pine cone, .01 g; 3 poke; 25 unidentifiable, .01 g; 21 unidentifiable seed
7037	65	395	T2h	LP	.65	.03	3	6, .04	119, .57		5	1 cheno-am; 3 pitch; 1 purslane; 18 unidentifiable, .01 g; 16 unidentifiable seed
7095	66	400	T2h	LP	3.36	.07	1	1, .01	222, 3.26		1	1 cheno-am; 4 pitch, .02 g; 3 unidentifiable; 3 unidentifiable seed
7135	67	405	T10	LP	.83	.19	1	5, .02	131, .60		17	15 chenopod cf.; 2 smartweed; 3 Walnut family nutmeat, .02 g; 27 unidentifiable; 8 unidentifiable seed
7172	68	410	T2g	LP	.51	.12	4	6, .04	52, .29	5, .02		5 Walnut family nutmeat, .04 g; 4 unidentifiable
7189	69	415	T10b	LP	.71	.09	1	9, .03	90, .56	4, .01	1	1 bedstraw; 3 pitch, .01 g; 8 unidentifiable, .01 g; 2 unidentifiable seed; 2 unidentified seed

Continued on the next page

Table 6.7. *Continued*

Unit: Bag Number	Level	Depth (cm)	Zone	Period*	Plant Weight (g)	Wood Weight (g)	Acorn Count, Weight (g)	Black Walnut Count, Weight (g)	Hickory Count, Weight (g)	Hackberry Count, Weight (g)	Hazel Count, Weight (g)	Chenopod Count, Weight (g)	Other
7250	70	420	T10b	LP	1.19	.01	1		8, .10	140, .94	8, .02		1 pitch; 29 Walnut family nutmeat, .06 g; 26 unidentifiable, .06 g; 2 unidentifiable seed; 3 unidentified seed
7288	71	425	U1	LP	.83	.14			19, .16	48, .40	17, .13	1	1 grape; 1 pitch; 6 unidentifiable; 1 unidentifiable seed; 1 unidentified seed
7314	72	430	U1	LP	.20	.07	6		4, .04	8, .03	1	1	1 acorn meat; 1 acorn meat cf.; 7 pitch, .05 g; 8 unidentifiable, .01 g; 7 unidentifiable seed; 1 unidentified seed
7356	73	435	U2a	LP	.89	.07	8	1, .02	29, .34	56, .38	1	2	8 pitch, .05 g; 11 unidentifiable, .02 g; 10 unidentifiable seed; 2 unidentified seed, .01 g
7396	74	440	U2	LP	.20	.04		2, .02	16, .11	6, .02			1 hazel cf.; 3 pitch, .01 g; 7 unidentifiable seed

7426	75	445	U2a	LP	.27	.05		2, .15	6, .05	3, .02		2	15 chenopod cf.; 1 pitch; 1 wild legume; 1 unidentifiable; 3 unidentifiable seed
7429	75	445	U2	LP	.05	.02		1, .01	3, .02			1	1 chenopod cf.
7443	76	450	U2a	LP	.11	.01		2, .05	6, .04	2, .01		4	8 chenopod cf.; 1 unidentifiable; 1 unidentifiable seed
7484	76	455	U2a	LP	.06	negl.		1, .01	7, .04	2, .01			10 chenopod cf.
7496	78	460	U2c	LP	negl.	negl.			1				2 unidentifiable; 1 unidentifiable seed
N62W64:													
944	32	430	T1	LP	.57	.16		1, .03	10, .05	69, .25		5	1 grape cf., .01 g; 1 thin hickory cf.; 18 unidentifiable, .07 g; 3 unidentifiable seed
965	33	435	T1a	LP	.29	.01			2	290, .26			1 acorn cf.; 3 pitch, .02 g; 15 unidentifiable seed
980	34	440	T1a	LP	.48	.02			1	116, .36			20 unidentifiable, .10 g; 2 unidentifiable seed
981	34	440	T1	LP	.25	.08		1, .01	11, .06	44, .05			4 pitch, .04 g; 12 poke cf.; 4 unidentifiable, .01 g; 5 unidentifiable seed
989	35	445	T1	LP	1.46	.13	1		107, 1.32		1, .01		1 unidentifiable
999	36	450	T1	LP	.17	.07			16, .10				1 purslane cf.; 3 unidentifiable seed; 2 unidentified

Continued on the next page

Table 6.7. *Continued*

Unit: Bag Number	Level	Depth (cm)	Zone	Period*	Plant Weight (g)	Wood Weight (g)	Acorn Count, Weight (g)	Black Walnut Count, Weight (g)	Hickory Count, Weight (g)	Hackberry Count, Weight (g)	Hazel Count, Weight (g)	Chenopod Count, Weight (g)	Other
1012	37	455	T1	LP	.34	.03			37, .28	10, .01			4 bark/pine cone; 1 pitch, .01 g; 7 poke cf.; 4 unidentifiable, .01 g; 1 unidentifiable seed
1022	38	460	U	LP	1.99	.10		39, .93	93, .92	12, .01			3 pitch, .03 g; 1 stargrass; 1 unidentifiable; 40 unidentifiable seed
1036	39	465	U2	LP	.32	.04	1		4, .02	152, .23			1 Beech family shell (chestnut or beechnut); 1 pitch, .03 g; 3 unidentifiable seed
1049	40	470	U2	LP	.03	.01			4, .02	3			1 pitch; 9 poke cf.; 2 unidentifiable seed
1049.1	40	470	U2	LP	.06	.01			4, .03	6, .01		1	10 hackberry cf.; 2 pitch, .01 g; 5 unidentifiable seed

*KS = Kirk Stemmed; ESN/KS = Early Side-Notched/Kirk Stemmed; ESN = Early Side-Notched; LP = Late Paleoindian.

Table 6.8. Ubiquity of Plant Remains in Column Samples from Dust Cave.

Taxon	Late Paleo. (N = 36)	E. Side-Notched (N = 12)	ESN/Kirk Stemmed (N = 10)	Kirk Stemmed (N = 8)
Acorn shell	39%	92%	100%	100%
Acorn meat	6%	8%	40%	13%
Black walnut	36%		20%	
Hazel	19%			25%
Hickory	100%	100%	100%	100%
Walnut family nutmeat	8%		10%	25%
Grape	3%	8%	20%	25%
Hackberry	75%	100%	100%	100%
Persimmon			10%	38%
Sumac		8%		38%
Chenopod	56%	75%	20%	13%
Wild legume	3%		10%	38%

black walnut is recovered in feature samples from these components (see below). Similarly, no straightforward trend is apparent for hazel.

Among fruit taxa, hackberry is 100 percent ubiquitous in all but the Late Paleoindian samples, where its ubiquity value is still high. The remaining fruits show a somewhat more plausible increase through time, from values below 10 percent for the Late Paleoindian and Early Side-Notched samples to 25 percent or above for the Kirk Stemmed component. Wild legume shows a similar increase through time, but the ubiquity of chenopod shifts in the opposite direction, dropping from above 50 percent to 20 percent or below after the Early Side-Notched component.

While differences in preservation between the components are probably not a significant factor (small seeds are found in all samples, and the excellent preservation of bone—even fish scales—in all zones speaks to this), different rates of deposition influence the ubiquity values for the column samples. As shown in Table 6.9, the components represent varying spans of time—from 300 to 1,500 years—and vary in average thickness from 15 to 54 cm. To better understand the ubiquity values, these sedimentation rates must be taken into account.

To estimate sedimentation rates for the Dust Cave components, I take the average depth of each and divide by its estimated time span to give "years per cm." These suggest that the mixed Early Side-Notched/Kirk Stemmed com-

Table 6.9. Sedimentation Rates for the Components at Dust Cave.

Component	Avg. thickness (cm)[a]	Date range (cal. B.P.)[b]	Years	Years/cm	Years/L
Kirk Stemmed	54	9570–7800	1770	32.7	13.1
Mixed ESN/KS	16	10,200–9570	630	40.0	16.0
Early Side-Notched	23	11,300–10,800	500	22.1	8.86
Late Paleoindian	40	12,650–11,300	1350	34.1	13.6

[a] Derived from the profile drawings given in Sherwood 2001:Figures 8.2, 8.3, and 8.12, and compared with Sherwood's (2001) estimated zone thickness.

[b] Derived from the calibrated radiocarbon dates for the zones given in Sherwood et al. 2004:Table 1.

ponent had a relatively slower sedimentation rate than the other zones. This is exaggerated, however, due to the nature of Zone Q. A disconformity in the deposits between Zone Q and the underlying Zone R (Early Side-Notched component) points to an event(s) that eroded sediments from the cave, apparently removing deposits dating between 10,800 and 10,200 cal B.P. (Sherwood 2001; Sherwood et al. 2004). Zone Q was thus presumably thicker at some point, and the sedimentation rate should probably be more similar to the other zones. The estimate given here is still informative, however.

The sedimentation rates for the Kirk Stemmed and Late Paleoindian components are similar, suggesting that their ubiquity values can be directly compared. The Early Side-Notched component has a slightly higher sedimentation rate, so that if plant remains are being deposited at the same rate as in previous components, fewer plant remains per volume of sediment should be expected. Thus the increases seen in ubiquity, for example for acorn and chenopod, may be understated.

Possible changes in plant use through time can be further explored in boxplots of plant density by component (Figure 6.4). These demonstrate a significant increase in the quantity of plant materials recovered per liter after the Late Paleoindian period, and particularly during the Kirk Stemmed occupation. However, density ratios do not take into account different sedimentation rates; a liter of sediment from one zone can represent a much different time span than a liter from another. Each of the column samples is hypothetically 50-x-50-x-5-cm in size, or 12.5 liters in volume. Dividing, this gives approximately 12.5 liters per 5 cm, or 2.5 liters/cm. "Years per liter" can be calculated by dividing "years per cm" (see above) by 2.5 liters/cm

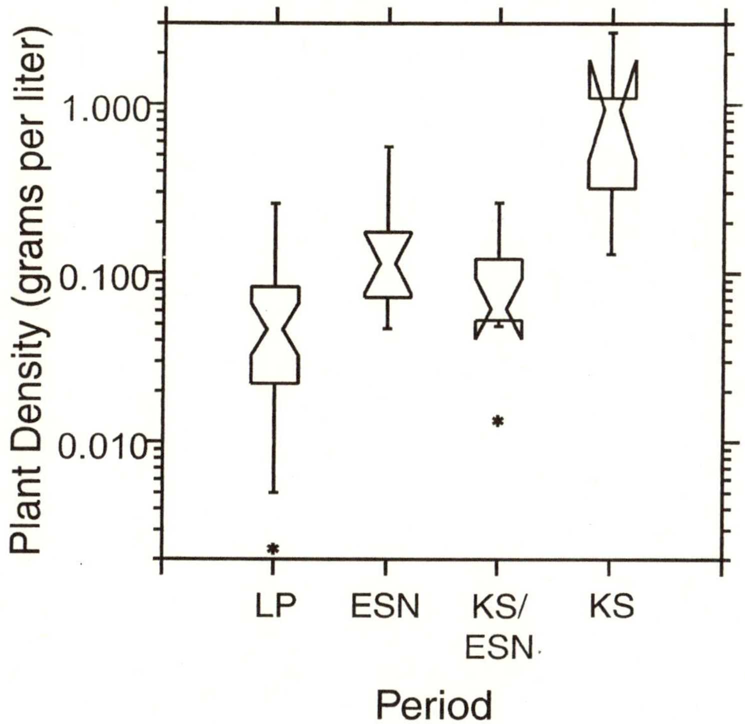

Figure 6.4. Boxplot comparing plant density by component in Dust Cave column samples.

(Table 6.9). The density of plant materials (plant weight in grams/volume in liters) can then be divided by "years per liter" to give an estimated "plants per year."

Boxplots of "plant density per year" by component (Figure 6.5) are quite similar to the plant density boxplots (Figure 6.4), but further emphasize differences between the components, particularly the Late Paleoindian and Early Side-Notched. A marked increase through time in the quantity of plants recovered is still apparent. The increase may be related to more intensive use of plant foods at the site, or more intensive occupation of the cave, which may include more frequent visits and/or longer stays. Also notable is the drop in the density of plant materials during the mixed Early Side-Notched/Kirk Stemmed component. This is likely related to the nature of this zone (Zone Q), which appears to represent a time of relatively sparse occupation (Sherwood 2001:360). However, it is also possible that the "years per cm," and therefore the denominator used in the ratio, is overestimated for

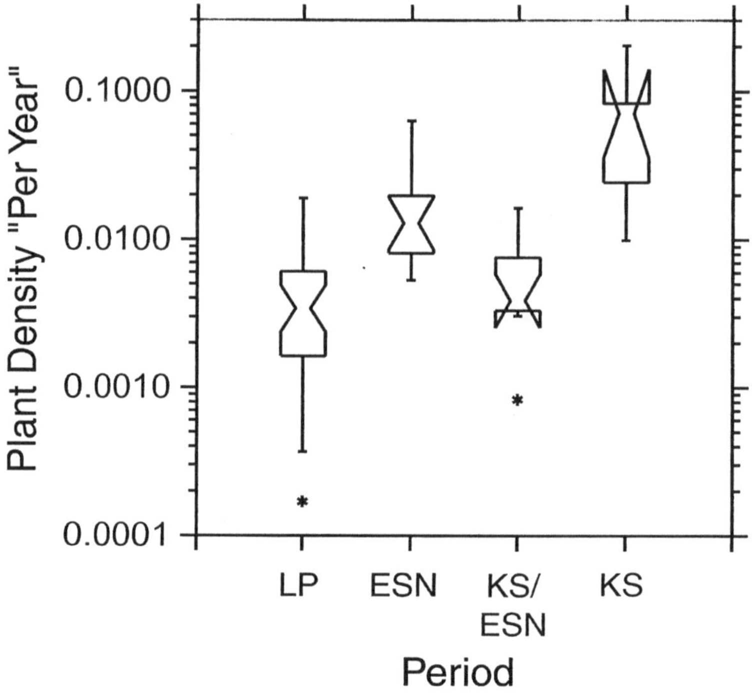

Figure 6.5. Boxplots comparing plant density "per year" by component in the Dust Cave column samples.

the mixed Early Side-Notched/Kirk Stemmed component, unduly exaggerating the differences between it and the other components.

The low density of plant remains recovered in the Late Paleoindian period may be related to differences in depositional history as much as intensity of cave occupation. Micromorphological studies of these deposits indicate significant fluvial activity at the site during the Late Paleoindian period (Sherwood 2001). As such, carbonized materials may have been redeposited within and/or swept out of the cave. The recovery of numerous small seeds from this component, however, is difficult to explain in light of this. If fluvial activities have significantly affected these early deposits, the presence of such a variety of seed taxa in the Late Paleoindian component is that much more remarkable.

It is also instructive to review the ubiquity values in light of the plant densities. Because the quantity of plant materials increases over time, the effective sample size increases, and the likelihood of finding rare items increases. The increase in ubiquity of "rare," or smaller and more fragile, items such as acorn shell and seeds may thus be related to the increase in plant materials re-

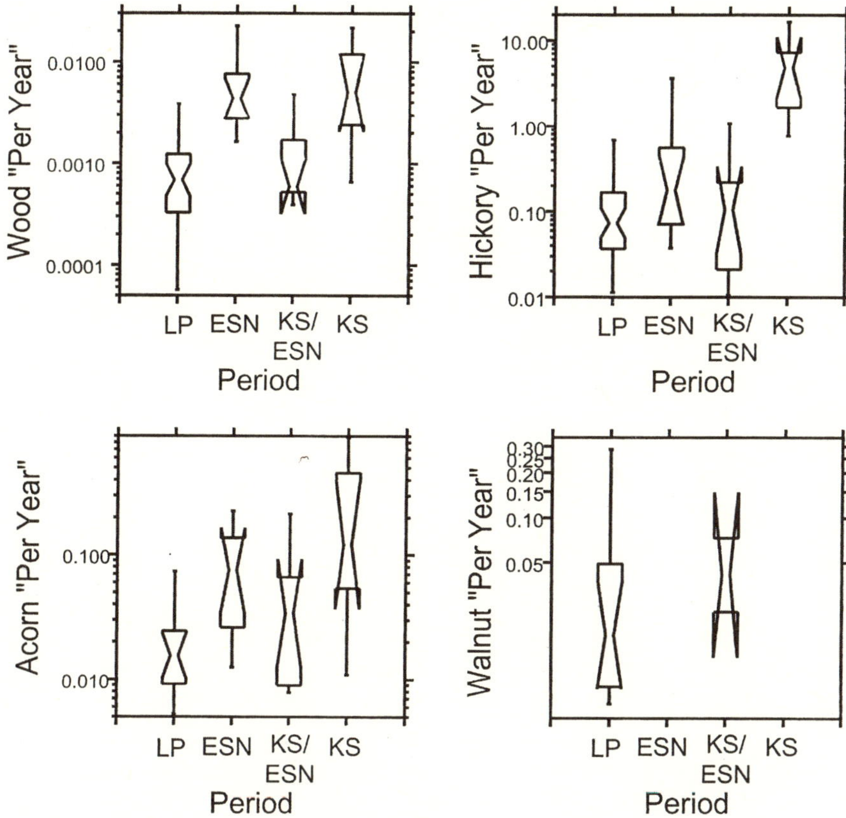

Figure 6.6. Boxplots comparing the density "per year" of wood, hickory, acorn, and black walnut in column samples from Dust Cave.

covered. The decrease through time of taxa such as chenopod is also notable, apparently unrelated to any increase in effective sample size.

The densities of various taxa also show an increase through time, which is not particularly surprising. The density of wood "per year" increases significantly in the Early Side-Notched and again in the Kirk Stemmed component, although there is overlap between the Late Paleoindian and mixed Early Side-Notched/Kirk Stemmed samples (Figure 6.6). A similar pattern is seen for acorn. As mentioned above, this pattern may be related in part to fluvial processes that may have washed these lighter, more fragile items away. Hickory, however, does not increase significantly until the Kirk Stemmed component, where its density rises by a degree of magnitude.

Changes in the density of black walnut are less clear, due in part to its recovery from only two components. Similarly, the low numbers of hazel, fruits,

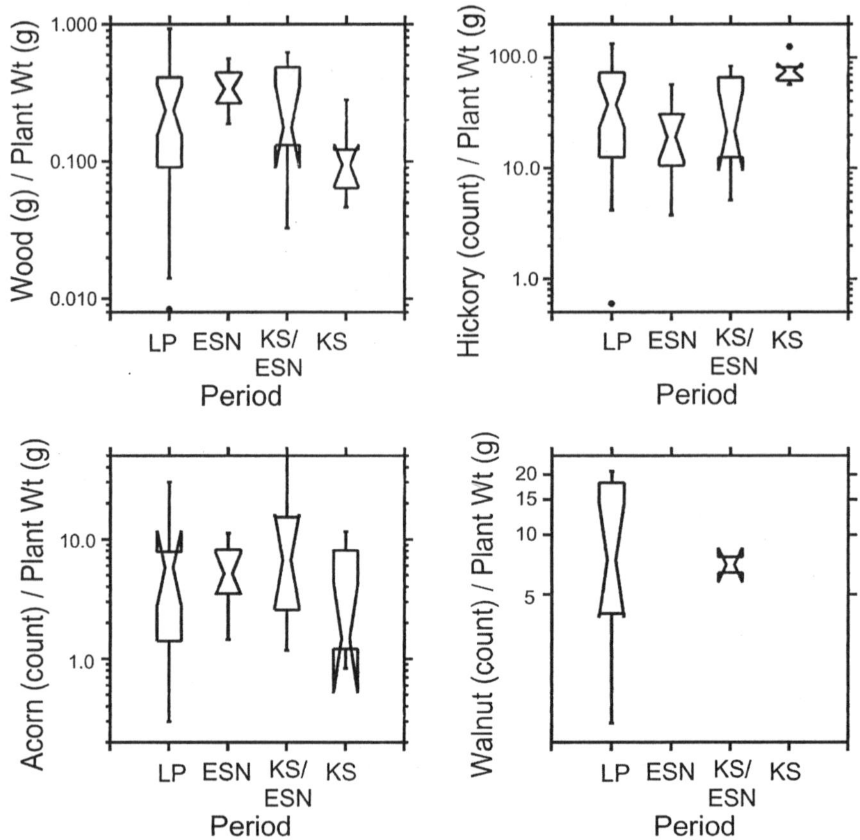

Figure 6.7. Boxplots comparing relative densities of wood, hickory, acorn, and black walnut in column samples from Dust Cave.

chenopod seeds, and other weedy seed taxa preclude boxplots from revealing notable patterns that are substantially different from the ubiquity measures.

Additional information about plant use at Dust Cave can be gleaned from the relative densities of the various plant taxa recovered from the column samples. Figure 6.7 demonstrates that relative to other plants, the recovery of wood decreases significantly in the Kirk Stemmed component. This coincides with a significant increase in hickory nutshell. It may be that hickory nutshell to some extent replaces wood as a fuel source at this time, perhaps related to more intensive use of hickory. Acorn use drops to some extent, although the notches overlap slightly. No changes through time are apparent for the use of black walnut, other than its absence from the Early Side-Notched and Kirk Stemmed samples.

The remaining plant taxa tend to decrease in the Kirk Stemmed component relative to other plants (Figure 6.8). A marked drop is seen for hazel, hackberry, and weedy seeds. Chenopod and fruits other than hackberry also appear to drop, although this decrease is not statistically significant for the fruits, and chenopod is represented by a single sample in the Kirk Stemmed component. This is likely due in large part to the increase in hickory, which has a sizeable impact on the denominator of this ratio. Possible changes in smaller taxa may thus be masked by the increase in hickory.

To summarize the trends seen in the Dust Cave column samples, plant use significantly increases through time at the site. Increases in nearly all taxa are apparent. The major exception is the mixed Early Side-Notched component, although the nature of this occupation, accompanied by significant erosion and possible slope wash of deposits, is at present unclear. The lower quantities of plant materials, particularly wood and acorn, in the Late Paleoindian deposits may be related to fluvial activity at the site during this time (Sherwood 2001), which may have washed these lighter fragments out of the sediments. However, the significant recovery of chenopod and other small seeds from these early samples is then difficult to explain. Alternatively, it is possible that recent seasonal inundation of these lower deposits may have adversely affected fragile wood and acorn shell fragments, with little impact on the preservation of seed coats.

The ways in which plant resources are used at the site do not change until the end of the Early Archaic, during the Kirk Stemmed component. At this time, hickory increases significantly while wood decreases. Other small taxa, generally recovered in low numbers, also decrease, including hazel, hackberry, chenopod, and weedy seeds, but this apparent drop may be heavily influenced by the increase in hickory. Acorn use relative to other plant foods, however, does not appear to change significantly over time.

Feature Samples

The plant materials recovered from Dust Cave feature samples are listed in Table 6.10. An initial glance reveals that the feature contents are similar to the column samples. Hickory is again the dominant taxon, although acorn shell is much better represented. Several samples in particular contain large quantities of acorn shell. These include a Kirk Stemmed hearth (Feature 350) with over 500 fragments, and a charcoal ring feature (Feature 363a) from the mixed Early Side-Notched/Kirk Stemmed component with over 1,000 acorn shell fragments. Black walnut is recovered from all four components, mostly in small quantities, with the exception of an expedient hearth (Feature 405) from which 51 shell fragments were recovered. Hazel appears in small quantities, and interestingly only in Kirk Stemmed samples.

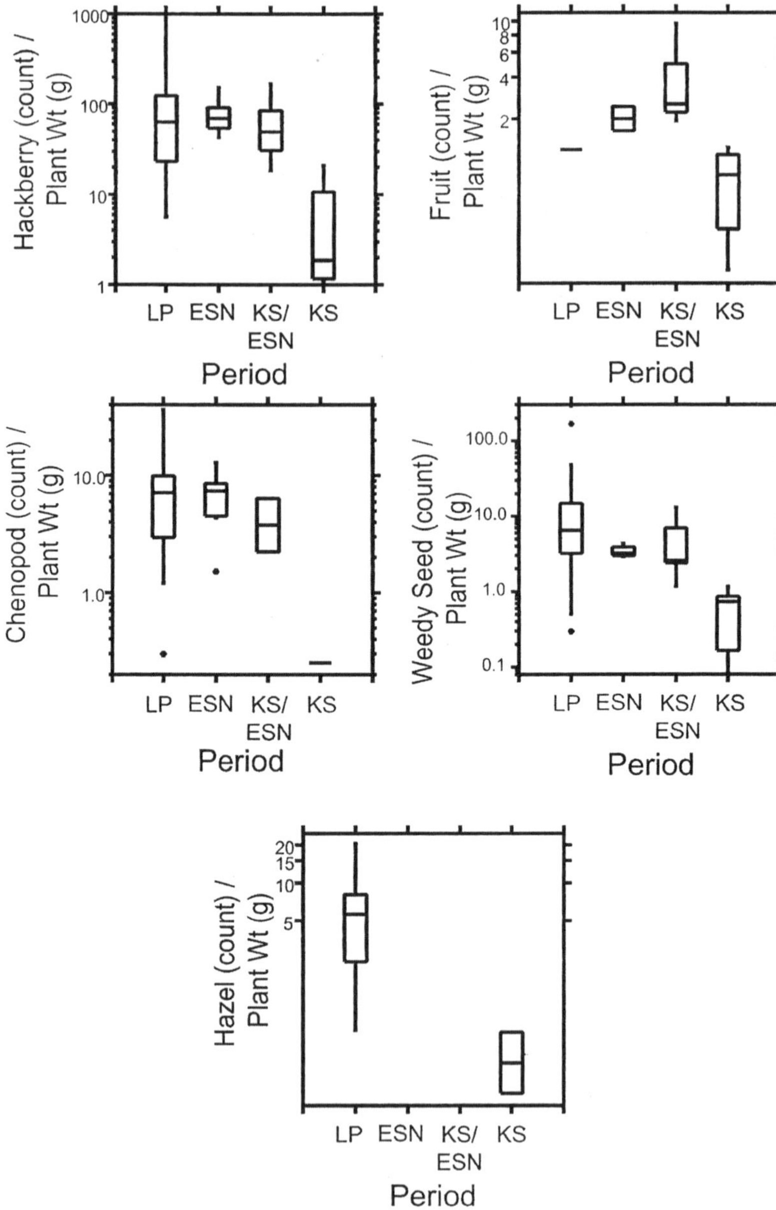

Figure 6.8. Boxplots comparing relative densities of hazel, hackberry, fruits other than hackberry, chenopod, and wild seeds in the column samples from Dust Cave.

Table 6.10. Plant Materials Recovered from Dust Cave Feature Samples.

Period: Bag Number	Unit	Level	Depth (cm)	Feature Number	Plant Weight (g)	Wood Weight (g)	Acorn Count, Weight (g)	Black Walnut Count, Weight (g)	Hickory Count, Weight (g)	Hackberry Count, Weight (g)	Chenopod Count, Weight (g)	Other
Kirk Stemmed:												
1702	N63W64	38	355	114	7.04	3.70	44, .09		353, 3.04	37, .15		2 persimmon, .01 g; 1 pine cone; 1 wild legume; 14 unidentifiable, .05 g
5209	N61W65	48	355	350	11.06	.69	505, 1.08		716, 8.99	20, .10		1 acorn cf.; 9 acorn meat, .04 g; 1 hazel; 16 persimmon, .04 g; 1 pitch; 2 sumac; 8 wild legume; 17 unidentifiable, .12 g; 5 unidentifiable seed
5444	N63W66	45	340	358	6.07	1.08	3		390, 4.89	9, .06		1 chenopod cf.; 9 unidentifiable, .04 g; 1 unidentifiable seed
5630	N60W66	44	335	368	8.55	4.77	16, .07		250, 3.31	18, .17		13 acorn meat, .08 g; 1 hazel; 4 pitch, .03 g; 14 unidentifiable, .12 g; 7 unidentifiable seed
5700	N60W66	45	340	375	14.81	2.93	59, .14	5, .23	932, 11.09	19, .12		1 acorn meat, .04 g; 1 bedstraw; 2 chenopod cf.; 8 persimmon, .04 g; 6 pitch, .03 g; 27 unidentifiable, .19 g; 3 unidentifiable seed

Continued on the next page

Table 6.10. *Continued*

Period: Bag Number	Unit	Level	Depth (cm)	Feature Number	Plant Weight (g)	Wood Weight (g)	Acorn Count, Weight (g)	Black Walnut Count, Weight (g)	Hickory Count, Weight (g)	Hackberry Count, Weight (g)	Chenopod Count, Weight (g)	Other
5967	N63W66	47	350	389	1.25	.14	48, .09		107, .73	24, .20		1 hazel; 3 persimmon, .02 g; 1 poke; 11 wild legume, .02 g; 11 unidentifiable, .05 g; 3 unidentifiable seed
6572	N62W62	50	320	444	1.65	1.32	1		33, .33			1 unidentifiable
6600	N62W62	52	330	448	.23	.06	1, .01		7, .07	5, .04		11 persimmon, .05 g; 1 unidentifiable seed
6622	N62W62	53	335	450	3.36	.40	2, .01	1, .02	242, 2.78	22, .14		1 unidentifiable, .01 g; 1 unidentifiable seed
6652	N60W62	49	315	451	8.57	5.70	4, .01		211, 2.72	11, .08	2	5 acorn meat, .02 g; 6 unidentifiable, .04 g; 2 unidentifiable seed; 1 unidentified seed
Early Side-Notched/Kirk Stemmed:												
4395	N60W68	53	380	330	1.12	.83	2		25, .23	10, .04		1 acorn cf.; 1 persimmon, .01 g; 4 unidentifiable, .01 g; 1 unidentifiable seed
5469	N62W65	52	375	360	.35	.09	2, .01		18, .14	23, .10		1 grape; 1 hazel cf.; 1 pitch, .01 g; 7 unidentifiable

5649	N60W65	50	365	363a	4.28	.93	1063, 1.89		172, 1.34	8, .07		2 pitch, .01 g; 2 sumac; 1 wild legume; 11 unidentifiable, .04 g
6082	N60W66	52	375	397	.04	.02	1	1	2, .01	1, .01		1 unidentifiable
6875	N60W62	59	365	459	1.39	.73	6, .01	1, .01	75, .46	36, .15		1 black walnut cf., .01 g; 1 grape; 4 persimmon, .01 g; 2 unidentifiable, .01 g; 1 unidentifiable seed
6943	N62W62	64	390	462	2.72	1.97	226, .45		4, .03	36, .24	1	1 acorn cf.; 1 pitch, .01 g; 5 unidentifiable, .02 g; 4 unidentifiable seed
Early Side-Notched:												
1509	N60W64	42	375	111	1.60	.25	15, .04	1, .01	142, .88	59, .36		1 acorn cf.; 1 pine cone; 5 pitch, .05 g; 3 unidentifiable, .01 g; 8 unidentifiable seed
1751	N59W64	51	420	115	.67	.21	12, .03		3, .02	44, .29		1 chenopod cf.; 7 pitch, .10 g; 5 unidentifiable, .02 g; 6 unidentifiable seed
5706	N63W65	56	385	377	1.92	.99	109, .20	7, .19	36, .24	35, .19		5 persimmon, .01 g; 3 pitch, .01 g; 1 Walnut family nutshell; 23 unidentifiable, .09 g
5732	N63W65	57	395	380	.51	.14	1		10, .05	34, .22		8 acorn meat, .07 g; 1 bark, .01 g; 1 pitch, .01 g; 2 unidentifiable, .01 g; 1 unidentifiable seed
6099	N60W65	53	380	402	2.10	.81	1	7, .22	109, 1.00	14, .07		3 unidentifiable seed

Continued on the next page

Table 6.10. *Continued*

Period: Bag Number	Unit	Level	Depth (cm)	Feature Number	Plant Weight (g)	Wood Weight (g)	Acorn Count, Weight (g)	Black Walnut Count, Weight (g)	Hickory Count, Weight (g)	Hackberry Count, Weight (g)	Chenopod Count, Weight (g)	Other
6111	N60W66	53	380	405	3.12	.36		51, .72	225, 1.85	25, .10		7 persimmon fruit, .08 g; 3 unidentifiable, .01 g
6118	N60W65	53	380	406	1.91	.48		6, .32	96, 1.00	24, .09		3 unidentifiable, .02 g; 1 unidentifiable seed coat
6129	N60W65	53	380	410	.58	.18	1		38, .20	34, .15	1	1 black walnut cf., .01 g; 1 pine cone, .01 g; 1 pitch; 1 pitch/pine cone, .01 g; 4 unidentifiable, .02 g
6144	N60W66	55	390	413	2.69	.51	1	3, .29	173, 1.41	102, .42		1 acorn cf.; 1 persimmon; 3 pitch, .02 g; 1 sumac; 18 unidentifiable, .04 g; 1 unidentifiable seed
6874	N61W62	53	375	458	.15	.11	1		1, .01	8, .03		
6972	N60W62	65	395	467	.03	.01	1		1	3, .01		6 pitch, .01 g; 2 poke; 1 unidentifiable; 9 unidentifiable seed
Late Paleoindian:												
293	N62W64	32	425	37	.03	.01			1, .01	8, .01	1	14 grape cf.; 1 pitch; 6 unidentifiable seed; 1 unidentified
1001	N62W64	37	455	99	.31	.08	8		22, .20	5, .03	1	1 poke cf.; 2 unidentifiable seed

1761	N60W64	50	415	116	.28	.22	5		4, .03	36, .03		1 pitch; 1 unidentified seed
1900	N60W64	58	455	118	.52	.01		5, .14	39, .37			1 black gum cf.; 1 pitch; 15 unidentifiable seed
5747	N62W65	56	390	382	.41	.21	1		19, .14	11, .05		4 acorn cf.; 13 unidentifiable, .01 g
5790	N62W66	57	395	384	.27	.06	2		17, .13	12, .07		1 pitch, .01 g; 1 unidentifiable
5826	N62W65	61	415	387	3.47	3.42	1		1, .02	1		1 bedstraw; 7 persimmon, .01 g; 14 unidentifiable, .02 g
6283	N60W66	58	405	420	.26	.18	2		4, .04	3, .01	1	1 bedstraw; 3 pitch, .02 g; 8 unidentifiable, .01 g; 5 unidentifiable seed
6308	N60W66	59	410	423	.87	.29	2, .01		32, .28	45, .25	5	11 chenopod cf.; 6 pitch, .04 g; 1 unidentifiable; 23 unidentifiable seed
6326	N60W65	59	410	117	.94	.25	1		2, .06	64, .32	1	3 chenopod cf.; 1 hickory cf.; 25 pitch, .29 g; 2 unidentifiable, .02 g; 31 unidentifiable seed
6493	N60W66	66	445	438	.11	.04			10, .07			
7068	N62W62	66	400	473	.77	.23	6, .01		13, .12	69, .37	5	1 cheno-am; 1 stargrass; 8 unidentifiable, .02 g; 116 unidentifiable seed, .02 g
7076	N62W62	66	400	474	.47	.13	2		4, .06	46, .27	9	1 cheno-am; 21 chenopod cf.; 1 morningglory cf.; 3 unidentifiable, .01 g
7438	N61W62	66	445	486	.21	negl.			18, .19	1		2 acorn cf.; 1 black walnut cf., .02 g; 1 wild legume; 2 unidentifiable

Among fruit taxa, hackberry is by far most frequently recovered. Persimmon is generally well represented, while grape and sumac are present in relatively few samples. Chenopod is recovered more frequently from Late Paleoindian features, and wild legumes from Kirk Stemmed features. Several cheno-ams were also found in Late Paleoindian samples. Weedy seeds present include bedstraw, poke, yellow stargrass, and a possible morning glory seed.

Quantitative comparisons of the Dust Cave feature samples are in some ways less complicated than the column samples. The features represent snapshots of activities at the cave. While the features may have been used over a number of years—and indeed some of the hearths, with their layers of ash and charcoal, appear to have been reused on a number of occasions (Homsey 2004)—this time span is relatively negligible. Unlike the column samples, differing sedimentation rates are not a concern for the features.

Of interest, however, is the range of activities that the features represent. A variety of feature types were chosen for analysis, from rings of charcoal to ash pits and rock-lined hearths. While all are associated with burning activities, these activities may include cooking, heating, and lighting the cave, as well as the sweeping of coals and ash out of hearths into separate pits. The contents of the features are likely to vary considerably, as the activities they represent vary. As such, I compare the feature samples by component as well as by type.

Trends through Time

Comparisons of ubiquity values by component for the various taxa demonstrate several possible trends through time (Table 6.11). Acorn shell increases in ubiquity from the Late Paleoindian through the Kirk Stemmed components, from 71 percent to 100 percent. Acorn meats show a similar increase through time. Unlike the column samples, black walnut is present in samples from all components and appears to peak in the Early Side-Notched rather than the Late Paleoindian period. Hazel is much more restricted, however, recovered only from Kirk Stemmed samples. In contrast, hickory is present in all samples. While hackberry has a high ubiquity in all components, the ubiquity of persimmon increases from 7 percent among Late Paleoindian features to 50 percent among Kirk Stemmed features. Grape and sumac display low ubiquities; grape is further restricted to mixed Early Side-Notched/Kirk Stemmed samples. Chenopod and wild legumes show opposite trends in ubiquity, with chenopod decreasing through time and wild legumes increasing.

Table 6.11. Ubiquity of Plant Remains in Feature Samples from Dust Cave.

Taxon	Late Paleo. (*N* = 14)	E. Side-Notched (*N* = 11)	ESN/Kirk Stemmed (*N* = 6)	Kirk Stemmed (*N* = 10)
Acorn shell	71%	82%	100%	100%
Acorn meat		9%		30%
Black walnut	7%	55%	33%	20%
Hazel				20%
Hickory	100%	100%	100%	100%
Grape			33%	
Hackberry	86%	100%	100%	90%
Persimmon	7%	27%	33%	50%
Sumac		9%	17%	10%
Chenopod	50%	9%	17%	10%
Wild legume			17%	30%

Similar to the column samples, the density of plant materials recovered from features also increases through time (Figure 6.9). Comparing the various taxa separately, it appears that wood and hickory account for this change (Figure 6.10). Mirroring the boxplots for all plant materials, wood and hickory both increase significantly in the Early Side-Notched features and continue to rise in quantity through the Kirk Stemmed component, although the later rise is not statistically significant. This trend through time may be related to postdepositional processes; it seems unlikely that Late Paleoindians are using less fuel in their fires than Early Archaic peoples. The fluvial activity in the cave during the Late Paleoindian period (Sherwood 2001) may have reworked the features, washing ash and charcoal from them (Homsey 2004). It is somewhat surprising, then, that acorn does not follow this trend in the feature samples, although it is present in significantly smaller quantities in Late Paleoindian column samples (see above). No simple explanation for lower quantities of plant materials in the Late Paleoindian features seems to suffice; a combination of fluvial reworking and less occupation of the site seems likely.

Boxplots of the densities of fruit and seed taxa do not reveal distinct patterning through time. The lack of significant differences for these taxa, represented by smaller seeds and seed fragments, is likely due to the fact that they are recovered in low quantities.

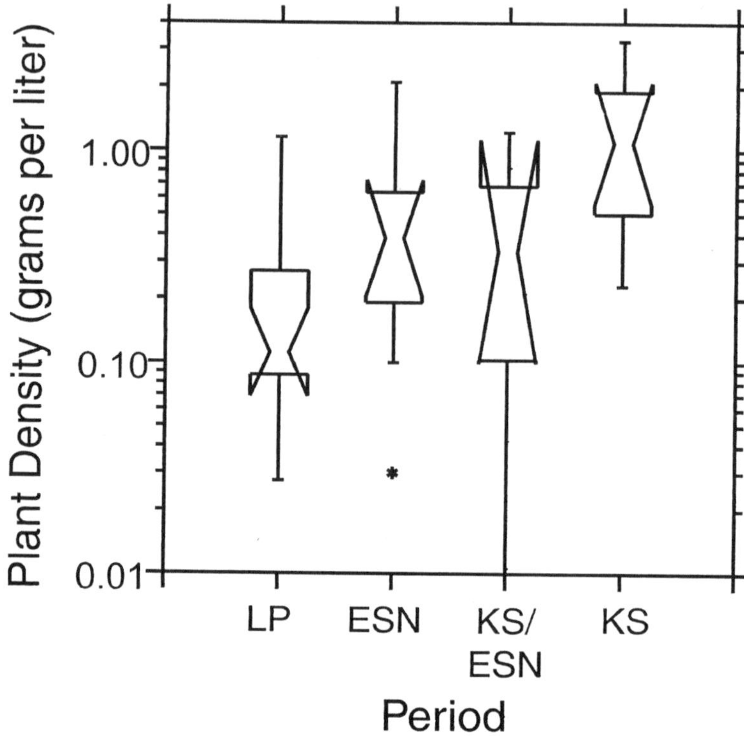

Figure 6.9. Boxplots comparing plant density in Dust Cave feature samples through time.

Although the density of wood and hickory recovered from features changes significantly through time, the relative densities of these taxa do not show similar patterns (Figure 6.11). Instead, the relative densities of wood and hickory, as well as acorn, are comparable in all components. This also contrasts with the column samples, which demonstrate a significant decrease in the relative density of wood and increase in hickory in the Kirk Stemmed component (Figure 6.7). If wood and acorn were indeed adversely affected by reworking of the deposits by floodwaters in the Late Paleoindian component and their presence is underrepresented, their relative densities for this component may well be understated. However, the significant shift in hickory and wood in column samples is seen in the Kirk Stemmed samples, not the Early Side-Notched component.

It may be that hickory nutshell is overrepresented in column samples relative to feature samples, particularly in the Kirk Stemmed component. This

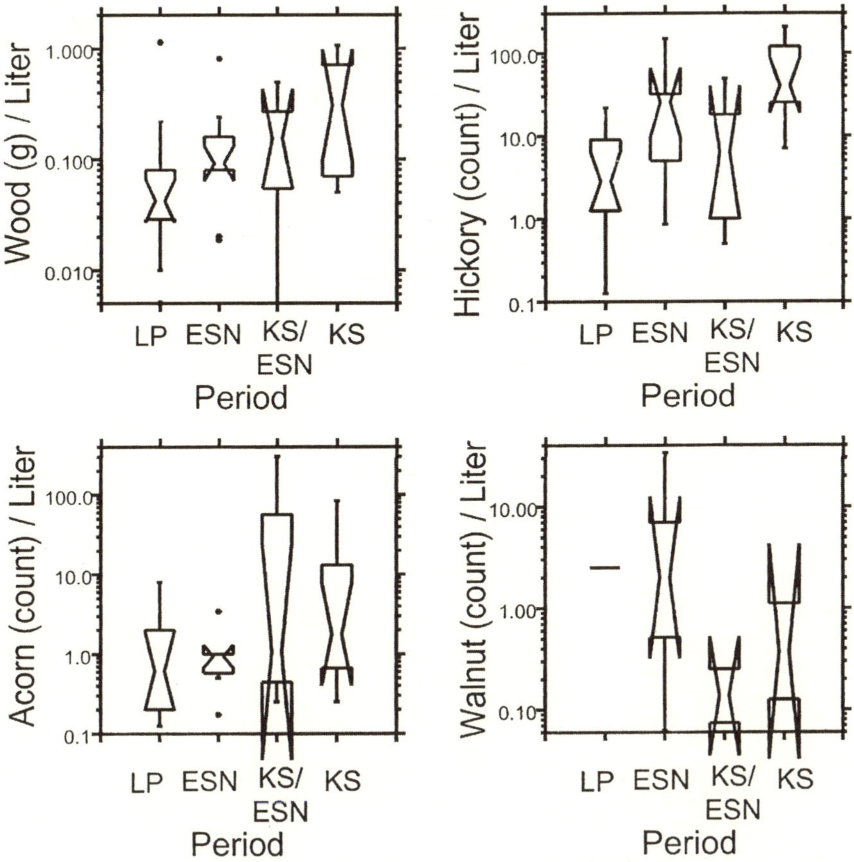

Figure 6.10. Boxplots comparing density of wood, hickory, acorn, and walnut in Dust Cave feature samples through time.

may be related to the increased occupation of the cave at this time, as suggested by increases in the density of plant remains. More fragile acorn shell and wood fragments may not have weathered the trampling, sweeping, and disturbance associated with peoples' occupation of the cave as well as denser hickory nutshells. Wood and acorn may therefore be underrepresented in the general living contexts associated with column samples, particularly at times when the cave was intensively occupied, such as the Kirk Stemmed component. The importance of acorn relative to other plant foods may thus be significantly understated.

Among the other taxa, black walnut does seem to decrease relative to other plants to some degree (Figure 6.11), as do hackberries, edible seeds,

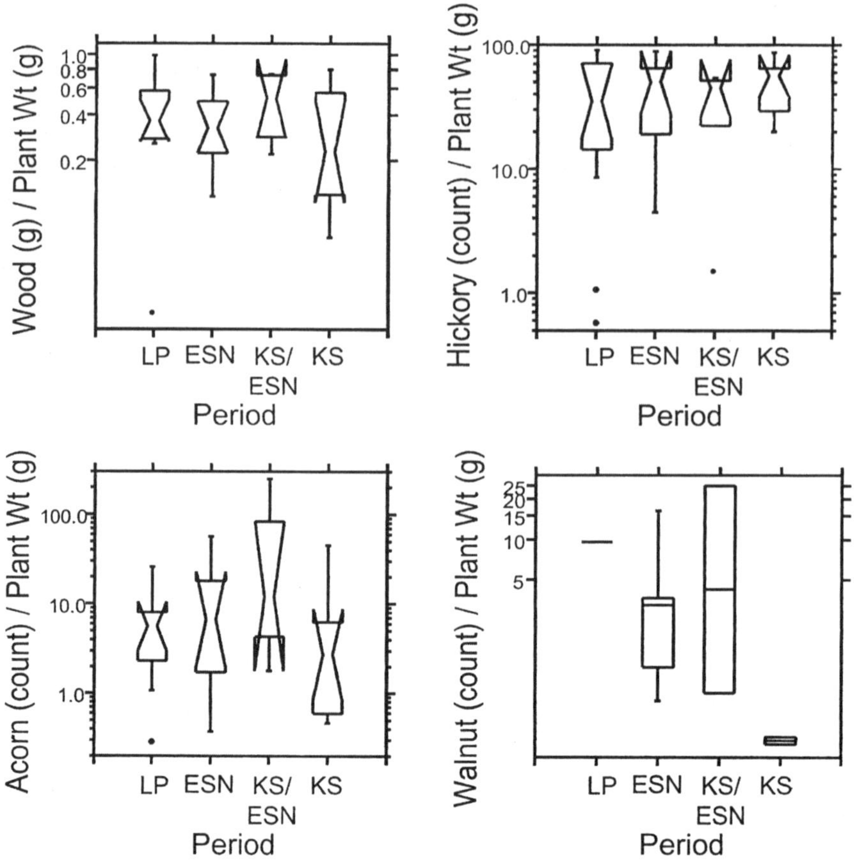

Figure 6.11. Boxplots comparing relative densities of wood, hickory, acorn, and black walnut in Dust Cave feature samples through time.

and other seeds (Figure 6.12). This trend is similar to that seen among column samples. It appears that hickory and perhaps acorn became targeted resources by the end of the Early Archaic, overshadowing use of these other food items. Fruits other than hackberries show no significant changes through time, however.

In sum, the feature samples show some patterning through time. The density of plant remains recovered increases through time, although this may be exaggerated as fluvial processes might have adversely affected plant materials in Late Paleoindian features. Most notable, however, is the lack of change in the relative densities of plant taxa recovered. Hickory does not increase significantly relative to other plant materials in the Kirk Stemmed compo-

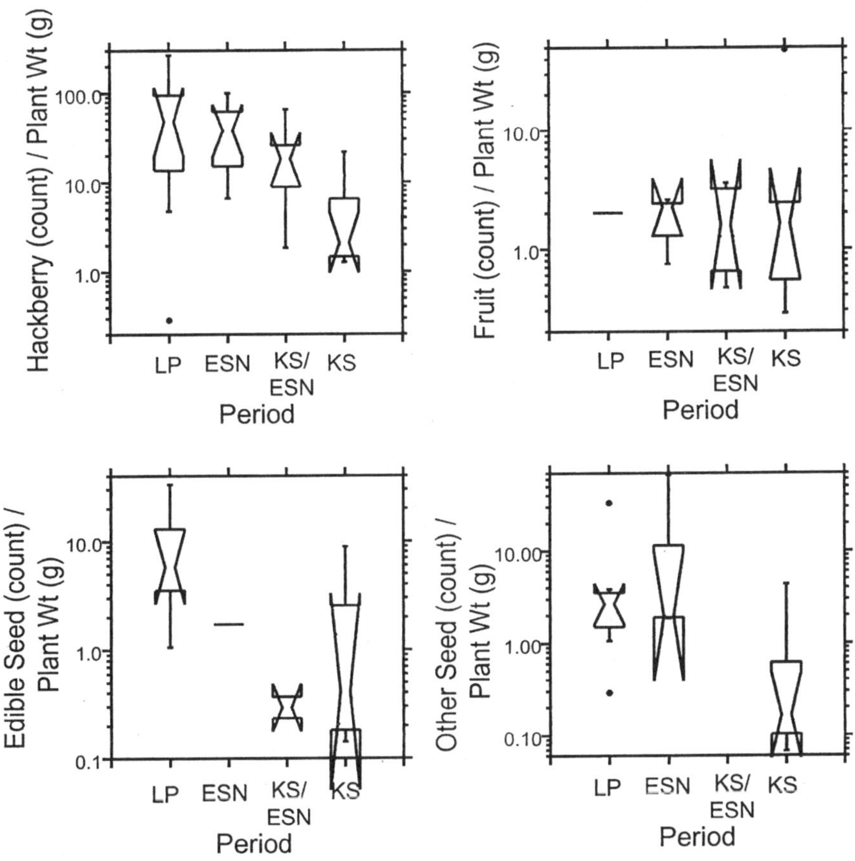

Figure 6.12. Boxplots comparing the relative densities of hackberry, fruits other than hackberry, edible seeds, and other seeds in Dust Cave feature samples.

nent. It is possible that the increase observed in column samples overstates the use of hickory. Along the same lines, the importance of acorn may be understated in column samples. Chenopod and wild legumes seem to complement each other, the former decreasing in use through time and the latter becoming more important. Fruits such as persimmon, grape, and sumac show little change in use, while use of hackberries may decrease by the end of the Early Archaic period.

Trends by Feature Type

Lara Homsey (2004) has created a typology for features at Dust Cave using geochemical, macro-, and micromorphological characteristics. The range

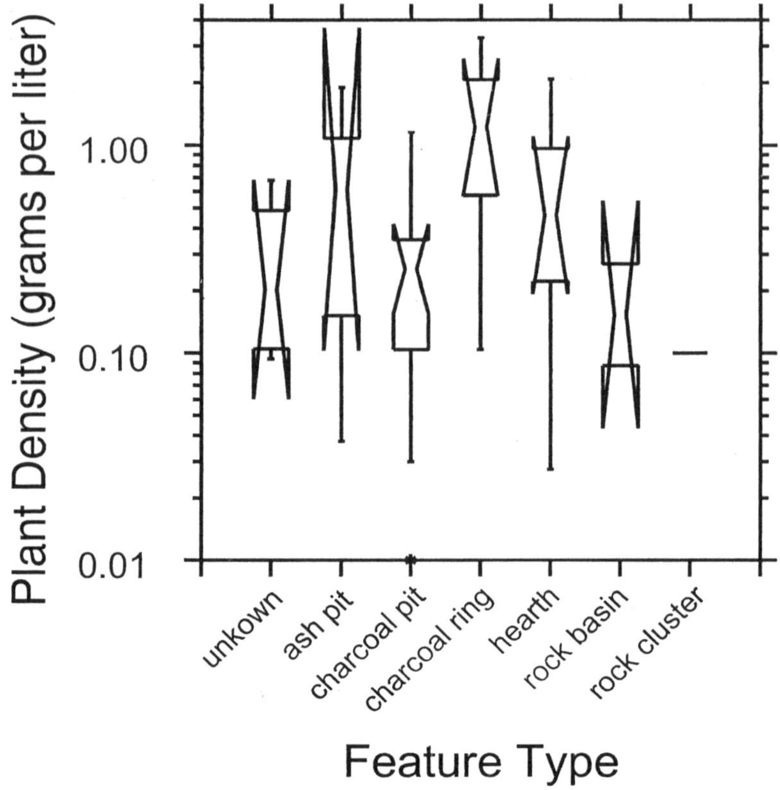

Figure 6.13. Boxplots comparing plant density by feature type in Dust Cave feature samples.

and organization of features at Dust Cave is discussed in greater detail in Chapter 5. Of importance here are the categories associated with the feature samples included in my analysis. These include features associated with burning activities: in situ fireplaces, or hearths and rock basins; and fireplace rake-outs, including ash pits, charcoal pits, and charcoal rings (Homsey 2004:Table 6.2). My feature samples also include one "rock cluster," which Homsey (2004:187) includes among unburned deposits and suggests may have served as cooking stones, piled and ready for use in hearths. Four of the features could not be assigned a feature type at this time, due to vagaries in field descriptions of these features.

Plant densities vary considerably among the feature types (Figure 6.13), although this variation could be due in large part to differences by component as well. In general, charcoal rings tend to have greater plant densities

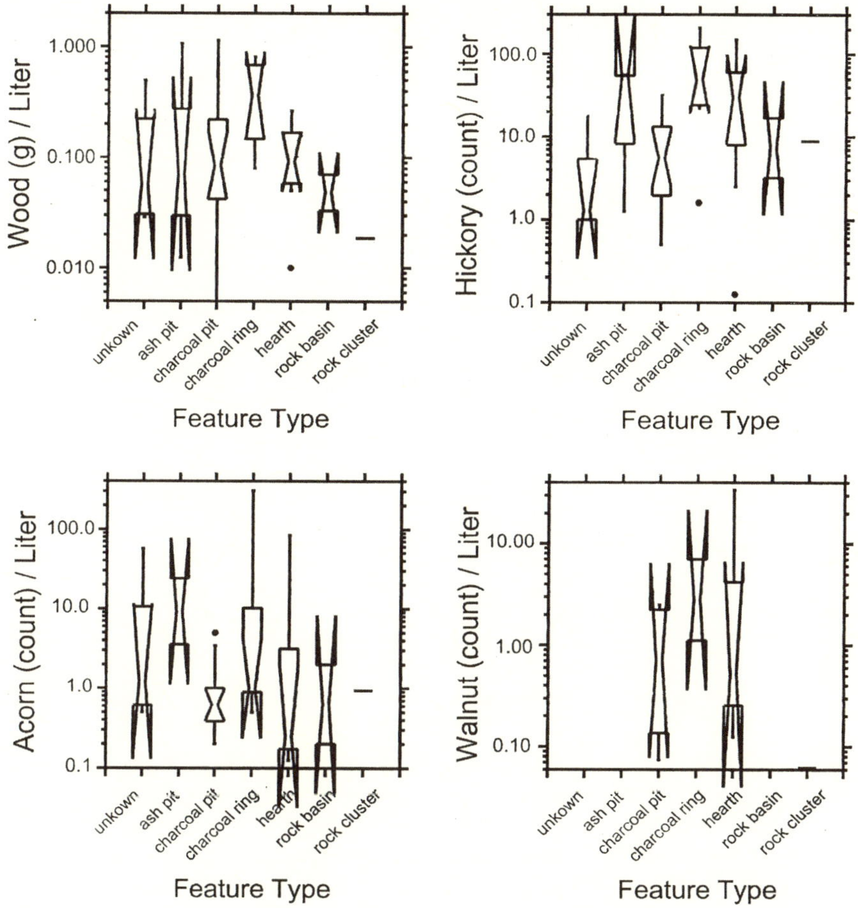

Figure 6.14. Boxplots comparing the densities of wood, hickory, acorn, and black walnut by feature type in Dust Cave feature samples.

than other feature types, particularly in comparison to charcoal pits. Perhaps not surprisingly, similar trends are seen among densities of wood and hickory plotted by feature type (Figure 6.14). No patterning is evident for acorn or black walnut, however. Fruit and seed taxa also show little patterning, with the exception of the significantly low value of "other seeds" among hearths (Figure 6.15).

Similar to comparisons by component, boxplots of relative densities of the various taxa sorted by feature type demonstrate little patterning. However, correspondence analysis proved much more useful, as it illustrates relationships among taxa within samples. I ran a correspondence analysis using the

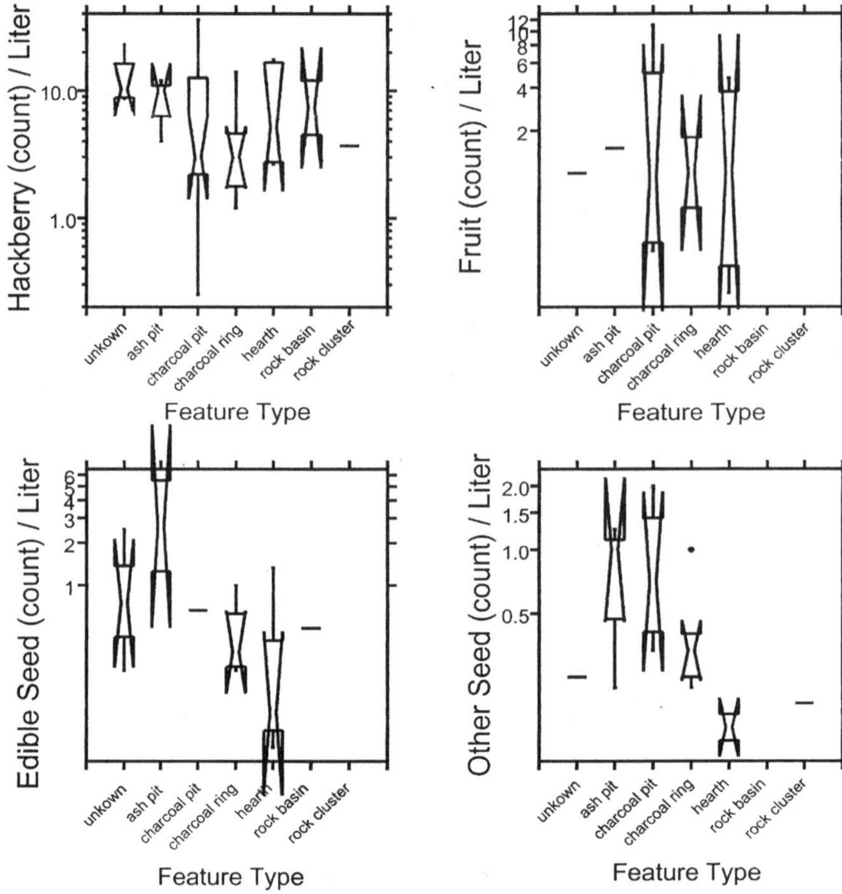

Figure 6.15. Boxplots comparing densities of hackberry, fruits other than hackberry, edible seeds, and other seeds by feature type in Dust Cave feature samples.

following variables: acorn, black walnut, edible seeds, hackberry, and hickory. The resulting plot explains the greatest amount of variation in the data (85 percent) along two axes (see Hollenbach 2005:Tables 6.13 and 6.14 for diagnostic statistics of the correspondence analysis and loadings of the variables). The first axis separates acorn from the other taxa; the second axis groups hickory and black walnut apart from hackberry and edible seeds (Figure 6.16).

By plotting the samples along these axes, the taxa that have the greatest influence on the samples are apparent (Figure 6.17). Most of the samples, regardless of type, tend to fall along the left side of the first axis, nearer hickory

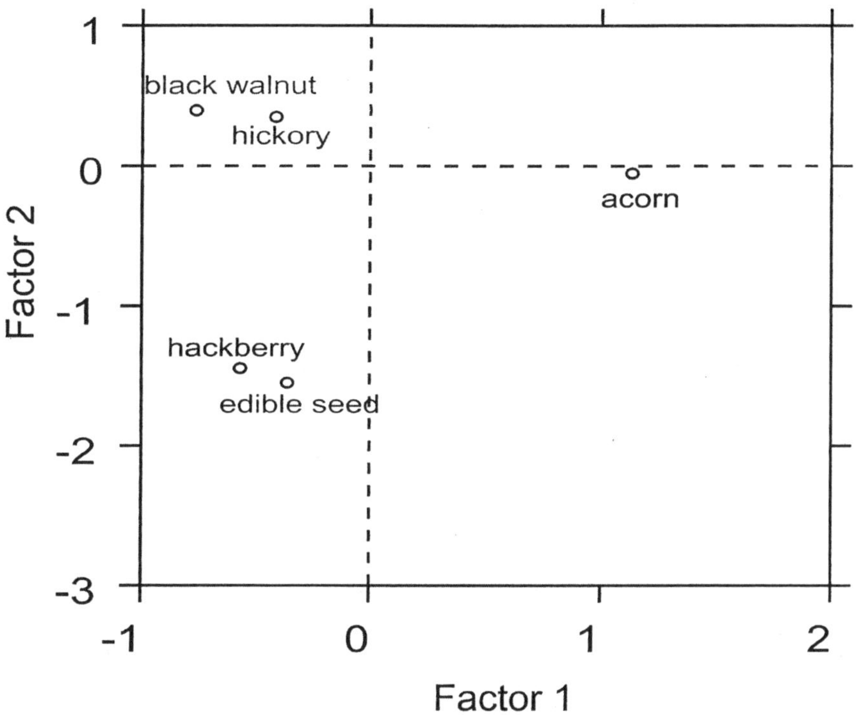

Figure 6.16. Correspondence map of plant taxa in Dust Cave features.

and black walnut. At least one sample from each type, except for ash pits and rock features, is influenced by acorn, falling on the right side of the graph. This includes a Kirk Stemmed hearth and an Early Side-Notched charcoal pit, as well as a charcoal ring and unknown feature type from the mixed Early Side-Notched/Kirk Stemmed component (Zone Q).

More of the samples separate along the second axis. Most of the hearths cluster near hickory and black walnut, with the exception of a Late Paleoindian sample, pulled distinctly toward the hackberry and edible seed end of the axis. Charcoal rings tend to cluster nearer the nut taxa, while a number of the Late Paleoindian and Early Side-Notched charcoal pits plot near the hackberry and edible seeds. Similarly, the Late Paleoindian ash pit, rock feature, and unknown features tend toward the lower end of the second axis.

Comparing the feature types, it appears that hearths and charcoal rings tend to include greater quantities of hickory and black walnut, while charcoal pits contain a greater range of seed and fruit taxa. The unknown features are more similar to charcoal pits, plotting farther from hickory and black walnut.

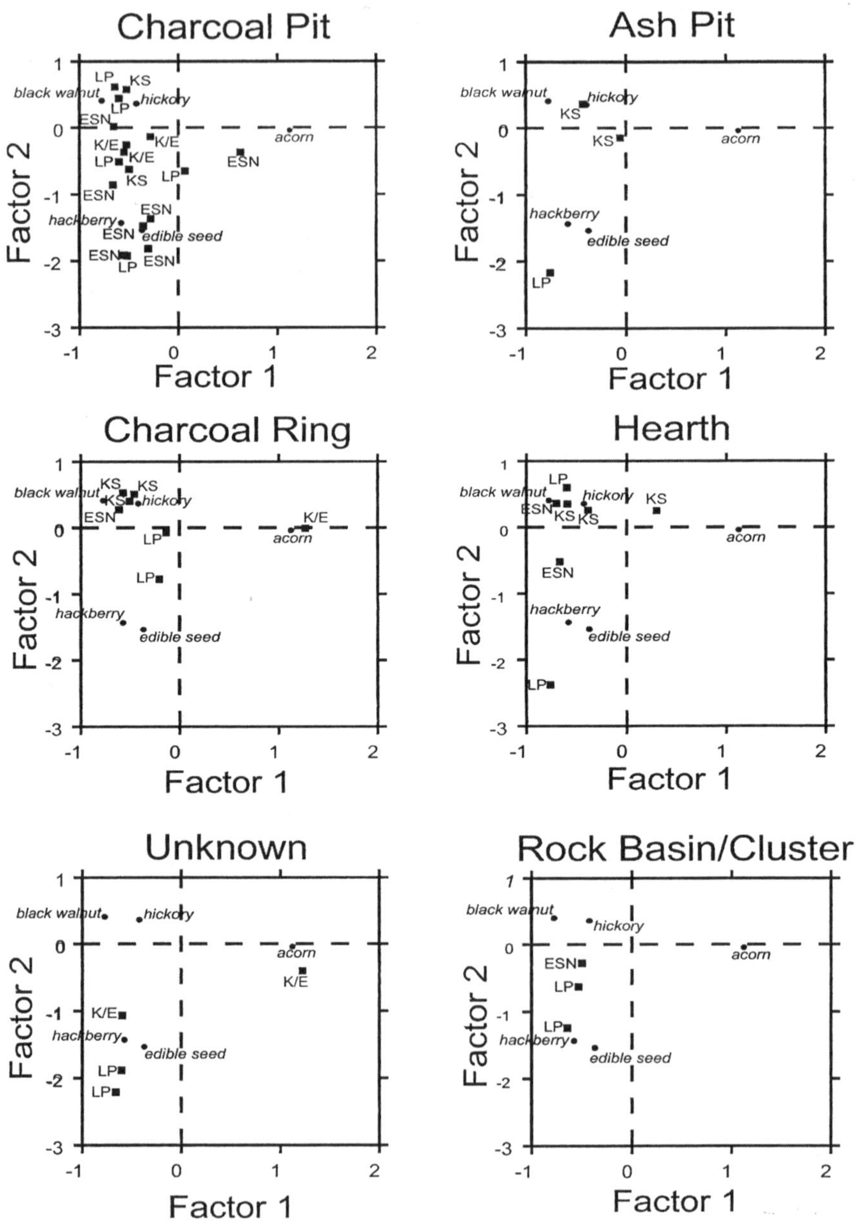

Figure 6.17. Correspondence map of Dust Cave features by type using five variables.

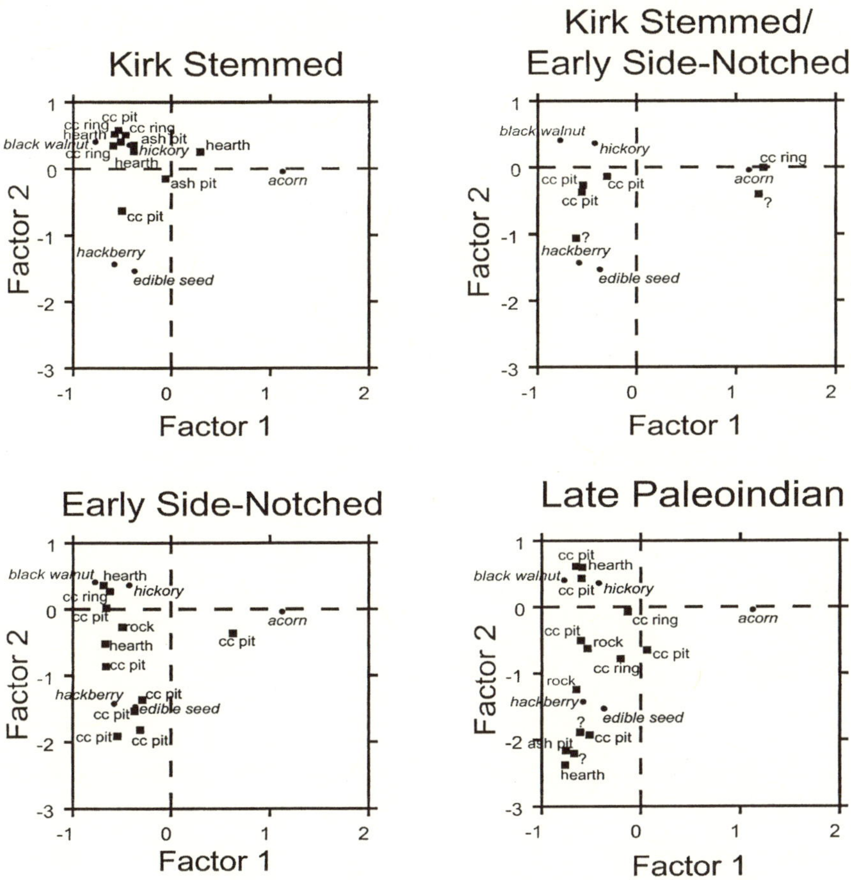

Figure 6.18. Correspondence map of Dust Cave features by component using five variables.

These patterns, however, are not as pronounced as differences by component (Figure 6.18). Among all feature types, Late Paleoindian and Early Side-Notched samples are drawn toward the hackberry and edible seeds; mixed Early Side-Notched (Zone Q) samples tend to plot nearer acorn; and samples from the Kirk Stemmed component cluster nearer hickory and black walnut. The feature samples group more by component than by type.

In sum, the macrobotanical contents of the various Dust Cave features are strikingly similar when compared by feature type. Charcoal rings are notable for their relatively high densities of plant remains, particularly wood and hickory. If these features are indeed created by fluvial redeposition, as Homsey (2004:176) suggests, the process is apparently efficient in accumulating carbonized remains. Hearths also display high quantities of hickory shell, particularly relative to other plant materials. This coincides nicely with Homsey's (2004) interpretation of these features associated with nut processing, particularly during the Kirk Stemmed occupation. Charcoal pits, features associated with the cleaning of hearths, contain markedly lower amounts of hickory.

A correspondence analysis of the feature samples reveals less patterning among the samples by type than by component. Late Paleoindian and Early Side-Notched features contain larger quantities of hackberries and edible seeds, particularly chenopod. Acorn is associated largely with samples from the mixed Early Side-Notched/Kirk Stemmed component, while Kirk Stemmed features are associated with hickory nutshell. Boxplots, however, suggest that the use of hickory and acorn relative to other plant materials changes little through time.

Summary

The plant remains from the Dust Cave samples present several interesting patterns. The column samples demonstrate an increase in plant remains through time, suggesting an increase in use of the site. Feature samples show a similar increase, however, which may reflect fluvial activity in the cave during the Late Paleoindian period that might have washed charcoal from features. Of note, however, is the fact that small seeds such as chenopod are regularly recovered from these lower deposits and features and appear to have been little affected by these fluvial activities. Regardless, plant density in column samples increases by an order of magnitude, and reflects, at least in part, more intensive use of the site. Increasing occupation is indicated as well by geochemical signatures of the cave's deposits (Homsey 2004).

Among feature samples, little change in use of nut taxa through time is suggested. This differs from column samples, in which hickory increases significantly in the Kirk Stemmed component. It is possible that hickory nutshell is overrepresented in these general context samples, being denser and therefore more resistant to the stresses of trampling, cleaning, and bioturbation associated with more intensive use of the cave. As indicated by the column samples, use of nuts increases in the Kirk Stemmed component, but the feature samples suggest that both hickory and acorn were targeted.

The use of fruit taxa changed little through time, perhaps decreasing relative to nut use during the Kirk Stemmed period. More notable is the decrease in chenopod and possible increase in wild legumes over time. The drop in chenopod is illustrated both by boxplots of column and feature samples, as well as the correspondence analysis of features. This decrease in use might be related to changes in availability of chenopod, perhaps due to changes in local ecology. Such changes may also have increased the availability of nut resources. If hickory nuts and acorns are higher-ranked (higher return rate) foodstuffs, then an increase in their availability may be related to a decrease in use of lower-ranked (lower return rate) items, such as chenopod seeds and wild legumes. Gatherers may have been better able to meet their dietary needs with nut resources in Kirk Stemmed times, but needed to turn to lower-ranked foods during the Late Paleoindian and Early Side-Notched periods. Alternatively, the use of the cave may have changed significantly, from a general purpose camp to a locus specifically for processing nuts. These possibilities will be further discussed in the following chapter.

INTERSITE COMPARISONS

While intrasite patterns can provide information regarding changes in plant use through time, intersite comparisons may indicate differences in plant use across ecological settings. Of particular interest are possible differences between sites within the uplands and those situated in or with access to the floodplain. Here I make broad comparisons among assemblages from the four sites using ubiquity measures as well as correspondence analysis. I do not include 1/4-inch screen samples in these intersite comparisons, nor do I include the Dust Cave feature samples, in an attempt to use samples that are most comparable. I also consider the different components of the sites separately where possible.

Ubiquity

The ubiquity values of the various plant taxa suggest broad patterns among the sites (Table 6.12). Of particular note is the nearly 100 percent ubiquity of hickory nutshell at all sites, during all time periods. Hickory was recovered from all but one sample, a "pinch" sample from Stanfield-Worley. Its ubiquity at the sites is indicative of the importance of hickory in the diets of early foragers, as well as its high potential for preservation. Acorn also displays a relatively high ubiquity, which seems to increase from Late Paleoindian/Dalton to Early Archaic occupations. This rise in ubiquity may reflect more intensive use of this mast resource in later periods.

Black walnut generally has higher ubiquity values at upland sites, which may be related to the availability of this species in the various ecological settings. In contrast, hazel appears to be more frequently recovered at sites with

Table 6.12. Ubiquity of Plant Materials at the Four Rockshelter Sites.

Taxon	Stanfield-Worley (N=20)	Rollins Dalton (N=12)	Rollins Early Archaic (N=16)	LaGrange Dalton (N=5)	LaGrange Early Archaic (N=6)	Dust Cave Late Paleo. (N=36)	Dust Cave E. Side-Notched (N=12)	Dust Cave ESN/ Kirk Stemmed (N=10)	Dust Cave Kirk Stemmed (N=8)
Acorn shell	45%	50%	94%	80%	100%	39%	92%	100%	100%
Acorn meat	60%	17%	19%		17%	6%	8%	40%	13%
Black walnut	85%	50%	25%	80%	50%	36%		20%	
Hazel	15%			60%	17%	19%			25%
Hickory	95%	100%	100%	100%	100%	100%	100%	100%	100%
Grape	5%	17%	13%	20%	50%	3%	8%	20%	25%
Hackberry						75%	100%	100%	100%
Persimmon	45%	25%	13%	20%	17%			10%	38%
Sumac	5%	17%		40%	17%		8%		38%
Chenopod				20%	33%	56%	75%	20%	13%
Wild legume			6%	20%	50%	3%		10%	38%
Other seeds	5%	17%	6%	60%	33%	47%	25%	40%	50%

access to the wide creek bottoms of the Tennessee Valley, namely Dust Cave and LaGrange. Its absence from Rollins Bluff Shelter, located farthest from the Tennessee Valley, is notable.

Hackberry stands out among the fruit taxa, present only at Dust Cave. This is undoubtedly related to the preference of this species for floodplain settings. Grape, persimmon, and sumac, however, are recovered at all sites, albeit in low numbers. The repeated recovery of these taxa likely reflects their regular use by early foragers in the area, as well as their general availability in a number of topographic settings.

Weedy seed taxa display higher ubiquity at sites with access to the Tennessee Valley. This is particularly true of chenopod, which was not recovered from the two upland sites, Stanfield-Worley and Rollins. Wild legumes are similarly more likely to occur at the Tennessee Valley sites, although a single wild legume was recovered from an Early Archaic sample at Rollins. "Other seeds" (including taxa not listed above, seeds identified to family level, and unidentified seeds) also have higher ubiquity values at the sites near the Tennessee Valley. The value for Stanfield-Worley may be underestimated, however, as floatation samples were not available for the site.

Comparisons of ubiquity suggest that black walnut may have been utilized to a greater degree at upland sites, while hazel seems to be more prevalent at sites near the Tennessee Valley. Weedy seeds, and in particular chenopod, are more likely to be recovered at Tennessee Valley sites, and hackberry is clearly limited to riverine sites. Widely used taxa include hickory, acorn, grape, persimmon, and sumac.

Correspondence Analysis

I further explore differences between site assemblages using correspondence analysis. In this analysis, the two axes explain 96 percent of the variation among the sites (see Hollenbach 2005:Tables 6.16 and 6.17 for diagnostic statistics of the correspondence analysis and loadings of the variables). The first axis is heavily influenced by hackberry, separating this taxon from hickory, as well as acorn, black walnut, persimmon, and other fruits (Figure 6.19). The second axis best represents black walnut, setting it apart from hickory and acorn. Hackberry, hazel, and edible seeds, all displaying higher ubiquity at floodplain sites, group together toward the left side of the graph. The generally ubiquitous hickory, acorn, and fruits (namely grape and sumac) cluster near the origin of the graph.

Plotting the various sites along these axes illustrates differences among the sites (Figure 6.20). Several of the assemblages cluster near hickory. These

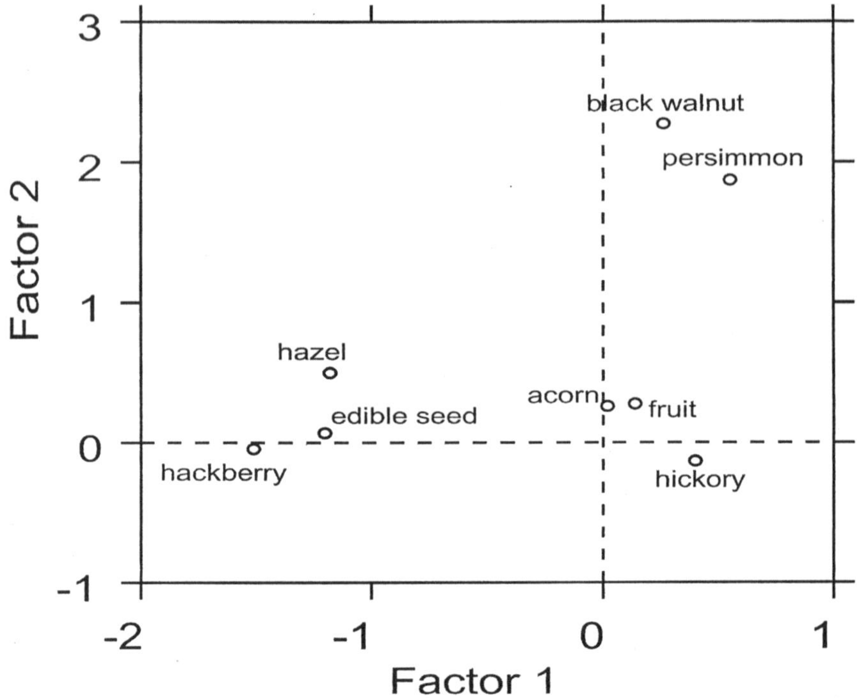

Figure 6.19. Correspondence map of plant taxa in the rockshelter assemblages.

include the Kirk Stemmed component at Dust Cave and both the Dalton and Early Archaic components at Rollins. The assemblages from Stanfield-Worley and LaGrange tend toward the black walnut and persimmon end of the second axis. Reviewing the counts of taxa in the LaGrange samples, the Dalton assemblage from the site is influenced more by black walnut than persimmon, while the opposite holds for the Early Archaic assemblage. The Dust Cave samples separate along the first axis, with the Late Paleoindian and Early Side-Notched assemblages clustering near hackberry and edible seeds. The Late Paleoindian samples also plot slightly higher than the Early Side-Notched, perhaps reflecting the greater recovery of hazel from the earlier component. The mixed Early Side-Notched/Kirk Stemmed assemblage from Dust Cave (Zone Q) plots between these earlier samples and the Kirk Stemmed samples, perhaps indicating the influence of fruit and acorn, or more likely the mixed nature of this component.

The correspondence analysis does indicate some trends through space. Black walnut is significant in assemblages from sites in or adjacent to the up-

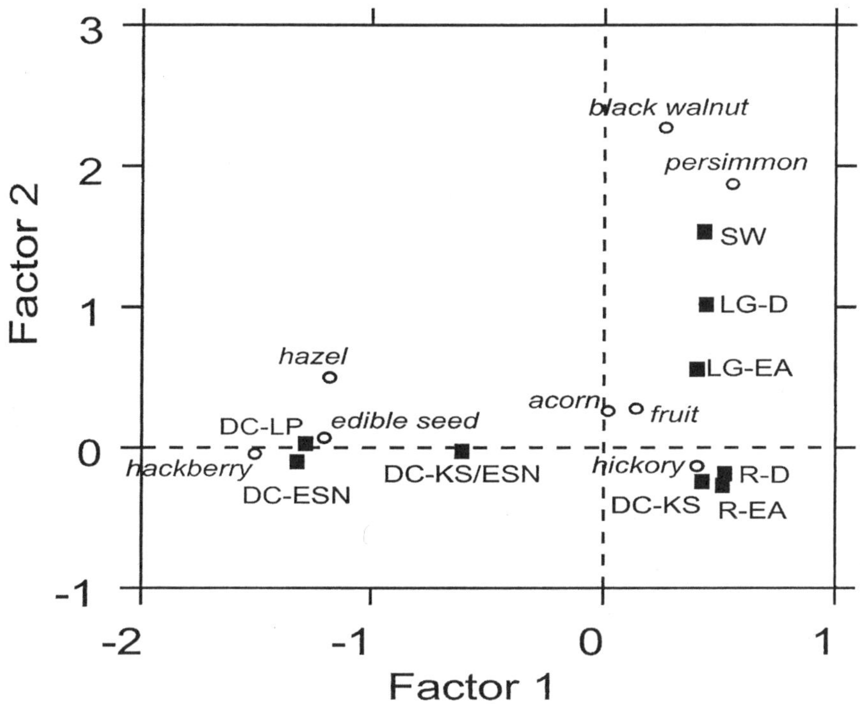

Figure 6.20. Correspondence map of rockshelter assemblages using eight variables.

lands, while hackberry, edible seeds, and hazel are of greater influence at a floodplain site. Also of note are the trends through time illustrated by the correspondence plots. Although the boxplots suggest a decrease in hickory and walnut in the Early Archaic component at Rollins, the correspondence analysis demonstrates much similarity between the Dalton and Early Archaic occupations at the site, both heavily influenced by hickory. In contrast, the boxplots indicate no significant shifts through time at LaGrange, although the correspondence analysis suggests a decrease in the importance of black walnut. The differences between the Dust Cave samples are well illustrated by the correspondence analysis, showing the increased use of hickory relative to other plant taxa by the end of the Early Archaic period.

SUMMARY

My analysis of plant remains from the four rockshelter sites elucidates several patterns regarding plant use through time and space in the region. Among the plant taxa, several stand out in that they are repeatedly recovered. Hickory was present in nearly every sample, illustrating its importance as a resource to early foragers. Acorn also occurred regularly in the samples, suggesting that this nut was also a dietary mainstay, likely underestimated in its importance because of the fragility of its shell. Persimmon, grape, and sumac, although recovered in low numbers, were present at every site in some form. These fruits, which seem to change little in use through time, appear to have been regularly consumed.

There are discernable trends among the data, but they vary considerably from site to site. Gatherers living at Stanfield-Worley apparently focused on black walnut and acorn as well as hickory, and supplemented these nut resources with various fruits. At Rollins, the dietary mainstay seems to have been hickory, while acorn and black walnut played less of a role. Plant use seems to change little through time at the site. At LaGrange, use of black walnut is greater in the Dalton period. In addition to hickory, acorn, and various fruits, edible seeds such as wild legumes and chenopod appear to have been regularly used at this site on the boundary between the sandstone hills and Tennessee Valley region. At Dust Cave, hickory and acorn are important nut resources that appear to have been used more intensively by the end of the Early Archaic period. Use of chenopod seems to decrease, however, although wild legumes may have replaced chenopod as an important edible seed in the diet of the site's occupants. There appears to be some trends across space, with black walnut a greater constituent of upland assemblages and edible seeds more frequently recovered at sites with access to the Tennessee Valley. In general, though, the patterns seem to be specific to each site. This is particularly true of changes through time: no single trend across sites is apparent.

NOTE

1. More detailed information about the materials recovered from the analyzed floatation samples from all four sites can be found in Hollenbach (2005).

7
Subsistence and Mobility in Northwest Alabama

Lists and quantitative comparisons of plant remains recovered from archaeological sites are descriptive but do not adequately detail plant use. In this chapter, I tie together the information presented in each of the previous chapters and develop a model of early foragers' mobility and subsistence strategies within the project area. First, I describe the nature of plant use in the region, comparing the results from the four rockshelter sites to analyses from other sites in the Southeast. Pulling from the various plant taxa recovered, I describe the decisions and practices undertaken by gatherers who exploit these resources. I then interpret the use of plants at each of the four rockshelter sites within the context of gathering, hunting, and procuring stone resources. I then use these data to sketch a model of seasonal rounds, pulling on the expectations derived from central place foraging theory. In light of the resulting model, I review the patterns of site distribution throughout the project area. Finally, I suggest ways in which the model derived here can expand our current understandings of early foragers in the broader Southeast and beyond.

THE NATURE OF PLANT USE IN THE LATE PALEOINDIAN AND EARLY ARCHAIC PERIODS

In line with conventional wisdom, the food plant assemblages at the four rockshelters reflect that early gatherers did indeed collect nuts in particular, as well as fruits. But the recovery of edible and other wild seeds also suggests that gatherers used an array of herbaceous plants, perhaps for their leafy greens and medicinal properties in addition to their edible seeds. I briefly recap the use of these various plant food categories suggested by the four rockshelter assemblages below.

Among the nut taxa, and among the plant remains in general, hickory nutshell was predominant. It was recovered from all but a single sample, and often in sizeable quantities. The frequent recovery of hickory may be related in large part to its robusticity; it certainly preserves better than more fragile acorn shell, wood, and smaller seeds. The prevalence of hickory may also be due to its use as a fuel, in addition to a foodstuff. Site occupants may have purposefully burned hickory nutshell, which is high in oil content, thereby further increasing its potential for preservation (Lopinot 1984). In any case, early foragers of the region appear to have significantly exploited hickory nuts, a foodstuff that is high in fat and calories, processed relatively quickly in bulk, and readily stored.

In contrast, black walnut shell was more limited in its recovery. Closely related to hickory, black walnut shell is also very robust, and the nutmeats are similarly high in fat and calories. However, gatherers do not appear to have used black walnuts to the same degree as hickory nuts. This may be due in part to more restricted availability of walnut trees, but is also likely related to the nut's high processing costs. Because a significant amount of energy is required to pick the meats from the nutshell, gatherers gain little for their efforts. Similar to walnuts, hazelnuts were infrequently recovered and have a relatively low return rate due to their high processing costs. Although the meat is easily pulled from the cracked shell, hazelnuts must be picked from shrubs. They also mature earlier in the fall and prefer different habitats than the other nuts, further suggesting that their use differed significantly.

Although present in smaller quantities than hickory, acorn shell was consistently recovered from the samples. Its shell is also more fragile than the other nuts, making it highly likely that acorns are underrepresented relative to their use. Yarnell and Black (1985:97) suggest that acorns were actually the most important foodstuff of some preceramic Southeastern groups prior to the practice of corn agriculture. However, acorns yield lower energetic return rates than do hickory nuts. Acorns demand more processing, due largely to the tannins that must be leached from the meats. They also have a lower fat content, and therefore provide fewer calories, than the other nuts. But acorns are also higher in carbohydrates. Often ground into a flour by historic native peoples, acorns might have played a distinctly different dietary role than the more oily nuts.

Fruits were recovered in much smaller numbers and less frequently than nutshell, but this more likely reflects their lower preservation potential than their dietary importance. Of the various fruit taxa recovered, persimmon, grape, and sumac repeatedly occurred in the samples, across all sites. This pattern of recovery suggests that these fruits in particular were regular components of early groups' diets but may also reflect the relatively large size of these seeds. The Dust Cave plant assemblage also contained significant numbers of hackberry seeds. In general, the fruits have lower caloric values than the nuts, but they also have significantly lower processing costs. As a result, their energetic return rates are sizeable, particularly when transported over short distances. It is likely that gatherers specifically targeted these low-cost resources during the height of their availability in summer.

A variety of edible seeds were recovered from the assemblages, particularly from sites with access to the Tennessee Valley. Of these edible seeds, most are represented by few specimens, often only in a single sample or a single site. These include smartweed and purslane seeds. Due to their infrequent recovery, these seeds may be incidental inclusions. Wild legumes were recovered more frequently, however, as were chenopod seeds. The latter demonstrate a much different pattern of recovery than the other edible seeds, particularly at Dust Cave, where they occurred in significantly more samples and in much greater quantities. Taken together, the patterns suggest that early gatherers did indeed utilize edible seeds. The relationship between gatherers and these taxa, particularly chenopod, is of notable interest, as gatherers in the Southeast eventually cultivated and in some instances domesticated these edible seeds in the Late Archaic period, around 3,500 years ago (Smith 1985; Yarnell 1993). The evidence presented here extends interactions between people and these plants into the Late Paleoindian period, some 9,000 years earlier.

Edible seeds are more similar to nuts than fruits in their nutritional value as well as their processing costs. Relatively high in fat and protein, and therefore in calories, the edible seeds also require significant processing to strip or thresh them from the seed heads. They generally have lower energetic return rates than nuts, suggesting that gatherers would collect dried seed heads in late fall or early winter, after the height of nut harvests.

The recovery of a number of the seed taxa hints at the use of leafy greens and spring shoots by early gatherers. These include chenopod, purslane, smartweed, pokeweed, and bedstraw. Although the seeds ripen in fall and the greens and shoots are generally only palatable in spring, it is not unreasonable to presume that gatherers would have utilized greens and shoots, particularly because they are the first plant foods, other than roots and tubers, available to foragers at the end of lean winters. Early peoples certainly interacted with these weedy plants. Even if the seeds were incidental inclusions rather that having been used by site occupants, these weedy plants must have grown close to the habitation sites. As such, early peoples were familiar with them. Although high in vitamins and minerals, leafy greens have relatively low energetic return rates, due primarily to their low caloric content. As such, gatherers likely did not travel far from habitation sites to collect these plant foods.

Few changes through time are apparent within the assemblages for which the Late Paleoindian and Early Archaic components could be separated. Use of black walnut and chenopod may decrease, while the opposite trend may be argued for wild legumes. However, there does not seem to be a significant shift in use of plants until the close of the Early Archaic period, when early groups appear to increase their use of hickory, and perhaps acorn. On the whole, however, the climatic and environmental transition from the Late Pleistocene to Early Holocene conditions appears to have had little impact on gathering within the project area.

The plant assemblages from the four rockshelter sites are generally comparable to those recovered from other sites in the Southeast (Table 7.1). Hickory nutshell is similarly predominant and ubiquitous, with acorn recovered regularly in smaller quantities. Black walnut and hazelnut occur more sporadically. Two members of the Beech family, beechnut and chestnut, were recovered from two Early Archaic sites in eastern Tennessee (Chapman and Shea 1981) but are poorly represented at the four rockshelter sites. Only several fragments from Dust Cave were identified as Beech family, but species could not be determined. Beechnut and particularly chestnut are not likely to be preserved and recovered, however, due to their thin, papery shells.

Similarities are also apparent among fruits. Most frequently recovered from Southeastern sites are grape, persimmon, sumac, and hackberry. Among edible seeds, chenopod was recovered from the most sites and in the greatest quantities, similar to the rockshelter samples. Other edible seeds include amaranth and knotweed, also eventually cultivated by Southeastern peoples around 3,500 years ago. Pokeweed and bedstraw are among the taxa with leafy greens and spring shoots represented by seed taxa. Weedy taxa not present at the four rockshelter sites include maygrass, peppervine, and copperleaf.

In general, then, the Late Paleoindian and Early Archaic plant assemblages from sites across the Southeast demonstrate greater similarities than differences. These similarities hold not only among the categories of plant foods recovered, but also within these categories. Hickory and acorn appear dominant among the nuts, with black walnut, hazel, and perhaps beechnut and chestnut playing lesser roles. Grape, persimmon, and sumac faithfully recur among fruits. Chenopod is more frequently recovered than other edible seeds. In addition, there are no glaring differences between the Late Paleoindian and Early Archaic assemblages, as the scarcity of taxa other than nuts

Table 7.1. Nonwood Plant Taxa Recovered from Late Paleoindian and Early Archaic Sites in the Southeast.

	Late Paleoindian Sites			Early Archaic Sites									
	Hester[a]	Rodgers[b]	Pearson[c]	Hester[a]	Patrick[d]	St. Albans[e]	Pearson[c]	1Gr1x1[f]	1Pi61[f]	1Gr50[f]	Lower Kirk IB[g]	Upper Kirk IB,BF[g]	Bifurcate IB/RI/CI/BF[g]
Acorn	x		1	x	x	x	3	.5g	.3g		9.7g	22.6g, 14.5g	18.7g,11.6g,37.1g,2.5g
Beechnut													< .2g,NA,NA,NA
Black walnut	x	x		x						.2g	< .1g	0g, .4g	.9g,NA,NA,NA
Chestnut												0g, .2g	9.6g,NA,NA,NA
Hazelnut													< .2g,NA,NA,NA
Hickory	x	x	265	x	x	x	1315	4.7g	50.1g	2.5g	49.5g	47.7g,38.2g	173.7g,76.4g,384.7g,15.8g
Walnut family	x										< .5g	NA, .4g	.9g,NA,NA,NA
Amaranth												1	
Asteraceae													16
Bedstraw													27
Bramble													1
Chenopod						x					3		14
Copperleaf												1	
Grape					x							4	10
Hackberry		x		x									

Continued on the next page

Table 7.1. *Continued*

	Late Paleoindian Sites			Early Archaic Sites									
	Hester[a]	Rodgers[b]	Pearson[c]	Hester[a]	Patrick[d]	St. Albans[e]	Pearson[c]	1Gr1x1[f]	1Pi61[f]	1Gr50[f]	Lower Kirk IB[g]	Upper Kirk IB,BF[g]	Bifurcate IB/RI/CI/BF[g]
Knotweed													1
Maygrass													1
Peppervine											1		
Persimmon				x					1			3	
Pokeweed					x							2	27
Sumac											2		2

[a] 22Mo569; Lentz 1986.
[b] Parmalee et al. 1976.
[c] Detwiler 2003.
[d] Schroedl 1978.
[e] Snider 1971.
[f] Caddell 1982.
[g] Chapman and Shea 1981. The abbreviations refer to the following: IB--Icehouse Bottom; BF--Bacon Farm; RI--Rose Island; CI--Calloway Island.

from Late Paleoindian sites is more likely due to sample size and perhaps preservation issues rather than shifts in gathering practices.

Although the assemblages are largely similar across time and space, we should not then conclude that gatherers performed the same tasks between 12,500 and 8,000 years ago at all sites in the Southeast. They do appear to have been presented with similar resources, the use of which entails particular costs and benefits. However, both the costs and benefits vary in relation to the landscape and the distribution of resources, including plants, animals, and stone materials, upon the landscape. Because they articulate with the exploitation of other resources, the decisions and activities associated with gathering surely varied in different landscapes. I further discuss such variations within the project area below, but first provide an overview of these decisions and activities faced by gatherers.

ACTIVITIES ASSOCIATED WITH GATHERING PLANT FOODS

An understanding of the decisions and actions involved in exploiting the various plant taxa described above is critical for two reasons. First, such information gives meaning to an otherwise rather uninteresting list of carbonized plants and their counts and weights, and encourages us to contemplate the peoples who used them. Second, it suggests activities that should be considered in models of early subsistence strategies and mobility patterns. Both botanical and ethnographic information can be used to better understand who might have collected the various plant taxa listed above, and where, when, and how they might have done so.

First and foremost, gatherers require knowledge of the habitats in which the various plants thrive and the seasons in which they ripen. This knowledge not only demands a catalogue of the plants that populate the landscape and their properties, but also a detailed mental map of the distribution of plants on the landscape, as well as a calendar of seasonal progressions and interannual cycles. Gatherers would take note of idiosyncratic events and accordingly adjust their "calendars" and emphasize particular areas on the "map." A cold spring would delay blooming and negatively impact nut yields, while an early frost might hasten the availability of nuts and seeds. A series of floods or a wildfire would depress the immediate availability of plant foods in the area affected, but would heighten yields in the following year.

In addition, a number of taxa do not produce sizeable harvests on a yearly basis. Oaks, hickories, and black walnuts only yield acorns and nuts in appreciable quantities every two to five years, depending on the species. In addition, these periodic yields are synchronized across species over a large geographic area, several hundred kilometers apart (Koenig and Knops 2000, 2005). During poor years, gatherers would not have simply been able to go to the next hickory grove. Short of moving their camp as much as 800 kilometers away, they would have had to make the best of that year's crop and fill in dietary voids with other foodstuffs such as edible seeds. Gatherers would thus need to adjust their strategies accordingly.

To stay abreast of both the location of productive stands and the timing of harvests, gatherers certainly monitored the growth of plants on the landscape around them. Such monitoring could have taken place during the course of other activities, such as collection of firewood or water, while hunting or checking traps, on the way to fishing spots or berry patches, or while moving camp from one spot to the next. This information might well have been shared among members of a group, or between groups during larger (macroband) aggregations.

Once plant foods ripened, group members would need to decide whom to send to patches to gather the plant foods. Across ethnographic foraging groups, the gathering of most plant foods falls largely to women. Rather than an agreement between men and women to complement their food tasks, this decision appears to be related to the need of women to obtain stable nutrition for themselves and their children. Generally predictable in time and space, particularly when monitored over the course of a season, plants serve as reliable sources of food. Children likely joined women in collecting and gathering, particularly of plant foods such as fruits that require little processing. Individuals likely gathered foods for themselves and their families, rather than sharing among larger groups. This is suggested not only by ethnographic accounts, but also by the fact that neither handling costs nor handling times for the plant foods considered here appear to decrease for task groups of two or more. This does not mean that gatherers performed their tasks alone. They might have gathered in groups, for camaraderie as much as safety or any other reason, particularly if the resource patch were large enough to support the efforts of multiple gatherers.

While the larger pattern suggests that women gathered and men hunted, there was likely a large degree of overlap, both among different individuals and for different food resources. Women may well have hunted, particularly smaller animals that are more reliably taken. They might also have joined men on longer hunting forays. And men may well have gathered, particularly those resources such as nuts that have a short period of availability, have high return rates, and might have served as important staples stored over the winter.

Whether men or women gathered plant foods, it is highly likely that women processed and prepared them. This allocation of food preparation to women similarly holds across ethnographic foraging groups, and includes both plant and animal foods (Hawkes 1996; Kelly 1995; Panter-Brick 2002). As such, the tools associated with food preparation likely belonged to women and might have been made by them as well (Bird 1993). In addition to knives and scrapers, these would include nutting stones. Bedrock mortars such as those at Stanfield-Worley might have belonged to a particular woman and her family, perhaps marking her/their usufruct rights to the shelter and the resources in its vicinity (e.g., Jackson 1991).

Once gathered and processed, early groups may have stored some of these plant foods. No evidence for underground storage by Late Paleoindian and Early Archaic peoples has been found in the region, particularly at the four rockshelter sites discussed here. Yet this does not preclude the use of bags, baskets, and other aboveground containers for storing foods. We should not rule out the possibility that early peoples gathered and processed plant foods for storage. Indeed, storage of plant foods is perhaps necessary to support the argument that groups invested heavily in the collection of resources such as nuts, seeds, and fruits by moving their campsites and engaging the labor of all group members. Such large-scale efforts would not generally be needed to meet an individual's daily nutritional requirements.

In addition to the above activities, early groups might also have actively shaped the distribution of plant resources on the landscape. They might have encouraged the growth of particular species, perhaps by pruning, transplanting, dropping seeds, or clearing away competition (e.g., Fowler 1996; Scarry and Yarnell 2006). Using controlled fires, they might also have created and/or maintained forest clearings (e.g., Fowler 1996). This would produce edge situations favored by shrubs such as sumac and hazel, and frequented by game like deer and rabbits. It would also allow the crowns of nearby nut-bearing trees to grow in a more open setting, thus increasing their yield (Munson 1986). Again, no direct evidence for such interactions between early Southeastern groups and the landscape is available, but given the intimate knowledge of the landscape that these early peoples likely had, such an intimate relationship is not improbable.

SUBSISTENCE PRACTICES IN THE LATE PALEOINDIAN AND EARLY ARCHAIC PERIODS

Because the foraging groups who lived at the four rockshelter sites used animal and stone resources in addition to plants, I consider the results of faunal and stone tool analyses for each of the sites. I use information from the faunal analyses to complement the plant analyses regarding both the habitats exploited by the sites' occupants and the seasons in which they occupied the sites. Stone tool analyses indicate an additional range of activities performed by early foragers while at the sites. The raw materials used to manufacture the stone tools further provide information about the distance over which groups routinely traveled to obtain such materials. The various strands of data weave together to suggest the subsistence strategies employed by Late Paleoindian and Early Archaic groups. Below I examine the activities performed at each site, and then explore the similarities and differences among them to determine how these activities vary through time and space.

Stanfield-Worley

Nuts and fruits dominate the plant remains from Stanfield-Worley, indicating that the site's wooded surroundings provided ample opportunity for gathering these resources. The occupants of the site likely targeted the autumn collection of nuts, particularly hickory, acorn, and black walnut, as well as ripened persimmons after the first frost. Other than one sample tentatively assigned to the Dalton zone from which large quantities of acorn meats were recovered, acorn is rather poorly represented relative to hickory and black walnut, although this is most likely due to differences in recovery.

The sizeable representation of black walnut bears further mention. This species occurs in numbers comparable to hickory, unlike the assemblages at Rollins and Dust Cave. Because black walnuts grow singly rather than in stands, gatherers generally cannot collect walnuts from multiple trees in a single location. The significant quantities of black walnut recovered suggest that either black walnut trees were more common in the surrounding area, and/or that gatherers visited black walnut trees with particularly high yields. The latter would include trees with large crowns that grew in relatively open conditions. Both possibilities speak to the nature of the local environment.

In comparison, gatherers appear to have collected hazelnuts more opportunistically than the other nut taxa. Fruits might also have been gathered as encountered, but prior to the ripening of nuts, gatherers may well have set out on forays to specifically collect grapes, and possibly sumac and honey locust. These fruits, as well as persimmons later in the fall, might have been collected for immediate consumption as well as to dry for future use.

In addition to gathering nuts, the women visiting Stanfield-Worley appear to have invested some time and energy in processing them. This is suggested by the presence of bedrock mortars at the site, including conical "hominy holes" at the edge of the drip line as well as cup-shaped depressions, or nutting stones, pecked into the bedrock encountered at the base of the Dalton zone. At least one hammerstone and pecked sandstone slab were also recovered from this component (DeJarnette et al. 1962:83–85; Goldman-Finn 1997:8, 10). The recovery of over 200 acorn meats from one sample also speaks to nut processing. These meats may have been accidentally burned while being parched or toasted, perhaps to reduce the tannin content and/or prepare them for storage by preventing germination and contamination by insects, mold, and mildew. The presence of what may be prepared surfaces near the bedrock nutting stones is also intriguing (Homsey 2004:269). These surfaces might have been ideal for spreading out nutmeats and coals for parching or toasting.

While nuts may be stored in the shell, these processing activities suggest that foraging groups occupied the site during autumn, likely during the peak of nut availability. Persimmons, sumac berries, grapes, and honey locust pods might have been brought to the site from previously visited locations as they can be dried and stored as well, but they are also available in late summer and early autumn. This does not rule out use of the site during other seasons. The occupants might have parched and stored nuts such as acorns within the rockshelter, planning to return in winter. No features suggesting underground storage were encountered, but this does not preclude use of aboveground storage in baskets or bags.

Hunting and hide preparation also appear to have been important activities performed by the site's occupants. White-tailed deer were a particular focus of hunting efforts, as they comprise the majority of identified bone from the Dalton zone. Squirrel is also well represented, as are turkey and turtles (Parmalee 1962). Meat cutting and hide preparation are indicated by the range of tools, as well as microwear polish on these tools (Goldman-Finn 1997).

Microwear analyses also indicate that the site occupants worked wood (Goldman-Finn 1997:26). Tool manufacture, however, is poorly represented at the site. The stone tool assemblage is characterized by resharpened and heavily reworked items and is notably lacking in early-stage bifaces (Goldman-Finn 1997:15; Randall 2002:100). In addition, the majority of tools are made from blue-gray Fort Payne chert, which outcrops along the Tennessee River some 10 kilometers from the site, rather than locally available materials. This leads Goldman-Finn (1997:29) and Randall (2002:103–105) to suggest that hunters visiting Stanfield-Worley prepared their toolkits prior to visiting the site, quite likely at locales within the river valley nearer chert outcrops.

Randall (2002:103–105) further proposes that the occupants at Stanfield-Worley did not manufacture tools at the site because it was not convenient for them to do so. Instead, men and women invested their time in hunting, particularly white-tailed deer, and collecting and processing nuts. Both of these activities have temporal and, to some extent, spatial limits. Ripened acorns, black walnuts, and hickory nuts are available in quantity for only several weeks during autumn. Deer and turkeys vie for these mast resources as well. Both are particularly attractive prey in the fall, in part because they carry extra fat for the upcoming winter. They are also bolder in their movements and therefore easier to hunt: deer are in the midst of mating season, and turkeys travel in larger flocks in autumn. Gatherers and hunters might have headed to the uplands near the site to take advantage of both nuts and the wildlife attracted to them.

In sum, the collection and processing of hickory nuts, black walnuts, and acorns appear to have been important activities at the site, supported not only by the plant remains but also by the presence of bedrock mortars, as well as a hammerstone and sandstone slab that might have been used to crack nuts. Prepared surfaces near the bedrock mortars might also have been manufactured for and used to prepare nuts for consumption or storage. The occupants supplemented hunted food and nuts with fruits, including persimmons, grapes, and sumac. This interpretation contrasts markedly with DeJarnette and colleagues' (1962:85–88) original conclusions that the Dalton peoples relied all but exclusively on hunting for their subsistence during their stays at Stanfield-Worley.

Rollins Bluff Shelter

Gatherers who visited Rollins Bluff Shelter appear to have pursued hickory nuts, and likely acorn as well, as both taxa had high ubiquities. Although hickory nutshell was recovered in much greater numbers than acorn, these differences are likely due to preservation. Interestingly, though, the two taxa display different trends through time. Use of acorn remains stable relative to other plants, while hickory use decreases. This suggests that the manner in which site occupants used, processed, and/or disposed of hickory nutshell seems to have changed. Gatherers appear to have collected black walnuts as the opportunity arose, but did not specifically target these nuts, as they are present only in low numbers.

Both Dalton and Early Archaic occupants supplemented their diets with fruit, which might have been fresh or dried. Women and children might have targeted fruits for collection prior to nut harvests, gathered for immediate consumption and/or to dry for future use. During the peak of nut gathering, groups probably gathered fruits opportunistically, with the majority of effort concentrated on collecting acorns and hickory nuts.

Edible seeds do not appear to have figured largely in the diets of the site's occupants, as evidenced by the recovery of a single wild legume from the Early Archaic component. The rarity of edible and weedy seeds in the Rollins samples may be related to the local setting, as well as sampling issues. Creeks and streams cut steep valleys into the sandstone hills of the uplands in the Fall Line Hills, creating relatively narrow zones of disturbance appropriate for the growth of weedy taxa. Significant stands of weedy taxa might have been lacking. The paucity of these taxa could well be related to sampling: although the samples were processed using floatation, they appear to be rather small in size and were passed through 1/4-inch mesh before being processed. Thus the small size of samples may have precluded significant recovery of such seeds, which are relatively infrequent to begin with, and/or the initial screening might have damaged small seeds, making them unidentifiable.

Gatherers processed nuts and perhaps fruits and seeds at the site, as evidenced by mortars, nutting stones, and mullers/hammerstones (Stowe 1970). One mortar and one nutting stone were recovered from the Dalton component, increasing in the Early Archaic component to two mortars and five mortar fragments, five nutting stones, three muller/hammerstones, one hammerstone, and one anvil stone (Stowe 1970:Tables 14–16). The increase in ground stone tools associated with processing plant foods coincides with the rise in the ubiquity of acorn shell, suggesting an increase in plant use at the site, whether due to more frequent or more intensive site use.

Although the various plant taxa may be stored, their availability overlaps in autumn. The fruits and wild legume ripen in summer, and squash in late summer, but are also present through the fall, when nut harvests peak. As mentioned above, the recovery of ground stone tools in the Dalton and Early Archaic components suggests that nut processing was an important activity at the site, further indicating an autumn occupation. Use of the site during other seasons cannot be ruled out, however.

Additional stone artifacts recovered from the site indicate that the occupants also hunted and prepared hides. This is suggested by the presence of points, unifacial blades, various forms of scrapers, and utilized flake tools. Unfortunately, preservation of bone at Rollins was poor, thus precluding faunal analyses. However, the small amount of bone present appears to be predominantly white-tailed deer (Stowe 1970:124).

In addition to hunting and hide preparation, the site's occupants also manufactured stone tools. This is evidenced by numerous waste flakes, particularly in the Early Archaic deposits. The increase in debitage, as well as in chipped stone tools, in the Early Archaic component may reflect increased intensity of site use. Ground stone tools also increase, as noted above. The stone tool assemblage thus complements the increase in plant use, suggesting that gatherers and hunters used the site more frequently or stayed for longer periods.

The lithic assemblage also demonstrates a decrease in the use of nonlocal blue-gray Fort Payne chert, out of which a slight majority of the Dalton points are made, in favor of locally available Tuscaloosa gravel. This suggests that Dalton occupants had stronger ties to the Tennessee River, where blue-gray Fort Payne chert outcrops, some 40 km from Rollins Bluff Shelter. They might have traveled to the river valley more often, or traded more extensively with groups in that region. Interestingly, though, the proportion of blue-gray Fort Payne debitage does not change between the two components. Rather than transporting raw materials with them, both Dalton and Early Archaic peoples brought finished blue-gray Fort Payne tools, including points, unifacial tools, and utilized flakes, with them to Rollins. They appear instead to be using local chert to make tools onsite, including expedient tools. Indeed, all of the cores from these early components are of Tuscaloosa gravel.

On the whole, the occupants of Rollins Bluff Shelter hunted, prepared hides, manufactured stone tools, and processed nuts, particularly hickory and acorn. Nut processing appears to have been an important activity at the site, as evidenced not only by the plant remains but also by the presence of mortars, nutting stones, and mullers. It is possible that these artifacts were stored at the site, reinforcing use of the site for processing nuts. The intensity of occupation, whether in terms of longer stays or more frequent visits, appears to have increased in the Early Archaic period. Concomitantly, the occupants' range of mobility seems to have decreased to some extent, as suggested by the decrease in use of nonlocal blue-gray Fort Payne chert. It is possible that Early Archaic hunter-gatherers adjusted their ranges in response to climatic and subsequent habitat changes, or to increases in population density. Ties with the Tennessee River Valley remained important, however, as occupants continued to use tools made from blue-gray Fort Payne chert.

LaGrange Bluff Shelter

Although few floatation samples were available from LaGrange, those few samples were rich in plant taxa. Gatherers exploited hickory and black walnut, which were most frequently recovered from the samples, as well as acorn, which recurred consistently, although in low numbers. This may reflect preservation differences between acorn and the more robust Walnut family nuts. Nut processing is also evidenced at the site by the presence of at least one nutting stone, associated with carbonized nutshells, in the Early Archaic deposits. The nut taxa suggest that the surrounding environment included rich woods, especially indicated by the black walnut. Similar to Stanfield-Worley, the quantity of black walnut recovered is comparable to hickory nutshell, suggesting either that black walnut trees were relatively common within the region, and/or that these trees grew in a relatively open environment, thus yielding significant nut crops. An open environment could include forest margins. Such edge situations are suggested by the presence of hazel and sumac. The faunal assemblage also includes animals that favor wooded and ecotone habitats. Among the former are opossum, raccoon, squirrel, and box turtle, and the latter include white-tailed deer, striped skunk, and fox (Curren 1976).

The wide range of weedy seed taxa recovered might have grown in clearings, but also may reflect use of disturbed habitats along streams. Dry Creek runs just two kilometers to the north of the shelter, and Brush Pond is located five kilometers to the northeast. Both are associated with soils that occasionally flood or pond, providing the best habitat for wetland plants within Colbert County (Bowen 1994). Gatherers might have exploited these disturbed settings to obtain edible seeds, and perhaps greens as well. They likely gathered seed heads of chenopod, but probably not until after hickory nuts, acorns, and black walnuts had been harvested. Similarly, they might have collected wild legumes, which mature as early as July or August, prior to and/or after the peak in nut gathering. If gathered in late summer by pulling up the whole plant, the occupants might have left them to dry before threshing them.

LaGrange's occupants also consumed a variety of fruits, which were recovered consistently although in low numbers. These fruits, including persimmon, grape, sumac, mulberry, and possibly maypop, can all be dried and stored, so that it is possible they were brought to the site already dried rather than gathered fresh while the site was occupied. While they might have gathered fruits opportunistically during the peak of the nut harvest, women and children might have targeted ripe fruits during late summer. The major exception is mulberry, which ripens as early as May and is available only through August. Because of intense competition with wildlife, gatherers likely concentrated their efforts on these fruits during the peak of their availability, similar to their strategies for collecting nuts.

Assuming that LaGrange's occupants collected mulberries rather than having transported dried berries to the rockshelter from previous campsites, then it is likely these groups visited the site during summer as well as autumn. Although it is difficult to extrapolate from just a few fruit seeds, it is possible that gatherers used the site as a camp during collection and processing of mulberries in summer; sumac berries, grapes, and perhaps maypops, as well as wild legumes and hazelnuts in late summer and early fall; persimmons, acorns, black walnuts, and hickory nuts in autumn; and chenopod and perhaps wild legumes in late autumn and/or early winter. It is unlikely that they continuously occupied the site from May through November; the artifact density and number of features at the site do not warrant such an interpretation. Instead, groups probably inhabited the site over the course of several days or perhaps weeks, a pattern of use that likely applies to the other three sites as well.

In addition to gathering and processing nuts, fruits, and edible seeds, the occupants of LaGrange also engaged in hunting, hide preparation, and to some extent tool manufacture. Hunting is suggested by the presence of bifacial and unifacial blades and knives, in addition to hafted points. Although the faunal assemblage is relatively small, it indicates that the site's occupants hunted white-tailed deer, opossum, raccoon, squirrel, and rabbit (Curren 1976). Hide preparation is evidenced by the recovery of bifacial and unifacial scrapers, as well as a bone awl from the Early Archaic component that may have served as a leather punch.

Toolmaking is suggested by the presence of cores, particularly a cache of nine blue-gray Fort Payne chert cores recovered from Zone C, which is associated with corner-notched Early Archaic points. Few artifacts were recovered from this zone other than the cores, which were associated with a significant concentration of waste flakes toward the rear of the shelter. DeJarnette and Knight (1976) otherwise conclude that the occupants made few stone tools at the site, as preforms are rare and the majority of debitage is less than 10 mm in size. They suggest that the debitage therefore derives from retouch rather than stone tool manufacture. DeJarnette and Knight (1976:29) speculate that a specialized unifacial toolkit, comprised of scrapers, flakes, and knives, found in the Early Archaic levels of Zone B might have been used for wood-, bone-, and/or hide-working, so occupants might have focused their efforts on making tools from materials other than stone at the site.

Although quantitative information is not provided, DeJarnette and Knight (1976:49) note that the stone tools and flakes from all components demonstrate "the practically exclusive dominance" of blue-gray Fort Payne chert.

Indeed, four of the five Dalton points and 14 of the 16 Early Side-Notched points are made from blue-gray Fort Payne. This contrasts with Stanfield-Worley, which apparently included greater quantities of locally available Tuscaloosa gravel, even though the two sites are located similar distances from outcrops of blue-gray Fort Payne chert. The stone tool assemblage at LaGrange further differs from Stanfield-Worley in that Dalton points in particular, and presumably Early Side-Notched points as well, show little evidence of resharpening, suggesting that they were relatively disposable rather than heavily curated. Taken together, this suggests that the occupants of LaGrange made the majority of their stone tools elsewhere, but also had relatively easy access to raw materials, namely blue-gray Fort Payne chert. Located on the escarpment between Little Mountain and the plateau of the Tennessee River Valley, rather than nestled into the mountain ridges as Stanfield-Worley is, LaGrange may simply have offered easier travel to and from the river floodplains. Alternatively, the chert may have been available farther up the smaller streams and creeks around LaGrange than Stanfield-Worley, reducing the distance that occupants traveled to obtain it.

Also of interest are numerous pieces of abraded red and yellow ocher recovered from the site. These include five fragments of red ocher from the Dalton deposits, 19 pieces of red ocher and four of yellow ocher in the Early Archaic levels of Zone D, and four red ocher and one yellow ocher fragment from Early Archaic levels of Zone B. DeJarnette and Knight (1976:47) suggest that these artifacts may have held ritual importance. Abraded ocher is notably absent from Zone C, from which few artifacts were recovered in general. However, in this zone excavators encountered a burial of a middle-aged adult, accompanied by four chert flakes, a chert core, and a fragment of limestone. It seems that use of the site changed significantly during this component, which is associated with two corner-notched points. Interestingly, none of the rockshelters investigated here claim significant Early Archaic Kirk Corner-Notched deposits, often in stark contrast to the preceding Early Side-Notched and succeeding Kirk Stemmed and Eva/Morrow Mountain periods. Although an erosional event(s) might have removed evidence of Kirk Corner-Notched occupations from Dust Cave (Sherwood 2001; Sherwood et al. 2004), marked changes in the place of rockshelters in peoples' social landscapes during this period are also possible.

Few features are associated with the Dalton and Early Archaic occupations at LaGrange. These include two small pits—one near the bottom of Zone B and another in Zone D—that might have served as fire basins. A large, hardened surface of dark gray, clayey soil was encountered in Zone D, along with charred plant remains, animal bone, an Early Side-Notched point, and a nutting stone. DeJarnette and Knight (1976:48) note that this surface showed signs of fire, and refer to it as an "occupational floor." It is possible that this "floor" served purposes similar to the prepared surfaces observed at Dust Cave, for toasting, grilling, and various cooking activities (Homsey 2004; Sherwood 2001; Sherwood et al. 2004). That it is associated with a nutting stone, similar to the hardened clay surface at Stanfield-Worley adjacent to a bedrock mortar, is further intriguing and informative of its possible function.

In sum, the assemblages at LaGrange suggest that the site's occupants not only gathered and processed nuts but also exploited fruits and edible seeds. Use of edible seeds in particular might have entailed trips to the nearby creek and/or pond, with their associated soils prone to flooding and ponding. In addition to gathering, the occupants hunted game and prepared hides, and might have made bone and wood tools, but seem to have primarily maintained rather than manufactured stone tools. They appear to have made their chipped stone tools elsewhere, perhaps nearer the chert source along the Tennessee River. These groups must have had ready access to blue-gray Fort Payne chert, as the vast majority of their tools derive from this raw material, although it outcrops some 10 km from the site. It appears that the occupants of LaGrange frequented the Tennessee River floodplain.

In addition to serving as a temporary shelter for foraging groups, LaGrange might also have held ritual importance. This noneconomic dimension is suggested by the recovery of numerous fragments of abraded red and yellow ocher from all components of the site, and more so by the burial of an individual within the shelter's deposits. Such use of the rockshelter reminds us that these sites, as well as open-air sites, figured as important places on a social landscape that intertwined with the economic ones that we readily map.

Dust Cave

The plant assemblage from Dust Cave is the richest of the four on several levels. More samples were available for study from this site, and these samples derive from both floatation columns and features. As such, they provide both an averaged view of plant use at the site, as well as use that is bounded in time and space. Certainly related, at least in part, to the fact that the sample size is larger, the greatest range of plant taxa was recovered from Dust Cave.

The collection and processing of hickory nuts, as well as acorns, appears to have been a major activity of gatherers at Dust Cave. The consistently low numbers of acorn shell recovered are likely related to differences in preservation rather than use. In fact, several features contained significant quantities of acorn shell; of these, all but one included markedly greater quantities of acorn than hickory nutshell. Significant use of acorn at the site must not be overlooked. Black walnut and hazelnut, however, are recovered infrequently, often in low numbers. Several samples do contain greater quantities, perhaps suggesting years in which bumper crops of these nuts were available. In general, however, it seems that the site's occupants collected these nuts opportunistically, rather than targeting them as they did hickory nuts and acorns.

The occupants also consumed a variety of fruits that likely supplemented their diets. These include hackberry, persimmon, grape, and sumac, and possibly black gum and nightshade berries. Women and children might have concentrated their efforts toward collecting these fruits in late summer, prior to the height of nut availability, or perhaps picked them opportunistically while collecting nuts. They also might have gathered these fruits, with the exception of grapes, after harvesting nuts in the fall, as they persist on trees into winter. In addition to eating them fresh, gatherers might have dried and stored the fruits for future use.

Edible seeds recur consistently at Dust Cave, identified in over half of the Late Paleoindian and Early Side-Notched samples. While wild legumes were recovered in 10 samples, cheno-ams in six, and smartweed in just a single Late Paleoindian sample, chenopod occurs in 42 of the 106 samples from the site. This includes nearly half of the column samples and one-fourth of the features. Smartweed and cheno-ams might have been used occasionally, but gatherers appear to have significantly exploited chenopod in particular, and perhaps wild legumes. It is likely that gatherers specifically targeted chenopod, perhaps cutting dried seed heads after the peak of nut harvesting and returning with them to the site to thresh and prepare the seeds.

A variety of weedy seeds were also identified among the plant assemblage. The spring leaves of several of these, including poke, bedstraw, and purslane, as well as chenopod, smartweed, nightshade, and sumac, might have been used for greens. However, the seeds recovered in the samples, of course, are available in autumn. Some of these weedy seeds are likely commensals, perhaps growing in the immediate vicinity of the site and blown in by wind or tracked in by people or animals. The presence of both commensals and edible weedy seeds suggests that the local surroundings of the site were significantly disturbed, either by recurrent flooding of the creek that flowed within 50 m of the cave's entrance, or perhaps as a result of frequent human habitation. In either case, it is possible that chenopod grew in the immediate vicinity of the site.

The nut taxa in particular suggest that groups used the site in autumn. While the fruits ripen as early as midsummer, they are also generally available through fall. Similarly, the weedy seeds may mature in summer but also persist through autumn and in some cases into late winter. The faunal assemblage provides additional information regarding seasonality of site use. The recovery of a white-tailed deer antler still attached to the frontal bone suggests fall or early winter occupation, prior to loss of antlers in late winter and early spring (Walker 1998:152). Passenger pigeons, a migratory species, would have been available in fall and winter (Walker 1998:148). The significant use of waterfowl suggests occupation of the site during the migration of geese and ducks in fall and perhaps spring (Walker 1998:150). A possible spring occupation is further suggested by the recovery of suckers. In spring, these fish leave the main river channel for smaller tributary streams in large numbers to spawn, and would have provided ample fishing for the site's occupants in this season (Walker 1998:152). Occupation in other seasons is also possible; freshwater mussels, regularly recovered from the samples, would have provided a stable, year-round food source (Parmalee 1994:159).

Although the plant assemblage from all components at the site is generally characterized by nutshell, the quantitative data indicate several shifts in plant use through time. General increases in plant remains recovered suggest more intensive use of the site over time, whether through more frequent visits, longer stays, or increased activity during those stays. In particular, use of nuts as a foodstuff seems to have intensified, namely during the Kirk Stemmed component. Hickory nutshell increases significantly relative to other plant remains. Acorn use may also increase, as suggested by its ubiquity values, but does not appear to keep pace with increases in hickory. Use of black walnut, however, appears to decrease during the Kirk Stemmed component, as does hazelnut. This drop is perhaps related to a decline in open-growth or edge settings, in which these species produce higher yields. This coincides with a decrease in the recovery of edible and weedy seeds. Chenopod in particular drops significantly, while wild legumes, in contrast, may increase in importance. Compared to the nut taxa, however, use of wild legumes also appears to drop. Use of fruits, however, seems to change little over time, with the exception of hackberries, which decrease significantly in the Kirk Stemmed component.

Given the significant increase in hickory nuts along with the drop in use of resources that prefer open or edge settings, including weedy seed taxa, hazelnut, and perhaps black walnut, the Kirk Stemmed occupants of Dust

Cave appear to be targeting forest resources. This shift may be driven by changes in local ecological conditions, cultural practices, or both. Warmer temperatures during the Hypsithermal period might have increased the yield of hickory and oak trees, or shortened the spacing between bumper crops (perhaps every other year rather than every two to five years), reducing the need for gatherers to turn to lower-ranked resources like edible seeds. Trends in the faunal assemblage also suggest an increase in use of resources from closed habitats, coinciding with a decrease in use of species from open habitats (Walker 1998; see Chapter 5). This coincides with an increase in the use of mammals and a decrease in bird species, particularly waterfowl (Walker 1998).

Use of aquatic resources, however, remains fairly consistent. Walker (1998: 139–141; Walker et al. 2001:179) notes that over 60 percent of the faunal remains (comparing the number of individual specimens) from the Late Paleoindian through Kirk Stemmed components derive from aquatic habitats. This dependence on aquatic species is highest in the Early Side-Notched component, comprising some 75 percent of the total faunal assemblage. This relative stability masks a significant increase in exploitation of fish after the Late Paleoindian, as well as a decrease in use of waterfowl. Reliance on aquatic habitats is also indicated by the recovery of mussels from the deposits, which appears to increase in the Kirk Stemmed component. The various species in the assemblage indicate that occupants of Dust Cave collected shellfish both from the main river channel and its smaller tributaries (Parmalee 1994).

Geoarchaeological analyses of the sediments and feature assemblage demonstrate a significant shift in the Kirk Stemmed component as well. The Kirk Stemmed deposits contain significant quantities of ash and appear to be primarily anthropogenic (Sherwood 2001). The number and diversity of features increase substantially in these deposits, and their spatial distribution leads Homsey (2004) to suggest that the occupants were conserving space by clustering different activities in particular areas of the site. Notably, Homsey's (2003, 2004) geochemical analyses indicate that certain feature types, namely charcoal pits, contain high levels of strontium, which may reflect burning of hickory nutshell. Although more numerous in the Kirk Stemmed component, it is important to note that charcoal pits, as well as prepared surfaces that might have been used for a variety of cooking tasks, occur in the Late Paleoindian and Early Side-Notched components as well.

Recovery of ground stone tools might also reflect increases in nut processing. While no nutting stones were recovered from the earlier deposits, five derive from the Kirk Stemmed component. It is possible, however, that excavators did not recognize nutting stones as such in earlier deposits, mistaking these limestone slabs for roof fall instead.

In general, the chipped stone tool and bone tool assemblages suggest considerable continuity through time in activities performed at the site. Stone tools include points and nonhafted bifaces, scrapers, drills, gravers, and utilized flakes. The Late Paleoindian toolkit also included a suite of unifacial tools, including blades, scrapers, and gravers. Morphological and microwear analyses of these various tools indicate that they were used in hunting, butchering, and hide preparation, as well as working bone and wood. Bone tools, including awls and needles, further suggest hide preparation (Walker et al. 2001). A bone point from the Early Side-Notched component and a bone fishhook from the Kirk Stemmed component indicate that bone tools were used in obtaining prey as well.

Stone tools with bone and wood polish suggest tool manufacture from organic materials, as does a cache of 23 goose humeri excavated from the Late Paleoindian component (Walker and Parmalee 2004). Manufacture of chipped stone tools appears to have been an important site activity as well. Middle- and late-stage preforms are regularly recovered from the deposits, and debitage analyses further suggest that the site's occupants were shaping as well as retouching stone tools. Conservation of tools does not appear to have been a major concern, however, likely related to the ready availability of blue-gray Fort Payne chert, which outcrops within a kilometer of the site. This raw material comprises the vast majority of the stone tools, debitage, and cores at the site. Randall (2002) suggests that the occupants refurbished their toolkits while at Dust Cave, gearing up for forays into the uplands.

Although the tools suggest significant continuity in the types of activities performed at the site, the amount of lithic debitage recovered from the floatation and screen samples indicates significant differences through time in the intensity of tool manufacture and maintenance. The density of lithic debitage is highest in the Early Side-Notched deposits, while comparable between the Late Paleoindian and Kirk Stemmed components (Figure 7.1). This is in marked contrast to plant materials, recovery of shell, and the feature assemblage, which all indicate a significant increase in intensity of site use in the Kirk Stemmed component. The contrast is even more pronounced when the ratios of lithic debitage to plant remains are compared (Figure 7.2). Interestingly, the recovery of bone from floatation samples demonstrates a similar decrease to the lithic debitage (Figure 7.1).

These conflicting trends are intriguing. On one hand, the assemblages at

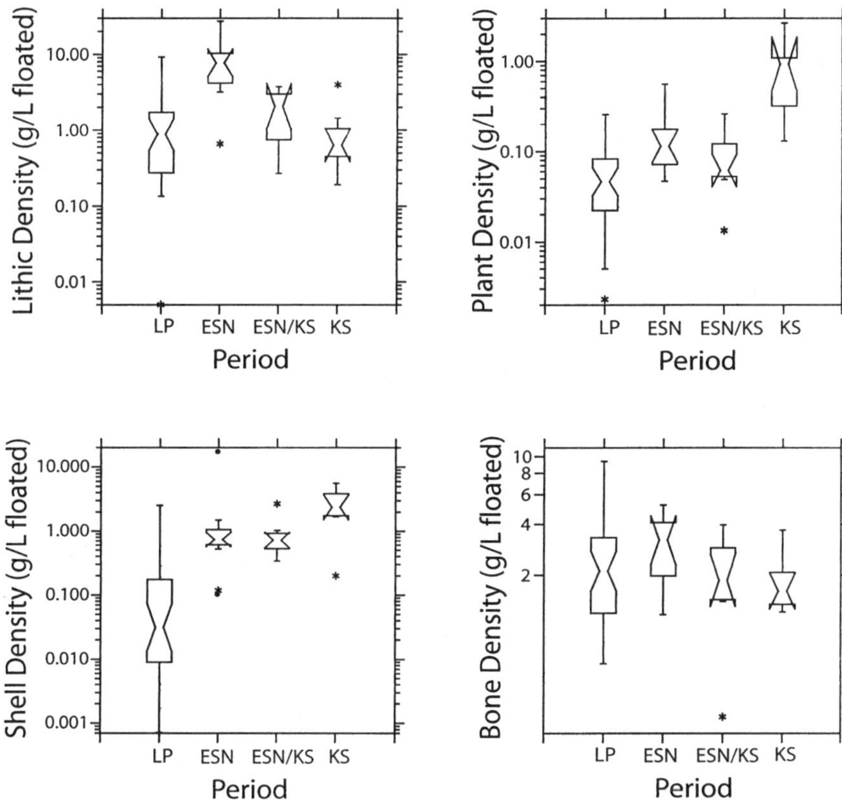

Figure 7.1. Boxplot comparing the ratio of lithic weight, plant weight, shell weight, and bone weight (g) to sample volume (liters) in Dust Cave column samples.

Dust Cave demonstrate continuity in the kinds of activities performed at the site: collection and processing of nuts and edible seeds, general use of fruits, hunting, fishing, butchering, hide preparation, and manufacture of bone and stone tools. On the other, they suggest subtle shifts in use of habitats and intensity of particular activities. Occupants of the site seem to increase their use of closed habitats by the Kirk Stemmed component, suggested by shifts in faunal resources, a significant increase in use of hickory relative to other plants, and an apparent decrease in use of edible seeds such as chenopod. They also increase their use of fish and mollusks during this period. At the same time, the site's occupants appear to engage less in the manufacture and/or maintenance of stone tools, and perhaps exploit fewer animal resources relative to plants than in previous components.

Taken together, these trends may suggest that the collection and pro-

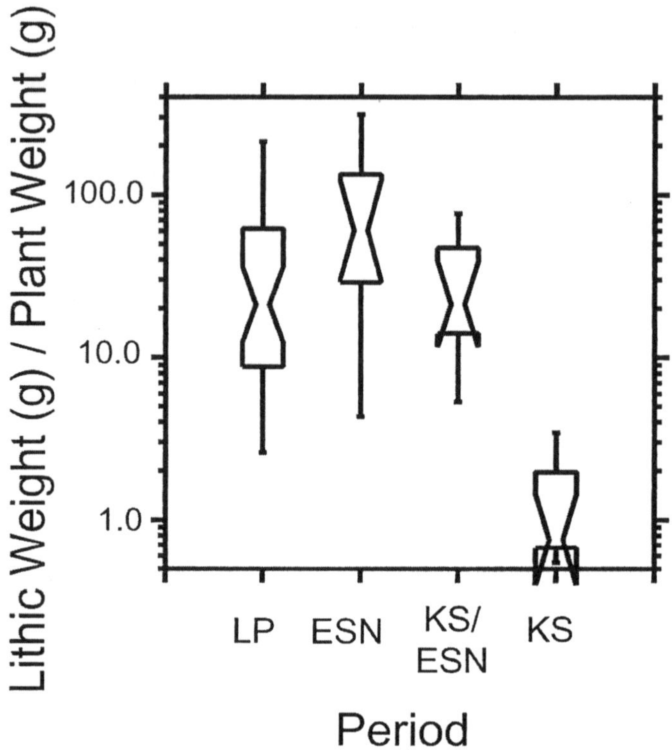

Figure 7.2. Boxplot comparing the ratio of lithic weight (g) to plant weight (g) in Dust Cave column samples.

cessing of hickory nuts, and maybe acorns, became a more important focus during the Kirk Stemmed occupation of Dust Cave. The question is why. Munson (1986) suggests that increases in hickory nutshell in the Middle Archaic in the Midwest are related to changes in technology, particularly the adoption of stone boiling for processing hickory nuts. As noted in Chapter 4, however, the costs of processing hickory nuts without boiling are sufficiently high that the nuts are unlikely to have been used extensively. The significant use of hickory nuts relative to other plant foods prior to the Middle Archaic is difficult to explain if these earlier groups did not use the boiling technique as well.

It is also possible that hickories became more prominent in the local landscape at this time, making Dust Cave an attractive site for exploiting hickory nuts. Broad environmental reconstructions suggest, however, that the percentage of hickories within forests remained relatively stable over the Pleistocene/

Holocene transition, although they may have decreased slightly around the "8.2 ka event" and rebounded shortly after. In contrast, the percentage of oaks in regional forests appears to have increased dramatically during the Pleistocene/Holocene transition. It is also possible that the effective yield of existing oak and hickory stands increased during the Hypsithermal period, as warmer temperatures likely decreased the periodicity between sizeable nut crops. The increase in use of animals living in wooded habitats seen from the faunal remains at Dust Cave does suggest that forests either expanded or became more productive. Finer-scale environmental reconstructions are required to corroborate this inference.

Another possibility is that the manner in which groups occupied the site changed in the Kirk Stemmed component. Given their more intensive occupation of the site, they may have disposed their stone and bone waste in different manners than previous groups. Staying for longer periods or expecting to return at shorter intervals, they might have cleaned the site to a greater degree. Hickory nuts, being more robust than other plant remains, might have better survived such cleaning. It is important to note, however, that very little cultural material was recovered from excavation units in the talus slope in front of the site. It seems that Kirk Stemmed occupants were not simply throwing their lithic debitage out the front of the cave, unless these materials were washed down slope into the creek.

Of the scenarios, I suspect that the reality of occupation at Dust Cave may have fallen somewhere between them. Intensive occupation certainly affected the final deposition of artifacts and ecofacts, and changes in local environment would have shaped subsistence strategies and the range of activities practiced while at the cave. In any event, the placement of Dust Cave within hunter-gatherers' economic, and likely social, landscapes changed significantly by the close of the Early Archaic period.

Summary

In a broad sense, the plant assemblages from the four rockshelter sites suggest that the occupants of each undertook a similar range of activities. Nut collection and processing appear to have been key at each, along with the supplemental use of fruits. In particular, significant quantities of hickory nutshell characterize each of the site assemblages. This likely reflects hickory nuts' dietary importance. It also suggests that the occupants of the sites used stone boiling, which is significantly more efficient than other methods, to process hickory nuts.

The plant assemblages indicate that occupants visited the sites at least during autumn, in part to collect and process nuts. While they might have brought fruits with them to the sites in dried form, they might also have gathered them opportunistically during nut harvests. It is also possible that gatherers visited the sites in late summer and earlier in the fall, not only to collect ripening fruits, such as mulberry, but also to monitor stands of oaks and hickories, as well as black walnuts, to determine where and when sizeable nut harvests would be available. At sites with nearby alluvial or open settings, gatherers might also have collected edible seeds in late autumn and early winter. The faunal assemblage at Dust Cave, which includes migratory waterfowl, fish that spawn in spring, and mollusks available throughout the year, suggests that this site might have been used during spring and other seasons as well.

These gathering activities were scheduled in concert with other subsistence activities at the sites, including hunting, butchering, and hide preparation. Groups might have targeted mammals and birds attracted to the same habitats and resources that gatherers exploited, including weedy seeds, sumac and hazel thickets along forest margins, and nut mast in forest communities. At Stanfield-Worley in particular, occupants appear to have traveled to the site to hunt deer, turkeys, and squirrels as well as harvest nuts, with little energy expended in the manufacture of stone tools. This contrasts with the other sites, where toolmaking appears to have been a common activity.

In spite of these broad similarities, the quantitative details of the plant assemblages suggest important differences at the sites across space and through time. Use of black walnuts seems to have been more important at the two sites in the Little Mountain region, Stanfield-Worley and LaGrange. This may be related to greater availability of the species in this area. Similarly, hackberry was recovered only at Dust Cave, situated on the Tennessee River, presumably because of hackberry's preference for riverbank settings. Occupants at rockshelters near the Tennessee River and/or sizeable streams, namely Dust Cave and LaGrange, appear to have exploited edible seeds to a greater extent than those ensconced in the uplands.

Changes in plant use through time are also particular to each site. Increased intensity of occupation, and of nut exploitation, is suggested at all three of the sites for which diachronic information is available. The recovery of mortars and nutting stones increases at each, and often the ubiquity of plant remains increases as well, suggesting higher rates of plant deposition. Use of black walnut seems to decrease at each of the sites over time, perhaps indicating a decrease in habitats that favor the productivity of this species. Overall, however, the manner in which plants are used changes little between the

Late Paleoindian and Early Archaic periods at Rollins, LaGrange, and Dust Cave. Not until the close of the Early Archaic, during the Kirk Stemmed component, does plant use change significantly at Dust Cave, marked by dramatic increases in the recovery of hickory nutshell.

The cultural role of rockshelters might also have changed significantly through time. As permanent fixtures on the landscape, the sites were important locales on the mental maps of hunter-gatherers. Groups cached goose humeri, raw material cores, mortars, and nutting stones; pecked mortars into the bedrock of sites; and prepared clay surfaces for cooking and other activities, suggesting not only planned returns to the sites, but perhaps usufruct rights to the shelters as well. The possible increase in intensity of site use during the Early Archaic period may relate to increases in population density or differences in the time spans associated with the Late Paleoindian and Early Archaic occupations, but may also indicate a shift in how early groups envisioned rockshelters within their social as well as economic landscapes. The social role of rockshelters is further suggested by the inclusion of burials at the sites, first evidenced by a corner-notched burial at LaGrange. This added dimension of site use continues into the Middle Archaic period, particularly the Eva/Morrow Mountain component, which includes several burials at Stanfield-Worley (DeJarnette et al. 1962) and Rollins (Stowe 1970), and several dozen burials at Dust Cave (Hogue 2003). These sites certainly served as more than temporary protection from the elements.

In sum, the focus of gathering and other subsistence and social activities, and changes in these activities through time, seem to be unique to each site. While the social importance of the sites can only be speculated, the economic activities appear to depend largely on the availability of resources on the local landscape.

MODELING EARLY FORAGING LIFEWAYS IN NORTHWEST ALABAMA

Mathematical models within evolutionary ecology address the influence of local resource structure on procurement strategies. In this project, I have applied a central place foraging theory model that evaluates the costs of transporting various plant, animal, and stone resources across the local landscape to the rockshelter sites. The salient features of the landscape include the topography, bedrock geology, and the seasonal and spatial distributions of plant resources. The latter can be inferred from a combination of historic General Land Office (GLO) survey descriptions of vegetation and paleoenvironmental reconstructions. I assume that the distribution and density of animal populations are dependent on the structure of local vegetative communities, in addition to water.

Using these variables within the mathematical model and mapping the results with the aid of a geographic information system, I calculated the return rates for a number of plant and animal resources used by Late Paleoindian and Early Archaic peoples. Several key observations can be made from the results. First, with respect to distances at which items can be profitably procured, resources are more usefully separated into categories of high versus low processing costs than high versus low return rates. Items with very high return rates but very low processing costs, such as mulberries and spawning fish, are likely to be exploited relatively close to camp as the benefits of obtaining them decrease rapidly with the distance traveled to obtain them. It is important to note that plant and animal resources do not simply divide into two separate categories. Instead, some plant foods, such as hickory, yield higher return rates and can be gainfully procured at greater distances than some animal foods, such as smaller animals.

Second, items with significant processing costs relative to caloric content have low return rates over any distance, as transport costs are small relative to handling costs. These include black walnut and hazelnut, which display markedly low return rates. Their scarcity in the samples may thus be related to their high processing costs rather than local availability. Third, the return rates of items with relatively low processing costs are rapidly affected by transport costs. These items, such as fruits, leafy greens, and line-caught fish, cannot be profitably transported over large distances. As such, foragers likely sited their camps near patches where they could readily procure these resources, which often yield high return rates over short distances. Fourth, field processing increases the distance over which items with significant byproducts, such as mussels and edible seeds, can be profitably transported.

Finally, seasonal and spatial differences in the availability of resources shape the return rates of resources in time and space. Plant food resources are clearly limited in their seasonal and spatial availability, fruiting at particular times and preferring particular habitats. Environmental reconstructions suggest that leafy greens and fruits likely preferred creek bottom habitats, while nut taxa were probably more plentiful in upland and slope settings.

Animal resources also have seasonal components. The distributions of some animal populations shift seasonally, as various plant foods become available. Game such as deer and wild turkeys likely frequented slopes and uplands in fall to take advantage of nut harvests, and creek bottoms in spring to exploit the tender leaves and shoots of the rich plant communities there. Migratory waterfowl would have been available only in spring and autumn; spring spawning runs would have significantly increased the density of some fish species. The caloric content of game also varies seasonally, as animals put on fat in autumn and draw on these stores through early spring.

Taken together, the transport-dependent return rates and seasonal and spatial availability of the various resources suggest a larger picture of early groups' mobility patterns. They likely visited river settings in spring, particularly to take advantage of spawning fish, migratory waterfowl, and game foraging on young sprouts and leaves. Gatherers likely collected leafy greens as well, particularly those close to camp. In summer, groups might have moved their camps to be near patches of ripening fruits, which yield significant return rates when transported over short distances. In contrast, hunters likely exploited game, which are relatively more dispersed in summer, over longer distances. Groups probably shifted their camps to the uplands and slopes in autumn, both to collect ripened nuts and to take advantage of game populations also attracted to mast resources. Toward the end of autumn and beginning of winter, they might have returned to creek bottom settings to collect edible seeds. Into winter, logistic hunting parties, and perhaps groups as a whole, concentrated their efforts on tracking game populations, which probably dispersed across the landscape as spruce yards disappeared in the region in the Early Holocene. People may have picked persisting fruits and seeds as they came across them, but probably did not seek out such plant foods due to their low densities. Knappers likely procured stone materials during the course of other activities, such as seasonal rounds and aggregation events, in order to offset the associated costs.

In addition to these seasonal subsistence activities, early groups likely aggregated for social purposes. Such events provided opportunities for exchanging goods, ideas, information, and stories; meeting mates; and maintaining social ties. They likely aggregated when and where resources were plentiful. Autumn seasons and creek bottom settings with nearby uplands are prime candidates. Late summer and early autumn fruits and nuts are available, while game animals carry an extra layer of fat. Migratory waterfowl frequent the area, wild turkeys travel in flocks, and rutting deer are less timid in their movements.

The plant, animal, and stone tool assemblages from the four rockshelter sites generally corroborate the above sketch of seasonal rounds. Dust Cave, sited along the Tennessee River, includes fish species that spawn, as well as migratory waterfowl available in spring. All four sites, which are located within or adjacent to slopes and uplands, claim plant assemblages rich in nut taxa and late fall fruits as well as faunal assemblages that include deer and wild turkeys, suggesting autumn occupations. The two sites with ready access to creek bottom communities (Dust Cave and LaGrange) include edible seeds in their plant assemblages, which gatherers likely collected in late fall or early winter. Furthermore, the significant density of sites located in the Seven Mile Island archaeological district may well reflect seasonal macroband aggregations. With notably rich river and floodplain resources, nearby upland communities, and a high quality chert available in the immediate vicinity, this district is a likely candidate for such aggregation events.

Let me take the opportunity here to point out that I do not argue that the same groups of peoples occupied these four rockshelter sites, moving from Dust Cave to Stanfield-Worley to LaGrange and back again. It is a possibility; foraging groups could cover the distance between Rollins and Dust Cave during the course of a year (Kelly 1995:Table 4.1), and apparently did, given the use of blue-gray Fort Payne chert at Rollins. However, it is quite likely that multiple bands resided within the region, and each may have used the various sites on different occasions. Moreover, each of the cultural components at the four sites spans several hundred years, if not close to a thousand. Any single group likely occupied a given site for only several days, or at most a couple weeks. As remarkable as the archaeological assemblages from rockshelter sites are, it is important to keep in mind that they represent generally brief occupations within a larger system of movements between sites across the landscape.

This larger system is reflected by the regional distribution of sites. The vast majority of the sites within the project area are located within the Tennessee Valley region, which may well be related to sampling bias. However, general trends through time can be discussed. After the close of the cooler Younger Dryas period, which roughly corresponds with Quad occupations in the project area, groups appear to have expanded their use of floodplain settings, relying less on upland sites. However, this pattern is shaped by movements of the Tennessee River. Any Clovis, Cumberland, and Quad sites within the floodplain would have been buried, eroded, or reworked by the shifting river (Collins et al. 1994; Sherwood 2001; Sherwood et al. 2004). These early groups exploited rich floodplain settings. Because the predominant resources within floodplains have low processing costs, including herbaceous plants, fruit taxa, fish, waterfowl, and mollusks, and therefore the return rates of these resources decrease exponentially as transport distances increase, early foragers likely placed camps within floodplains, at least during seasons of high resource availability, such as spring.

After the Younger Dryas period, early foraging groups also began using areas outside of the Tennessee Valley to a greater degree. The expansion of Dalton and Early Archaic groups into other physiographic districts may reflect the filling up of the Tennessee Valley and therefore an increase in population pressure within this district, as much as amelioration of harsher climatic conditions.[1] Early Archaic peoples also began to increasingly use local cherts to fashion stone tools, further suggesting a decrease in the importance of living near the river and a strengthening of relationships to more local landscapes.

These farther-flung groups still maintained close ties with the Tennessee Valley, however, returning to the Muscle Shoals area at least on occasion to obtain blue-gray Fort Payne chert, out of which they manufactured most of their formal stone tools. The large number of archaeological sites located along the river near the shoals, particularly in the Seven Mile Island Archaeological District, may well represent the aggregation of multiple bands in the immediate vicinity to retool, share information, and enjoy the company of friends and relatives. These large aggregations may have taken place in early autumn, when fruits were ripe, nuts just mature, and animals fat and bold with their preparations for the coming winter. It is also possible that bands met along the river in spring, to take advantage of spawning fishes and migrating waterfowl. But because game would still be lean and plant foods other than low-value leafy greens would have been scarce, such hypothetical spring meetings likely would have been relatively small and subdued.

The trend toward expansion of sites into new topographic and physiographic districts is reversed by groups using Bifurcate tools, who appear to have been very conservative in their choice of site location. This conservatism may be related to another global cooling event that occurred around 8,200 years ago. Afterward, peoples who made Kirk Stemmed bifaces used the landscape in significantly different manners than their predecessors. They more frequently sited camps in floodplain settings and increased their use of areas beyond the Tennessee Valley. This shift in site placement coincides with a significant increase in nut processing and a trend toward greater use of animals associated with closed habitats at Dust Cave. Analysis of organic assemblages from additional sites would elucidate whether these subsistence trends extend beyond Dust Cave.

GATHERING BEYOND NORTHWEST ALABAMA

The results of this project have several important implications beyond providing information about the lifeways of Late Paleoindian and Early Archaic peoples in northwest Alabama. These implications can be drawn from the plant assemblages, the application of central place foraging theory, and the regional model of seasonal rounds. They speak not only to the ways in which we approach archaeological foraging groups in the Southeast, but also to studies of hunter-gatherer lifeways in other times and places.

Implications from the Archaeobotanical Data

Several important points stem from the plant assemblages recovered from the four rockshelter sites. First, the assemblages do not reflect the entirety of early peoples' plant use. This is suggested by the recovery of miscellaneous seeds that are not in themselves edible, but are produced by plants that have edible leaves, shoots, or tubers, and/or plants that may exhibit medicinal properties. There are entire categories of foods and plant uses that fall outside the visibility of archaeologists. This is also true of uses of plants for material culture. Stone tools likely accounted for a relatively small percentage of the items made and used by early hunter-gatherers. This inherent bias should not discourage us from studying plant remains, but instead remind us to consider the possibility of use of foods, such as leafy greens, and material culture for which we are unlikely to have evidence.

Second, although the plant assemblages span the transition from the Late Pleistocene to Early Holocene environmental conditions, no significant differences among the assemblages are apparent. This is somewhat surprising, given the marked shifts in vegetation associated with this climatic transition. Because most of the assemblages begin with Dalton occupations, spanning the last significant climatic oscillation, it is possible that earlier peoples changed their subsistence strategies in response to the changing environment. However, significant differences are also not detected at Dust Cave, which includes a Quad occupation, coincident with the Younger Dryas oscillation. It is possible that the most dramatic shifts in local environments occurred prior to this event, that the basic postglacial resource structure of the region had already been established. It is also possible that early hunter-gatherers were very conservative in their subsistence strategies, particularly in use of plants. The plant assemblages serve as a reminder that we cannot simply assume that environmental changes directly evoke cultural changes, or that cultural changes are necessarily direct responses to environmental shifts.

Third, although there are large similarities in the taxa recovered from the various sites, occupants appear to have performed different suites of activities at each site. The nature of these activities, largely related to subsistence and manufacture of material culture, appears to depend on the distribution of resources relative to the location of the site on the landscape. This is not too surprising; for example, people are more likely to utilize aquatic resources when living near rivers. We frequently make this distinction when discussing exploitation of animal resources, but often gloss over differences in use of plant resources. The apparent assumption is that plant foods are generally ubiquitous, particularly in the temperate forests of the Southeast. The data presented here, however, indicate that hunter-gatherers do not simply opportunistically gather plant foods that they come across during the course of their day, but instead monitor the availability of plant resources, move their camps to gain better access to some plant foods, and specifically target particular species and particular patches. Gatherers engage in different activities at different sites, adjusted to the structure of local resources.

The latter two implications point to the need for more detailed paleoenvironmental reconstructions. Regional reconstructions of vegetation developed from pollen analyses are valuable, but do not provide information at the scale required to reconstruct the distributions of local plant and animal resources. The analysis of gastropods and microfauna that are sensitive to temperature changes, as well as phytolith and additional pollen analyses on a local level, might enable such fine-scale reconstructions. These would greatly enhance our understandings of early peoples' interactions with local landscapes.

Implications from the Model of Seasonal Rounds

One of the most striking characteristics of the model of settlement and subsistence strategies that I have sketched for northwest Alabama is that it does not differ dramatically from those proposed by researchers for other regions in the Southeast. Similar to others, I suggest that early groups resided in rich alluvial communities in spring and summer, moved into uplands in the fall to harvest nuts and target fattened deer, and dispersed in winter to hunt game and to subsist on what plant foods could be found. My model differs slightly in that I suggest that gatherers returned to creek bottoms in late fall or early winter to collect edible seeds.

By expressly considering how the use of plant foods influences and is influenced by travel across landscapes, however, my model reorients the focus of early foragers' settlement and subsistence strategies. Rather than focusing on hunting pursuits, stone procurement for toolmaking, and perhaps the collection of nuts, the model I have presented here places the temporal and spatial availability of reliable, predictable foodstuffs with relatively low processing costs at the center of mobility decisions. These foodstuffs include fruits, seeds, and fish, items targeted by gatherers rather than hunters. This model suggests that gatherers—namely women, children, and the elderly—had significant influence over the placement of camps, especially during periods of availability of valued resources that are spatially limited.

Use of plants appears to have been a consideration in movements to and from sites. This is evidenced by investment in plant-processing tools and features at the rockshelter sites. Mortars and nutting stones have been recorded at all four sites. Occupants pecked nutting stones into the bedrock at Stanfield-Worley and constructed prepared clay surfaces for processing foods both at this site and at Dust Cave (DeJarnette et al. 1962; Homsey 2004; Sherwood 2001). Site occupants clearly visited and revisited the sites with the intention of collecting and processing plant foods, as much as to hunt game, fish, or collect mussels.

It is notable, however, that within the project area there is little spatial incongruity between animal and plant resources. For example, river floodplains are particularly rich habitats in spring, in terms of both plant and animal resources. Leafy greens are abundant in these disturbed settings and would attract hungry animals as well as people. Spawning fish and migratory waterfowl provide an additional seasonal draw. In autumn, deer, turkey, and other animals are drawn to the uplands and slopes to exploit ripened nuts, which early gatherers also prized. Similar situations exist for fruits and edible seeds. In settings where there is greater incongruity in the location of plant and animal resources, such as the Great Basin (e.g., Zeanah 2000), the picture should be different.

In the Southeast, the question might be raised whether groups moved to particular settings to be closer to plant resources and subsequently took advantage of animals similarly attracted to those patches, or whether they moved to be near denser populations of animals and then gathered those plants that were nearby. I would argue that this question is relatively fruitless. As noted previously, animal and plant resources are not necessarily dichotomous. Relevant categories of resources do not appear to be those that do or do not have roots, but instead those that have low or high processing costs. Animal resources with low processing costs tend to be those that have shorter pursuit times, such as fish and rutting deer.

This redefining of resources on the basis of costs and return rates rather than plant versus animal fits well with ethnographic descriptions of women who may hunt as well as gather. Women do not appear to target simply plant resources, but instead those resources that provide a stable food supply for their children and themselves (Bird 1999; Panter-Brick 2002). In northwest

Alabama, this would include fish and mussels, and perhaps rutting deer and flocking turkeys, as well as greens, fruits, nuts, and seeds. It may be that we archaeologists too narrowly define and use the terms *hunting* and *gathering*, and should instead think of them as a continuum (Ingold 1986), as we have begun to consider human interactions with the landscape as a continuum between foraging and cultivation (e.g., Terrell et al. 2003).

These results have implications beyond the Late Paleoindian and Early Archaic periods in northwest Alabama. We should expect the activities of gatherers to direct mobility decisions of foraging groups living in environments with sufficient plant and/or low-cost resources—in other words, in any nonarctic environment. This includes not only the entire prehistoric Southeast, but also much of North America from the close of the Pleistocene onward. Thus in addition to rethinking previous models about Paleoindian and Early Archaic peoples in the Southeast, perhaps we should also reconsider whether the first peoples of North America pursued large mammals to the far ends of the continent or whether they followed available plant foods, as well as reliable and predictable animal resources like fish and waterfowl, along the continent's major river valleys. Surovell (2000) has modeled the Clovis expansion based on the assumption that foragers move their camps so as not to overlap female (gatherers') foraging radii, although he does not expressly consider the role of gathered foods within early subsistence strategies.

We could also apply a broader understanding of gathering practices to later Archaic foraging groups and give a situated context for the interactions between gatherers (women, children, and the elderly) and weedy plants in disturbed, floodplain settings. These interactions ultimately led to the cultivation, and in some instances domestication, of several native plants, marking a significant change in subsistence strategies and ultimately mobility patterns.

Implications from the Application of Central Place Foraging Theory

Along with various other archaeological problems, from site placement to field processing, this study demonstrates the utility of central place foraging theory for understanding the settlement and subsistence strategies of early foraging groups living in the Southeast. In contrast to examples from the Great Basin, Southeastern cases must address considerable overlap in the spatial availability of resources. The outcomes of the mathematical model are thus perhaps not as clear cut, but are suggestive. At the very least, the algorithm reveals the influence of variables on the problem at hand. For example, it highlights the relationship between processing costs and transport costs of particular resources, and the impact of this relationship on the degree and manner in which these resources might be used. Such information assists in interpretation of the archaeological data.

This study also illustrates the benefit of applying central place foraging theory within a geographic information system. The use of GIS facilitates the detection of patterning within the data by graphically displaying the results. It also juxtaposes these results with key landscape features, such as topography and site placement, enhancing the ability of the researcher to think of the problem in terms of a multidimensional landscape. Such dimensions include not only elevation and spatial coordinates but also ground cover, paths of travel, resource patches, or anything else that can be mapped.

In addition to field processing and site placement, I have also used central place foraging theory to consider the composition of workgroups sent out to obtain particular resources. It appears that cooperation is economically beneficial only when the package is too large for a single person to carry back to camp. These primarily include large animal prey, particularly within the study region. This also has implications for sharing; foragers rarely share small animal prey (Tucker 2001) or plant foods (Kelly 1995). People may travel and work together for companionship or perhaps safety, particularly when resources are abundant enough to allow multiple people to hunt or gather in a single patch. However, gatherers in particular do not appear to gain economically from working in groups, although they almost certainly gain socially. The exception may be the participation of children in the use of plant resources that they cannot collect at the same rate as adults. Hawkes and colleagues (1995) provide an example of children staying in camp to crack open mongongo nuts as their older female relatives head out to collect them. Although they cannot collect them as efficiently as adults do, children can process the nuts at a rate more comparable to adults. By dividing the efforts of the "team" in this way, mothers can maximize the return rate of their teams (Hawkes et al. 1995).

Such considerations also serve as reminders that the individuals making decisions modeled by these evolutionary ecology algorithms are people who engage in social interactions with others. They have identities and genders, as well as social roles. Even though we can never know the exact nature, or perhaps even some semblance of these roles and identities, such speculations are fruitful for expanding our ideas and interpretations, and hopefully our understanding of early societies. At the very least, they engage both archaeologists and the public, and enhance our ability to perceive early hunter-gatherers as fully modern humans with intellectual, physical, and social capacities equivalent to our own.

CONCLUDING THOUGHTS

In closing, I would like to highlight what I consider to be the most important conclusions that can be drawn from this project, as well as future areas of research that would expand on the results I have presented. First, the plant assemblages from the four rockshelter sites suggest that gathering activities are tailored to local landscapes. Furthermore, gathering activities comprise more than collecting nuts and fruits while walking. They include monitoring and perhaps managing the landscape, and require an intimate knowledge of the landscape and its resources. In addition, gathering articulates with other subsistence as well as social activities.

As such, the model I have formed here cannot be applied directly to other regions in the Southeast, in that local environments are likely to be different. However, my results do suggest that theories from evolutionary ecology, particularly central place foraging theory, can be successfully applied to address the subject of settlement and subsistence strategies in the Southeast. The mathematical models of evolutionary ecology distinguish salient variables within the problem at hand and organize the data for use in interpretation.

Within models of mobility patterns, central place foraging theory suggests that researchers need to consider the nature of local resource distribution. This includes not only the location of stone outcrops and presumed hunting grounds but also the spatial and temporal availability of plant resources and how this availability might affect the seasonal density of animal populations as well as plant foods. When these are taken into account, it appears that early foragers' settlement patterns reflect the use of reliable, predictable resources rather than hunting technologies and pursuits.

Evolutionary ecology, with its focus on the individual, also reminds us that the archaeological record is the result of the decisions and actions of individuals. These individuals had identities, different genders, were of different ages, and assumed different social roles. These identities and social roles shaped and were shaped by individuals' decisions and actions.

The project also highlights the interactions of peoples, plants, animals, and the landscape. The landscape has been anthropogenic for at least 13,000 years, influenced by the gathering, hunting, and dwelling activities of human groups. It was also anthropogenic in that early peoples ascribed meaning to the landscape. For example, Late Paleoindian and Early Archaic occupants of

LaGrange brought ocher with them to the site, presumably ritual in its use, and on at least one occasion buried their dead at the shelter (DeJarnette and Knight 1976). The sites were more than simply functional overnight stops.

As with most projects, this one suggests a number of topics to be further explored. The nature of early hunter-gatherer subsistence is not answered once and for all by this research. Additional analyses of plant and animal remains, studied in concert with each other and material culture, are key to indicating whether some of the larger patterns noted here, such as the marked shift in subsistence at the close of the Early Archaic period, hold both at other sites within the project area as well as other sites in the Southeast. Such analyses would also further our understanding of the diversity of subsistence strategies by early peoples in the region. More detailed reconstructions of local resources are also needed to understand how subsistence activities articulate with larger uses of and movements across the landscape.

The application of the central place foraging theory within GIS can also be refined. For example, variables such as processing costs could be better approximated through experimental studies. Additional variables could also be included, such as ease of travel through areas with different ground cover or for use of waterways.

Also intriguing are questions about the relationships between hunters and gatherers in areas where not only hunted and gathered resources overlap, but also the activities associated with one are closely related to the other. One might approach this by combing cultural studies of ethnographic groups for which this is the case, paying close attention to how individuals refer to themselves as hunters or gatherers. In addition to what it means to be a hunter or gatherer, the meaning that the landscape might hold for hunter-gatherers is also of interest. Much of this meaning is surely related to their intimate knowledge of and interaction with the landscape and the peoples, animals, and plants that it supports (Ingold 1996). The landscape is not only inscribed with their daily practices but also with their histories.

Given this, I believe that we still have much to learn about Paleoindian and Archaic peoples. This project adds significantly to our understanding of the economic pursuits of early foraging groups in the Southeast, largely because I present much-needed botanical data. Yet so much remains to be known about how groups living in landscapes beyond northwest Alabama made a living, both gathering and hunting. If organic materials are not preserved, then we must be more creative about how we think about subsistence activities, perhaps relying more heavily on environmental reconstructions until better dietary evidence is available. We also must be more creative about envisioning the social identities of foraging individuals, and the social interactions among foragers and with the landscape. There are many archaeological, environmental, and ethnographic clues about such interactions that have yet to be gathered and processed.

NOTE

1. This is an example of "ideal free distribution," another concept in human ecology, which argues that individuals will occupy the best sites or patches first; as these fill up and resources become depressed, subsequent groups move into locales that originally were less desirable (Fretwell and Lucas 1970).

References Cited

Adams, Jonathan (compiler)
2002 North America during the Last 150,000 Years. Electronic document, http://members.cox.net/quaternary/nercNORTHAMERICA.html, accessed January 22, 2005.

Adams, J. M., and H. Faure
1997 Palaeovegetation Maps of the Earth during the Last Glacial Maximum, and the Early and Mid Holocene: An Aid to Archaeological Research. *Journal of Archaeological Science* 24:623–647.

Alabama Maps
2005 Contemporary and Historical Map Index. Electronic document, http://alabamamaps.ua.edu/index.html, accessed March 12, 2005.

Alabama Secretary of State
2005 Lands Records Inquiry. Lands and Trademarks Division. Electronic document, http://arc-sos.state.al.us/CGI/SOSLND00.MBR/MENU, accessed February 12, 2005.

Alabama State Site File
2005 Alabama Online Cultural Resource Database. Electronic document, http://appserver.oas.ua.edu/assf/Login.jsp, accessed February 16, 2005.

Anderson, David G.
1995 Recent Advances in Paleoindian and Archaic Period Research in the Southeastern United States. *Archaeology of Eastern North America* 23:145–176.

Anderson, David G., and Glen T. Hanson
1988 Early Archaic Settlement in the Southeastern United States: A Case Study from the Savannah River Valley. *American Antiquity* 53:262–286.

Anderson, David G., Lisa D. O'Steen, and Kenneth E. Sassaman
1996 Environmental and Chronological Considerations. In *The Paleoindian and Early Archaic Southeast,* edited by David G. Anderson and

Kenneth E. Sassaman, pp. 3–15. University of Alabama Press, Tuscaloosa.

Anderson, David G., and Kenneth E. Sassaman

1996 Modeling Paleoindian and Early Archaic Settlement in the Southeast: A Historical Perspective. In *The Paleoindian and Early Archaic Southeast,* edited by David G. Anderson and Kenneth E. Sassaman, pp. 16–57. University of Alabama Press, Tuscaloosa.

Anderson, David G., and Joseph Schuldenrein

1983 Early Archaic Settlement on the Southeastern Atlantic Slope: A View from the Rucker's Bottom Site, Elbert County, Georgia. *North American Archaeologist* 4(3):177–210.

Asch, David L., Richard I. Ford, and Nancy B. Asch

1972 *Paleoethnobotany of the Koster Site: The Archaic Horizons.* Reports of Investigations No. 24, Illinois State Museum, Springfield.

Barlow, K. Renee, and Duncan Metcalfe

1996 Plant Utility Indices: Two Great Basin Examples. *Journal of Archaeological Science* 23:351–371.

Baxter, M. J.

1994 *Exploratory Multivariate Analysis in Archaeology.* Edinburgh University Press, Edinburgh.

Beck, Michael W.

1996 On Discerning the Cause of Late Pleistocene Megafaunal Extinctions. *Paleobiology* 22(1):91–103.

Belovsky, Gary E.

1988 An Optimal Foraging-Based Model of Hunter-Gatherer Population Dynamics. *Journal of Anthropological Archaeology* 7:329–372.

Bettinger, Robert L.

1991 *Hunter-Gatherers: Archaeological and Evolutionary Theory.* Plenum Press, New York.

Bettinger, Robert L., Ripan Malhi, and Helen McCarthy

1997 Central Place Models of Acorn and Mussel Processing. *Journal of Archaeological Science* 24:887–899.

Binford, Lewis R.

1979 Organization and Formation Processes: Looking at Curated Technologies. *Journal of Anthropological Research* 35:255–273.

1980 Willow Smoke and Dogs' Tails: Hunter-Gatherer Settlement Systems and Archaeological Site Formation. *American Antiquity* 45:4–20.

Bird, Rebecca

1999 Cooperation and Conflict: The Behavioral Ecology of the Sexual Division of Labor. *Evolutionary Anthropology* 8(2):65–75.

Bourdo, Eric A., Jr.

1956 A Review of the General Land Office Survey and of Its Use in Quantitative Studies of Former Forests. *Ecology* 37:754–768.

Bowen, Charles D.

1994 *Soil Survey of Colbert County, Alabama.* U.S. Department of Agriculture, Soil Conservation Service, in cooperation with Alabama Agricultural Experiment Station and Alabama Department of Agriculture and Industries, Washington, D.C.

Brannan, James A.

1992 On Modeling Resources Transport Costs: Suggested Refinements. *Current Anthropology* 33(1):56–60.

Brightman, Robert

1996 The Sexual Division of Foraging Labor: Biology, Taboo, and Gender Politics. *Society for Comparative Study of Society and History* 38:687–729.

Broyles, Bettye J.

1971 *Second Preliminary Report: The St. Albans Site, Kanawha County, West Virginia, 1964–1968.* Report of Archaeological Investigations No. 3, West Virginia Geological and Economic Survey, Morgantown.

Bryant, William S., William C. McComb, and James S. Fralish

1993 Oak-Hickory Forests (Western Mesophytic/Oak-Hickory Forests). In *Biodiversity of the Southeastern United States: Upland Terrestrial Communities,* edited by William H. Martin, Stephen G. Boyce, and Arthur C. Echternacht, pp. 143–202. John Wiley and Sons, New York.

Bryson, Reid A.

1999a Modeled Precipitation History: Muscle Shoals, Alabama. Manuscript on file at the Center for Climatic Research, University of Wisconsin, Madison.

1999b Modeled Temperature History: Muscle Shoals, Alabama. Manuscript on file at the Center for Climatic Research, University of Wisconsin, Madison.

Burns, Russell M., and Barbara H. Honkala (technical coordinators)

1990 *Silvics of North America: 1. Conifers; 2. Hardwoods.* Agriculture Handbook 654, U.S. Department of Agriculture, Forest Service, Washington, D.C.

Bush, Leslie L.

2004 *Boundary Conditions: Macrobotanical Remains and the Oliver Phase of Central Indiana, A.D. 1200–1450.* University of Alabama Press, Tuscaloosa.

Cable, John S.

1996 Haw River Revisited: Implications for Modeling Terminal Late Glacial and Early Holocene Hunter-Gatherer Settlement Systems in the Southeast. In *The Paleoindian and Early Archaic Southeast,* edited by David G. Anderson and Kenneth E. Sassaman, pp. 107–148. University of Alabama Press, Tuscaloosa.

Caddell, Gloria M.

1982 *Plant Resources, Archaeological Plant Remains, and Prehistoric Plant-Use Patterns in the Central Tombigbee River Valley.* Bulletin No. 7, University of Alabama Museum of Natural History, University.

1983 Charred Plant Remains from the Cedar Creek and Upper Bear Creek Reservoirs. In *Archaeological Investigations in the Cedar Creek and Upper Bear Creek Reservoirs,* edited by Eugene M. Futato, pp. 335–350. University of Alabama Office of Archaeological Research Report of Investigations 29; Tennessee Valley Authority Publications in Anthropology 32.

Caldwell, Joseph R.

1958 *Trend and Tradition in the Prehistory of the Eastern United States.* Memoirs of the American Anthropological Association No. 88, Menasha, Wisconsin.

Cambron, James W.

1955 Preliminary Report on the Stone Pipe Site in North Alabama. *Tennessee Archaeologist* 11(2):54–62.

1956 The Pine Tree Site—A Paleo-Indian Habitation Locality. *Tennessee Archaeologist* 12(2):1–10.

Cambron, James W., and David C. Hulse

1960 An Excavation on the Quad Site. *Tennessee Archaeologist* 16(1):14–26.

Cambron, James W., and Spencer A. Waters

1959 Flint Creek Rock Shelter (Part I). *Tennessee Archaeologist* 15(2):72–87.

Carey, Jennifer H.

1994 Vitis aestivalis. In *Fire Effects Information System.* U.S. Department of Agriculture, Forest Service, Rocky Mountain Research Station, Fire Sciences Laboratory (Producer). Electronic document, http://www.fs.fed.us/database/feis/, accessed January 31, 2005.

Carmen, Ma

2001 Sorex palustris. Animal Diversity Web. Electronic document, http://animaldiversity.ummz.umich.edu/site/accounts/information/Sorex_palustris.html, accessed January 3, 2005.

Chapman, Jefferson

1973 *The Icehouse Bottom Site (40MR23).* Report of Investigations 13, Department of Anthropology, University of Tennessee, Knoxville.

1975 *The Rose Island Site and the Bifurcate Point Tradition.* Report of Investigations 14, Department of Anthropology, University of Tennessee, Knoxville.

1976 Early Archaic Site Location and Excavation in the Little Tennessee River Valley: Backhoes and Trowels. *Southeastern Archaeological Conference Bulletin* 19:31–36.

1977 *Archaic Period Research in the Lower Little Tennessee River Valley, 1975: Icehouse Bottom, Harrison Branch, Thirty Acre Island, Calloway Island.* Report of Investigations 18, Department of Anthropology, University of Tennessee, Knoxville.

1978 *The Bacon Farm Site and a Buried Site Reconnaissance.* Report of Investigations 23, Department of Anthropology, University of Tennessee, Knoxville.

Chapman, Jefferson, and Andrea Shea

1981 The Archaeobotanical Record: Early Archaic to Contact in the Lower Little Tennessee River Valley. *Tennessee Anthropologist* 6:61–84.

Chapman, Jefferson, and Patty Jo Watson

1993 The Archaic Period and the Flotation Revolution. In *Foraging and Farming in the Eastern Woodlands,* edited by C. Margaret Scarry, pp. 27–38. University Press of Florida, Gainesville.

Claggett, Stephen R., and John S. Cable

1982 *The Haw River Sites: Archaeological Investigations at Two Stratified Sites in the North Carolina Piedmont.* Report R-2386, Commonwealth Associates, Jackson, Michigan.

Clausen, C. J., A. D. Cohen, Cesare Emiliani, J. A. Holman, and J. J. Stipp

1979 Little Salt Spring, Florida: A Unique Underwater Site. *Science* 203:609–614.

Cleland, Charles E.

1976 The Focal-Diffuse Model: An Evolutionary Perspective on the Prehistoric Cultural Adaptations of the Eastern United States. *Midcontinental Journal of Archaeology* 1(1):5–38.

Cobb, Richard M.

1987 A Speleoarchaeological Reconnaissance of the Pickwick Basin in Colbert and Lauderdale Counties of Alabama. Manuscript on file at the Office of Archaeological Research, University of Alabama, Tuscaloosa.

Cobb, Richard M., Boyce Driskell, and Scott Meeks

1995 Speleological Reconnaissance and Test Excavations in the Pickwick Basin. In *Cultural Resources in the Pickwick Reservoir,* edited by Catherine C. Meyer, pp. 219–262. Report of Investigations 75. Division of Archaeology, University of Alabama, Tuscaloosa.

Coe, Joffre L.
1964 *The Formative Cultures of the Carolina Piedmont.* Transactions of the American Philosophical Society 54(5), Philadelphia.

COHMAP Members
1988 Climatic Changes of the Last 18,000 Years: Observations and Model Simulations. *Science* 241(4869):1043–1052.

Collins, Michael B., Wulf A. Gose, and Scott Shaw
1994 Preliminary Geomorphological Findings at Dust and Nearby Caves. *Journal of Alabama Archaeology* 40(1–2):35–56.

Cowan, C. Wesley
1997 Evolutionary Changes Associated with the Domestication of *Cucurbita pepo*: Evidence from Eastern Kentucky. In *People, Plants and Landscapes,* edited by Kristen J. Gremillion, pp. 63–85. University of Alabama Press, Tuscaloosa.

Curren, Cailup B.
1976 Appendix I: Zooarchaeological Analysis of LaGrange Bluff Shelter, 1Ct90. *Journal of Alabama Archaeology* 22(1):56–60.

Daniel, I. Randolph
1998 *Hardaway Revisited: Early Archaic Settlement in the Southeast.* University of Alabama Press, Tuscaloosa.
2001 Stone Raw Material Availability and Early Archaic Settlement in the Southeastern United States. *American Antiquity* 66(2):237–266.

Delcourt, Hazel R.
1975 Reconstructing the Forest Primeval, West Feliciana Parish, Louisiana. *Melanges* 10:1–13.
1976 Presettlement Vegetation of the North of Red River Land District, Louisiana. *Castanea* 41:122–139.

Delcourt, Hazel R., and Paul A. Delcourt
1974 Primeval Magnolia-Holly-Beech Climax in Louisiana. *Ecology* 55:638–644.
1985 Quaternary Palynology and Vegetational History of the Southeastern United States. In *Pollen Records of Late-Quaternary North American Sediments,* edited by V. M. Bryant, Jr., and R. G. Holloway, pp. 1–37. American Association of Stratigraphic Palynologists Foundation, Dallas.

Delcourt, Paul A., and Hazel R. Delcourt
1981 Vegetation Maps for Eastern North America: 40,000 Yr B.P. to the Present. In *Geobotany II,* edited by Robert C. Romans, pp. 123–166. Plenum Press, New York.
1987 *Long-Term Forest Dynamics of the Temperate Zone: A Case Study of*

Late-Quaternary Forests in Eastern North America. Springer-Verlag, New York.

Delcourt, Paul A., Hazel R. Delcourt, Cecil R. Ison, William E. Sharp, and Kristen J. Gremillion

1998 Prehistoric Human Use of Fire, the Eastern Agricultural Complex, and Appalachian Oak-Chestnut Forests: Paleoecology of Cliff Palace Pond, Kentucky. *American Antiquity* 63(2):263–278.

DeJarnette, David L., and Vernon J. Knight, Jr.

1976 LaGrange. *Journal of Alabama Archaeology* 12(1):1–60.

DeJarnette, David L., Edward B. Kurjack, and James L. Cambron

1962 Stanfield-Worley Bluff Shelter Excavations. *Journal of Alabama Archaeology* 8(1&2).

Detwiler, Kandace R.

2001 Plant Use during the Late Paleoindian/Early Archaic Transition at Dust Cave. Paper presented at the 58th Annual Meeting of the Southeastern Archaeological Conference, Chattanooga.

2003 Botanical Remains from the Autaugaville Sites: 1Au383 and 1Au397. Manuscript on file at University of Alabama Museums, Office of Archaeological Services, Tuscaloosa.

Detwiler-Hollenbach, Kandace

2003 Nuts and More Nuts: Archaic Plant Use at Dust Cave. Paper presented at the 60th Annual Meeting of the Southeastern Archaeological Conference, Charlotte.

Dimbleby, G. W.

1967 *Plants and Archaeology.* John Barker, London.

Dragoo, Don W.

1976 Some Aspects of Eastern North American Prehistory: A Review. *American Antiquity* 41:3–27.

Driskell, Boyce N.

1996 Stratified Late Pleistocene and Early Holocene Deposits at Dust Cave, Northwestern Alabama. In *The Paleoindian and Early Archaic Southeast,* edited by David G. Anderson and Kenneth E. Sassaman, pp. 315–330. University of Alabama Press, Tuscaloosa.

2001 Field Investigations at Dust Cave, Northwest Alabama, 1989–2000. Paper presented at the 58th Annual Meeting of the Southeastern Archaeological Conference, Chattanooga.

Elston, Robert G., and David W. Zeanah

2002 Thinking Outside the Box: A New Perspective on Diet Breadth and Sexual Division of Labor in the Prearchaic Great Basin. *World Archaeology* 34(1):103–130.

Environmental Systems Research Institute (ESRI)
1998 *ArcView GIS: Geographic Information Software.* Environmental Systems Research Institute, Redlands, California.

FAUNMAP Working Group
1996 Spatial Response of Mammals to Late Quaternary Environmental Fluctuations. *Science* 272:1601–1606.

Fisher, Timothy G., Derald G. Smith, and John T. Andrews
2002 Preboreal Oscillation Caused by a Glacial Lake Agassiz Flood. *Quaternary Science Reviews* 21:873–878.

FitzGibbon, Clare
1998 The Management of Subsistence Harvesting: Behavioral Ecology of Hunters and Their Mammalian Prey. In *Behavioral Ecology and Conservation Biology,* edited by Tim Caro, pp. 449–473. Oxford University Press, New York.

Fowler, Catherine S.
1996 Historical Perspectives on Timbisha Shoshone Land Management Practices, Death Valley, California. In *Case Studies in Environmental Archaeology,* edited by Elizabeth J. Reitz, Lee A. Newsom, and Sylvia J. Scudder, pp. 87–101. Plenum Press, New York.

Fowler, Melvin L.
1959 *Summary Report of Modoc Rockshelter: 1952, 1953, 1955, 1956.* Report of Investigations 8, Illinois State Museum, Springfield.

Freeman, Sharon
2003 Prepared Surfaces: A First Impression. Paper presented at the 60th Annual Meeting of the Southeaster Archaeological Conference, Charlotte, North Carolina.

Fretwell, S. D., and H. L. Lucas
1970 On Territorial Behavior and Other Factors Influencing Habitat Distribution in Birds. *Acta Biotheoretica* 19:16–36.

Fritz, Gayle J.
2000 Native Farming Systems and Ecosystems in the Mississippi River Valley. In *Imperfect Balance: Landscape Transformations in the PreColombian Americas,* edited by David L. Lentz, pp. 225–249. Columbia University Press, New York.

Fritz, Gayle J., Virginia Drywater Whitekiller, and James W. McIntosh
2001 Ethnobotany of Ku-Nu-Che: Cherokee Hickory Nut Soup. *Journal of Ethnobiology* 21(2):1–27.

Futato, Eugene M.
1982 Some Notes on the Distribution of Fluted Points in Alabama. *Archaeology of Eastern North America* 10:30–33.

1983 *Archaeological Investigations in the Cedar Creek and Upper Bear Creek Reservoirs.* University of Alabama Office of Archaeological Research Report of Investigations 29; Tennessee Valley Authority Publications in Anthropology 32.

1995 Archaeological Site Distribution in the Pickwick Lake Area. In *Cultural Resources in the Pickwick Reservoir,* edited by Catherine C. Meyer, pp. 263–286. Report of Investigations 75, Division of Archaeology, University of Alabama, Tuscaloosa.

1996 A Synopsis of Paleoindian and Early Archaic Research in Alabama. In *The Paleoindian and Early Archaic Southeast,* edited by David G. Anderson and Kenneth E. Sassaman, pp. 298–314. University of Alabama Press, Tuscaloosa.

Gardner, Paul S.

1994 Carbonized Plant Remains from Dust Cave. *Journal of Alabama Archaeology* 40(1–2):192–211.

1997 The Ecological Structure and Behavioral Implications of Mast Exploration Strategies. In *People, Plants, and Landscapes: Studies in Paleoethnobotany,* edited by Kristen J. Gremillion, pp. 161–178. University of Alabama Press, Tuscaloosa.

Gardner, William M.

1974 *The Flint Run Paleo-Indian Complex: A Preliminary Report 1971 through 1973 Seasons.* Occasional Paper No. 1, Archaeology Laboratory, Catholic University of America, Washington, D.C.

1977 Flint Run Paleoindian Complex and Its Implications for Eastern North American Prehistory. *Annals of the New York Academy of Sciences* 288:251–263.

1983 Stop Me If You've Heard This One Before: The Flint Run Paleoindian Complex Revisited. *Archaeology of Eastern North America* 11:49–59.

Gero, Joan M.

1995 Railroading Epistemology: Paleoindians and Women. In *Interpreting Archaeology: Finding Meanings in the Past,* edited by Ian Hodder, Michael Shanks, Alexandra Alexandri, Victor Buchli, John Carman, Jonathan Last, and Gavin Lucas, pp. 175–178. Routledge, London.

Gilmore, Melvin R.

1932 *Some Chippewa Uses of Plants.* Papers of the Michigan Academy of Science, Arts, and Letters 17:119–143.

Goldberg, Paul, and Sarah C. Sherwood

1994 Micromorphology of Dust Cave Sediments: Some Preliminary Results. *Journal of Alabama Archaeology* 40(1–2):57–65.

Goldman-Finn, Nurit S.

1994 Dust Cave in Regional Context. *Journal of Alabama Archaeology* 40(1–2):212–231.

1995a *Archaeological Survey in the Middle Tennessee River Uplands, Colbert and Lauderdale Counties, Alabama.* University of Alabama Office of Archaeological Services, Report of Investigations 74.

1995b The Natural and Cultural Setting. In *Cultural Resources in the Pickwick Reservoir,* edited by Catherine C. Meyer, pp. 11–44. University of Alabama Division of Archaeology, Report of Investigations 75.

1997 Analysis of Collections from Stanfield-Worley Bluff Shelter, Northwest Alabama. Manuscript on file at the Office of Archaeological Services, University of Alabama Museums, Moundville.

Goldman-Finn, Nurit S., and Boyce N. Driskell

1994 Introduction to Archaeological Research at Dust Cave. *Journal of Alabama Archaeology* 40(1–2):1–16.

Goldman-Finn, Nurit S., and Renee B. Walker

1994 The Dust Cave Bone Tool Assemblage. *Journal of Alabama Archaeology* 40(1–2):107–115.

Goodyear, Albert

1974 *The Brand Site: A Techno-Functional Study of a Dalton Site in Northeast Arkansas.* Research Series 7, Arkansas Archaeological Survey Research, Fayetteville.

1982 The Chronological Position of the Dalton Horizon in the Southeastern United States. *American Antiquity* 47:382–395.

1989 A Hypothesis for the Use of Cryptocrystalline Raw Materials among Paleoindian Groups of North America. In *Eastern Paleoindian Lithic Resource Use,* edited by Christopher Ellis and J. C. Lothrop, pp. 1–9. Westview Press, Boulder.

Gose, Wulf A.

2000 Palaeomagnetic Studies of Burned Rocks. *Journal of Archaeological Science* 27:409–421.

Graham, Joseph B., and Fred Lamar Pearson

1964 Stanfield-Worley Bluff Shelter Excavations. Partial manuscript on file at the Office of Archaeological Services, University of Alabama Museums, Moundville.

Grayson, Donald K., and David J. Meltzer

2003 A Requiem for North American Overkill. *Journal of Archaeological Science* 30:585–593.

Gremillion, Kristen J.

2006 Central Place Foraging and Food Production on the Cumberland Plateau, Eastern Kentucky. In *Behavioral Ecology and the Transition to Agriculture,* edited by Douglas J. Kennett and Bruce Winterhalder, pp. 41–62. University of California Press, Berkeley.

Griffin, John W.

1974 *Investigations at Russell Cave.* National Park Service Publications in Archaeology 13. U.S. Government Printing Office, Washington, D.C.

Grover, Jennifer

1994 Faunal Remains from Dust Cave. *Journal of Alabama Archaeology* 40(1–2):116–134.

Hames, Raymond B., and William T. Vickers

1982 Optimal Diet Breadth Theory as a Model to Explain Variability in Amazonian Hunting. *American Ethnologist* 9:358–378.

Hammett, Julia E.

1997 Interregional Patterns of Land Use and Plant Management in Native North America. In *People, Plants, and Landscapes,* edited by Kristen J. Gremillion, pp. 195–216. University of Alabama Press, Tuscaloosa.

Harper, Roland M.

1913 *Economic Botany of Alabama, Part I.* Monograph 8, Geological Survey of Alabama, University.

1942 *Natural Resources of the Tennessee Valley Region in Alabama.* Special Report 17, Geological Survey of Alabama, University.

Hart, John P., David L. Asch, C. Margaret Scarry, and Gary W. Crawford

2002 The Age of the Common Bean (*Phaseolus vulgaris* L.) in the Northern Eastern Woodlands of North America. *Antiquity* 76:377–385.

Hastorf, Christine A., and Virginia S. Popper

1988 *Current Paleoethnobotany: Analytical Methods and Cultural Interpretations of Archaeological Plant Remains.* University of Chicago Press, Chicago.

Hawkes, Kristen

1993 Why Hunter-Gatherers Work: An Ancient Version of the Problem of Public Goods. *Current Anthropology* 34(4):341–361.

1996 Foraging Difference between Men and Women: Behavioral Ecology of the Sexual Division of Labor. In *The Archaeology of Human Ancestry: Power, Sex, and Tradition,* edited by James Steele and Stephen Shennan, pp. 283–305. Routledge, New York.

Hawkes, Kristen, Kim Hill, and James F. O'Connell

1982 Why Hunters Gather: Optimal Foraging and the Aché of Eastern Paraguay. *American Ethnologist* 9:379–398.

Hawkes, K., J. F. O'Connell, and N. G. Blurton Jones

1995 Hadza Children's Foraging: Juvenile Dependency, Social Arrangements, and Mobility among Hunter-Gatherers. *Current Anthropology* 36(4):688–700.

Haynes, Gary

2002 The Catastrophic Extinction of North American Mammoths and Mastodonts. *World Archaeology* 33(3):391–416.

Hogue, S. Homes

1994 Human Skeletal Remains from Dust Cave. *Journal of Alabama Archaeology* 40(1–2):173–191.

2003 Bioarchaeology at Dust Cave. Paper presented at the 60th Annual Meeting of the Southeastern Archaeological Conference, Charlotte.

Hollenbach, Kandace D.

2005 Gathering in the Late Paleoindian and Early Archaic Periods in the Middle Tennessee River Valley, Northwest Alabama. Unpublished Ph.D. dissertation, Department of Anthropology, University of North Carolina, Chapel Hill.

2007 Gathering in the Late Paleoindian: Archaeobotanical Remains from Dust Cave, Alabama. In *Foragers of the Terminal Pleistocene,* edited by Renee B. Walker and Boyce N. Driskell, pp. 132–147. University of Nebraska Press, Lincoln.

Hollingsworth, Caryn Yeager

1989 The Archaeology of Sheeps Bluff Shelter (1Fr324), Franklin County, Alabama. Master's thesis, Department of Anthropology, University of Alabama, Tuscaloosa.

Homsey, Lara K.

2003a Feature Variability in the Early and Middle Archaic Components at Dust Cave, Alabama. Paper presented at the 60th Annual Meeting of the Southeastern Archaeological Conference, Charlotte.

2003b Geochemical Characterization of Archaeological Sediments at Dust Cave, Alabama. Master's thesis, Department of Geology and Planetary Sciences, University of Pittsburgh, Pittsburgh.

2003c The Spatial Organization of the Late Paleoindian through Middle Archaic Occupation at Dust Cave, Alabama. Paper presented at the 68th Annual Meeting of the Society for American Archaeology, Milwaukee.

2004 The Form, Function, and Organization of Anthropogenic Deposits at Dust Cave, Alabama. Unpublished Ph.D. dissertation, Department of Anthropology, University of Pittsburgh, Pittsburgh.

Homsey, Lara K., and Rosemary C. Capo

2006 Integrating Geochemistry and Micromorphology to Identify Feature Use at Dust Cave, a Paleoindian through Middle Archaic Site in Northwest Alabama. *Geoarchaeology* 21:237–269.

Hubbard, R. N. L. B.

1980 Development of Agriculture in Europe and the Near East: Evidence from Quantitative Studies. *Economic Botany* 34(1):51–67.

Hubbert, Charles

1989 Paleo-Indian Settlement in the Middle Tennessee Valley: Ruminations from the Quad Paleo-Indian Locale. *Tennessee Anthropologist* 14(2):148–164.

2004 Cotton Field Meditations II. *Alabama Archaeology Society Stones and Bones* 46(5):11–12.

Ingold, Tim

1986 Gatherer-Hunter, Forager-Predator: Modes of Subsistence in Human Evolution. In *Essays on Human Ecology and Social Relations,* edited by Tim Ingold, pp. 79–100. Manchester University Press, Manchester.

1996 Hunting and Gathering as Ways of Perceiving the Environment. In *Redefining Nature: Ecology, Culture, and Domestication,* edited by Roy Ellen and Katsuyoshi Fukui, pp. 117–155. Berg, Oxford.

Jackson, Thomas L.

1991 Pounding Acorn: Women's Production as Social and Economic Focus. In *Engendering Archaeology: Women and Prehistory,* edited by Joan M. Gero and Margaret W. Conkey, pp. 301–325. Basil Blackwell, Oxford.

Johnson, Hunter B., and Scott C. Meeks

1994 Source Areas and Prehistoric Use of Fort Payne Chert. *Journal of Alabama Archaeology* 40(1–2):66–78.

Johnson, Jay K.

1985 Upland Subsistence Data from Colbert Ferry Park, Northwest Alabama. *Journal of Alabama Archaeology* 31(1):48–63.

Jones, George T., Donald K. Grayson, and Charlotte Beck

1983 Artifact Class Richness and Sample Size in Archaeological Surface Assemblages. In *Lulu Linear Punctated: Essays in Honor of George Irving Quimby,* edited by Robert C. Dunnell and Donald K. Grayson, pp. 55–73. Anthropological Papers 72. University of Michigan, Ann Arbor.

Jones, K. T., and D. B. Madsen

1989 Calculating the Cost of Resource Transportation: A Great Basin Example. *Current Anthropology* 30:529–534.

Kadane, Joseph B.

1988 Possible Statistical Contributions to Paleoethnobotany. In *Current Pa-*

leoethnobotany: Analytical Methods and Cultural Interpretations of Archaeological Plant Remains, edited by Christine A. Hastorf and Virginia S. Popper, pp. 206–214. University of Chicago Press, Chicago.

Kaplan, Hillard, and Kim Hill

1992 The Evolutionary Ecology of Food Acquisition. In *Evolutionary Ecology and Human Behavior,* edited by Eric Alden Smith and Bruce Winterhalder, pp. 167–202. Aldine de Gruyter, New York.

Kaplan, Hillard, Kim Hill, A. Magdalena Hurtado, and Jane Lancaster

2001 The Embodied Capital Theory of Human Evolution. In *Reproductive Ecology and Human Evolution,* edited by Peter T. Ellison, pp. 293–318. Aldine de Gruyter, New York.

Kaplan, Hillard, Kim Hill, Jane Lancaster, and A. Magdalena Hurtado

2000 A Theory of Human Life History Evolution: Diet, Intelligence, and Longevity. *Evolutionary Anthropology* 9:156–185.

Keeley, Lawrence H.

1999 Use of Plant Foods among Hunter-Gatherers: A Cross-Cultural Study. In *Prehistory of Agriculture,* edited by P. Anderson, pp. 6–14. Monograph 40, Institute of Archaeology, University of California, Los Angeles.

Kelly, Robert L.

1983 Hunter-Gatherer Mobility Strategies. *Journal of Anthropological Research* 39:277–306.

1995 *The Foraging Spectrum.* Smithsonian Institution Press, Washington, D.C.

1997 Hunter-Gatherer Foraging and the Colonization of the New World. In *The Human Tide: Human Colonisation and the Palaeolithic Record,* edited by A. Velichko, E. Kurenkova, and Y. Gribchenko, pp. 211–255. Moscow Institute of Geography, Moscow.

Kelly, Robert L., and Lawrence C. Todd

1988 Coming into the Country: Early Paleoindian Hunting and Mobility. *American Antiquity* 53(2):231–244.

Kindscher, Kelly

1987 *Edible Wild Plants of the Prairie.* University Press of Kansas, Lawrence.

Koenig, Walter D., and Johannes M. H. Knops

2000 Patterns of Annual Seed Production by Northern Hemisphere Trees: A Global Perspective. *American Naturalist* 155:59–69.

2005 The Mystery of Masting in Trees. *American Scientist* 93(4):340–347.

Kroening, Eric

2004 Microtus xanthognathus. Animal Diversity Web. Electronic document, http://animaldiversity.ummz.umich.edu/site/accounts/information/Microtus_xanthognathus. html, accessed January 3, 2005.

Kuhnlein, Harriet V., and Nancy J. Turner
1991 *Traditional Plant Foods of Canadian Indigenous Peoples: Nutrition, Botany, and Use.* Gordon and Breach Science Publishers, Philadelphia.

Kurz, Don
1997 *Shrubs and Woody Vines of Missouri.* Missouri Department of Conservation, Jefferson City.

Kutzbach, J. E., P. J. Guetter, P. J. Behling, and R. Selin
1993 Simulated Climatic Changes: Results of the COHMAP Climate-Model Experiments. In *Global Climates since the Last Glacial Maximum,* edited by H. E. Wright, Jr., J. E. Kutzbach, T. Webb, III, W. F. Ruddiman, P. A. Street-Perrott, and P. J. Bartlein, pp. 24–93. University of Minnesota Press, Minneapolis.

Kvamme, Kenneth L.
1999 Recent Directions and Developments in Geographic Information Systems. *Journal of Archaeological Research* 7(2):153–201.

Lee, Richard B.
1968 What Hunters Do for a Living, or, How to Make Out on Scarce Resources. In *Man the Hunter,* edited by Richard B. Lee and Irven DeVore, pp. 30–48. Aldine, Chicago.

Lee, Richard B., and Irven DeVore
1968 Problems in the Study of Hunters and Gatherers. In *Man the Hunter,* edited by Richard B. Lee and Irven DeVore, pp. 3–12. Aldine, Chicago.

Lee, Wendy
2001 Sorex cinereus. Animal Diversity Web. Electronic document, http://animaldiversity.ummz.umich.edu/site/accounts/information/Sorex_cinereus.html, accessed January 3, 2005.

Lentz, David L.
1986 Archaeobotanical Remains from the Hester Site: The Late Paleoindian and Early Archaic Horizons. *Midcontinental Journal of Archaeology* 11:269–279.

Lewis, Thomas M. N., and Madeline K. Kneberg
1959 The Archaic Culture in the Middle South. *American Antiquity* 25(2):161–183.

Little, Elbert L.
1995 *National Audubon Society Field Guide to North American Trees.* Knopf, New York.

Logan, Wilfred D.

1952 *Graham Cave: An Archaic Site in Montgomery County, Missouri.* Missouri Archaeological Society Memoir No. 2, Columbia.

Lopinot, Neal H.

1984 Archaeobotanical Formation Processes and Late Middle Archaic Human-Plant Interrelationships in the Midcontinental U.S.A. Ph.D. dissertation, Department of Anthropology, Southern Illinois University, Carbondale. University Microfilms, Ann Arbor, Michigan.

Martin, Alexander C., and William D. Barkley

1961 *Seed Identification Manual.* University of California, Berkeley.

Mason, Ronald J.

1962 The Paleo-Indian Tradition in Eastern North America. *Current Anthropology* 3:227–283.

McMillan, Katherine, Kandace D. Hollenbach, and Renee B. Walker

2007 Socioeconomic Perspectives on the Late Paloeoindian at Dust Cave, Alabama. Paper presented at the 64th Annual Meeting of the Southeastern Archaeological Conference, Knoxville.

Meeks, Scott C.

1994 Lithic Artifacts from Dust Cave. *Journal of Alabama Archaeology* 40(1–2):79–106.

1997 Archaeological Test Excavations at the Refuge Site (1Lu356): A Multicomponent Site in the Seven Mile Island Wildlife Management Area, Lauderdale County, Alabama. Report prepared for the City of Florence. University of Alabama Museums, Office of Archaeological Services, Moundville.

1998 The Use and Function of Late Middle Archaic Projectile Points in the Midsouth. Master's thesis, Department of Anthropology, University of Alabama, Tuscaloosa.

2001 The Younger Dryas Event in the Southeastern United States: Implications for Understanding Late Pleistocene/Early Holocene Human Ecodynamics in the Highland Rim, Northern Alabama. Manuscript on file at the Department of Anthropology, University of Tennessee, Knoxville.

Meltzer, David J., and Bruce D. Smith

1986 Paleoindian and Early Archaic Subsistence Strategies in Eastern North America. In *Foraging, Collecting, and Harvesting: Archaic Period Subsistence and Settlement in the Eastern Woodlands,* edited by Sarah W. Neusius, pp. 3–31. Center for Archaeological Investigations, Southern Illinois University, Carbondale.

Metcalfe, Duncan, and K. Renee Barlow

1992 A Model for Exploring the Optimal Trade-Off between Field Processing and Transport. *American Anthropologist* 94:340–356.

Meyer, Catherine C.

1995 *Cultural Resources in the Pickwick Reservoir.* University of Alabama Division of Archaeology, Report of Investigations 75.

Miller, Carl F.

1956 Life 8,000 Years Ago Uncovered in an Alabama Cave. *National Geographic* 110(4):542–558.

Miller, Naomi

1988 Ratios in Paleoethnobotanical Analysis. In *Current Paleoethnobotany: Analytical Methods and Cultural Interpretations of Archaeological Plant Remains,* edited by Christine A. Hastorf and Virginia S. Popper, pp. 72–85. University of Chicago Press, Chicago.

Mintz, Sidney W.

1985 *Sweetness and Power: The Place of Sugar in Modern History.* Viking, New York.

Mithen, Steven J.

1989 Modeling Hunter-Gatherer Decision Making: Complementing Optimal Foraging Theory. *Human Ecology* 17(1):59–83.

Morey, Darcy F.

1994 *Canis* Remains from Dust Cave. *Journal of Alabama Archaeology* 40(1–2):163–172.

Morse, Dan F.

1973 Dalton Culture in Northeast Arkansas. *Florida Anthropologist* 26:23–38.

1975a Reply to Schiffer. In *The Cache River Archaeological Project: An Experiment in Contract Archaeology,* edited by B. Schiffer and J. J. House, pp. 113–120. Research Series 8, Arkansas Archaeological Survey, Fayetteville.

1975b Paleo-Indian in the Land of Opportunity: Preliminary Report on the Excavations at "Dalton Hill" (3GE94). In *The Cache River Archaeological Project: An Experiment in Contract Archaeology,* edited by B. Schiffer and J. J. House, pp. 135–146. Research Series 8, Arkansas Archaeological Survey, Fayetteville.

1997a An Overview of the Dalton Period in Northeastern Arkansas and in the Southeastern United States. In *Sloan: A Paleoindian Dalton Cemetery in Arkansas,* edited by Dan F. Morse, pp. 123–139. Smithsonian Institution Press, Washington, D.C.

1997b Summary. In *Sloan: A Paleoindian Dalton Cemetery in Arkansas,* edited by Dan F. Morse, pp. 123–139. Smithsonian Institution Press, Washington, D.C.

Morse, Dan F., and Phyllis A. Morse
1983 Archaeology of the Central Mississippi Valley. Academic Press, New York.

Munson, Patrick J. (editor)
1984 *Experiments and Observations on Aboriginal Wild Plant Food Utilization in Eastern North America.* Indiana Historical Society, Prehistory Research Series 2, Indianapolis.

Munson, Patrick J.
1986 Hickory Silviculture: A Subsistence Revolution in the Prehistory of Eastern North America. Paper presented at Emergent Horticultural Economies of the Eastern Woodlands Conference, Southern Illinois University, Carbondale.

Neusius, Sarah W.
1982 Early-Middle Archaic Subsistence Strategies: Changes in Faunal Exploitation at the Koster Site. Unpublished Ph.D. dissertation, Department of Anthropology, Northwestern University.

Nicholas, Danielle
2001 Synaptomys borealis. Animal Diversity Web. Electronic document, http://animaldiversity.ummz.umich.edu/site/accounts/information/Synaptomys_borealis.html, accessed January 3, 2005.

Oakley, Carey B., and Eugene M. Futato
1975 *Archaeological Investigations in the Little Bear Creek Reservoir.* Research Series No. 1, Office of Archaeological Research, University of Alabama, Moundville.

O'Connell, James F.
1995 Ethnoarchaeology Needs a General Theory of Behavior. *Journal of Archaeological Research* 3:205–255.

O'Hear, John W., and David L. DeJarnette
1974 *Cypress Creek Watershed Archaeological Site Survey.* Report submitted to the U.S. Soil Conservation Service, Auburn, by the University of Alabama, Department of Anthropology, University.

Orians, Gordon H., and Nolan E. Pearson
1979 On the Theory of Central Place Foraging. In *Analysis of Ecological Systems,* edited by D. J. Horn, G. R. Stairs, and R. D. Mitchell, pp. 155–177. Ohio State University Press, Columbus.

Osborne, W. Edward, Michael W. Szabo, Charles W. Copeland, Jr., and Thornton L. Neathery
1989 *Geologic Map of Alabama.* Geological Survey of Alabama, Tuscaloosa.

Overpeck, Jonathan T., Robert S. Webb, and Thompson Webb, III
1992 Mapping Eastern North America Vegetation Change of the Past 18 ka: No-Analogs and the Future. *Geology* 20:1071–1074.

Panter-Brick, Catherine
2002 Sexual Division of Labor: Energetic and Evolutionary Scenarios. *American Journal of Human Biology* 14:627–640.

Panter-Brick, Catherine, Robert H. Layton, and Peter Rowley-Conwy
2001 Lines of Enquiry. In *Hunter-Gatherers: An Interdisciplinary Perspective,* edited by Catherine Panter-Brick, Robert H. Layton, and Peter Rowley-Conwy, pp. 1–11. Cambridge University Press, Cambridge.

Parmalee, Paul W.
1962 Faunal Remains from the Stanfield-Worley Bluff Shelter. *Journal of Alabama Archaeology* 8:112–114.
1994 Freshwater Mussels from Dust and Smith Bottom Caves, Alabama. *Journal of Alabama Archaeology* 40(1–2):135–162.

Parmalee, Paul W., R. Bruce McMillan, and Frances B. King
1976 Changing Subsistence Patterns at Rodgers Shelter. In *Prehistoric Man and His Environments: A Case Study in the Ozark Highland,* edited by W. Raymond Wood and R. Bruce McMillan, pp. 141–162. Academic Press, New York.

Pearsall, Deborah M.
2000 *Paleoethnobotany: A Handbook of Procedures.* 2nd ed. Academic Press, San Diego.

Peterson, Frederick A., and Patrick J. Munson
1984 Amaranth as a Food Resource in the Prehistoric Midwestern United States. In *Experiments and Observations on Aboriginal Wild Plant Food Utilization in Eastern North America,* edited by Patrick J. Munson, pp. 317–337. Indiana Historical Society, Prehistory Research Series 6(2), Indianapolis.

Peterson, Lee Allen
1977 *Edible Wild Plants of Eastern and Central North America.* Houghton Mifflin, New York.

Petruso, Karl M., and Jere M. Wickens
1984 The Acorn in Aboriginal Subsistence in Eastern North America: A Report on Miscellaneous Experiments. In *Experiments and Observations on Aboriginal Wild Plant Food Utilization in Eastern North America,* edited by Patrick J. Munson, pp. 360–378. Indiana Historical Society, Prehistory Research Series 6(2), Indianapolis.

Pike, Meta
2003 Comparing Feature Types from a Middle Archaic Component at Dust

Cave. Paper presented at the 60th Annual Meeting of the Southeastern Archaeological Conference, Charlotte.

Pike, Meta G., Kandace D. Hollenbach, and Lara K. Homsey

2005 Changing Patterns in Plant Use and Processing Technologies at Dust Cave, Alabama. Poster presented at the 70th Annual Meeting of the Society for American Archaeology, Salt Lake City.

Popper, Virginia S.

1988 Selecting Quantitative Measurements in Paleoethnobotany. In *Current Paleoethnobotany: Analytical Methods and Cultural Interpretations of Archaeological Plant Remains,* edited by Christine A. Hastorf and Virginia S. Popper, pp. 53–71. University of Chicago Press, Chicago.

Prentice, Guy

1986 Origins of Plant Domestication in the Eastern United States: Promoting the Individual in Archaeological Theory. *Southeastern Archaeology* 5:103–119.

Price, James, and James Krakker

1975 *Dalton Occupation of the Ozark Border.* University of Missouri, Museum Briefs 20, Columbia.

Radford, Albert E., Harry E. Ahles, and C. Ritchie Bell

1964 *Manual of the Vascular Flora of the Carolinas.* University of North Carolina Press, Chapel Hill.

Randall, Asa R.

2001 Untangling Late Paleoindian and Early Side-Notched Stone Tool Assemblages at Dust Cave, Alabama. Paper presented at the 58th Annual Meeting of the Southeastern Archaeological Conference, Chattanooga.

2002 Technofunctional Variation in Early Side-Notched Hafted Bifaces: A View from the Middle Tennessee River Valley in Northwest Alabama. Master's thesis, Department of Anthropology, University of Florida, Gainesville.

2003 Archaic Technological Practice at Dust Cave. Paper presented at the 60th Annual Meeting of the Southeastern Archaeological Conference, Charlotte.

Randall, Asa R., and Kandace R. Detwiler

2002 Reinvestigating Stanfield-Worley Bluff Shelter. Paper presented at the 59th Annual Meeting of the Southeastern Archaeological Conference, Biloxi.

Redfield, Alden, and John H. Moselage

1970 The Lace Place, a Dalton Project Site in the Western Lowlands in Eastern Arkansas. *Arkansas Archaeologist* 11(2):21–44.

Reidhead, Van A.

1981 *A Linear Programming Model of Prehistoric Subsistence Optimization: A Southeastern Indiana Example.* Indiana Historical Society, Prehistory Research Series 6(1), Indianapolis.

Rose, Jim

1999 Sorex arcticus. Animal Diversity Web. Electronic document, http://animaldiversity.ummz.umich.edu/site/accounts/information/Sorex_arcticus.html, accessed January 3, 2005.

Scarry, C. Margaret

1986 Change in Plant Procurement and Production during the Emergence of the Moundville Chiefdom. Unpublished Ph.D. dissertation, Department of Anthropology, University of Michigan, Ann Arbor.

Scarry, C. Margaret, and Richard A. Yarnell

2006 Domestication and Husbandry of Indigenous Plants in Eastern North America. Manuscript prepared for *Handbook of North American Indians, Volume 3: Environment, Origins, and Population.* Smithsonian Institution Press, Washington, D.C.

Schiffer, Michael B.

1975 Some Further Comments on the Dalton Settlement Pattern Hypothesis. In *The Cache River Archaeological Project: An experiment in contract archaeology,* edited by B. Schiffer and J. J. House, pp. 103–112. Research Series 8. Arkansas Archaeological Survey, Fayetteville.

Schopmeyer, C. S. (technical coordinator)

1974 *Seeds of Woody Plants in the United States.* Agriculture Handbook 450. U.S. Department of Agriculture, Forest Service, Washington, D.C.

Schroedl, Gerald F.

1978 *The Patrick Site (40MR40), Tellico Reservoir, Tennessee.* Report of Investigations No. 25, Department of Anthropology, University of Tennessee, Knoxville.

Seeman, Mark F., and Hugh D. Wilson

1984 The Food Potential of *Chenopodium* for the Prehistoric Midwest. In *Experiments and Observations on Aboriginal Wild Plant Food Utilization in Eastern North America,* edited by Patrick J. Munson, pp. 299–316. Indiana Historical Society, Prehistory Research Series 6(2), Indianapolis.

Sherwood, Sarah C.

2001 The Geoarchaeology of Dust Cave: A Late Paleoindian through Middle Archaic Site in the Western Middle Tennessee River Valley. Unpublished Ph.D. dissertation, Department of Anthropology, University of Tennessee, Knoxville.

Sherwood, Sarah C., and Jefferson Chapman

2003 Prepared Clay Surfaces at Dust Cave and Icehouse Bottom. Paper presented at the 68th Annual Meeting of the Society for American Archaeology, Milwaukee.

2005 The Identification and Potential Significance of Early Holocene Prepared Clay Surfaces: Examples from Dust Cave and Icehouse Bottom. *Southeastern Archaeology* 24(1):70–82.

Sherwood, Sarah C., and Boyce N. Driskell

2003 A Chronostratigraphic Framework for the Early and Middle Archaic at Dust Cave. Paper presented at the 60th Annual Meeting of the Southeastern Archaeological Conference, Charlotte.

Sherwood, Sarah C., Boyce N. Driskell, Asa R. Randall, and Scott C. Meeks

2004 Chronology and Stratigraphy at Dust Cave, Alabama. *American Antiquity* 69(3):533–554.

Shuman, Bryan, Patrick Bartlein, Nathaniel Logar, Paige Newby, and Thompson Webb, III

2002 Parallel Climate and Vegetation Responses to the Early Holocene Collapse of the Laurentide Ice Sheet. *Quaternary Science Reviews* 21:1793–1805.

Shuman, Bryan, Thompson Webb, III, Patrick Bartlein, and John W. Williams

2002 The Anatomy of a Climatic Oscillation: Vegetation Change in Eastern North America during the Younger Dryas Chronozone. *Quaternary Science Reviews* 21:1777–1791.

Skeen, James N., Phillip D. Doerr, and David H. Van Lear

1993 Oak-Hickory-Pine Forests. In *Biodiversity of the Southeastern United States: Upland Terrestrial Communities,* edited by William H. Martin, Stephen G. Boyce, and Arthur C. Echternacht, pp. 1–34. John Wiley and Sons, New York.

Smith, Bruce D.

1985 *Chenopodium berlandieri* ssp. *jonesianum*: Evidence for a Hopewellian Domestication from Ash Cave, Ohio. *Southeastern Archaeology* 4:107–133.

Smith, H. Clay

1990a Bitternut Hickory. In *Silvics of North America, Volume II: Hardwoods,* edited by Russell M. Burns and Barbara H. Honkala. Agriculture Handbook 654, U.S. Department of Agriculture, Forest Service, Washington, D.C. Electronic document, http://www.na.fs.fed.us/spfo/pubs/silvics_manual/volume_2/carya/cordiformis.htm, accessed January 29, 2005.

1990b Mockernut Hickory. In *Silvics of North America, Volume II: Hard-*

woods, edited by Russell M. Burns and Barbara H. Honkala. Agriculture Handbook 654, U.S. Department of Agriculture, Forest Service, Washington, D.C. Electronic document, http://www.na.fs.fed.us/spfo/pubs/silvics_manual/volume_2/carya/tomentosa.htm, accessed January 30, 2005.

Smith, Eric Alden

1988 Risk and Uncertainty in the 'Original Affluent Society': Evolutionary Ecology of Resource-Sharing and Land Tenure. In *Hunters and Gatherers, Volume I: History, Evolution and Social Change,* edited by T. Ingold, D. Riches, and J. Woodburn, pp. 222–251. Berg, New York.

Smith, Eric Alden, and Bruce Winterhalder

1992 Natural Selection and Decision Making: Some Fundamental Principles. In *Evolutionary Ecology and Human Behavior,* edited by Eric Alden Smith and Bruce Winterhalder, pp. 25–60. Aldine de Gruyter, New York.

Snider, George E., Jr.

1971 An Analysis of Hearths from the St. Albans Site. In *Second Preliminary Report: The St. Albans Site, Kanawha County, West Virginia, 1964–1968,* edited by Bettye J. Broyles, pp. 93–95. Report of Archaeological Investigations No. 3, West Virginia Geological and Economic Survey, Morgantown.

Snyder, Lynn M., and Paul W. Parmalee

1992 An Archaeological Faunal Assemblage from Smith Bottom Cave, Lauderdale County, Alabama. Reprinted in *Cultural Resources in the Pickwick Reservoir,* edited by Catherine C. Meyer, pp. 377–422. Report of Investigations 75 (1995), Division of Archaeology, University of Alabama, Tuscaloosa.

Snyder, S. A.

1991 Odocoileus virginianus. In *Fire Effects Information System.* U.S. Department of Agriculture, Forest Service, Rocky Mountain Research Station, Fire Sciences Laboratory. Electronic document, http://www.fs.fed.us/database/feis/, accessed September 24, 2007.

Soday, Frank J.

1954 The Quad Site: A Paleo-Indian Village in Northern Alabama. *Tennessee Archaeologist* 10:1–20.

SPSS

1999 SYSTAT Statistical Package, Version 9.0 SPSS, Chicago.

Stafford, C. Russell

1991 Archaic Period Logistical Foraging Strategies in West-Central Illinois. *Midcontinental Journal of Archaeology,* 16:212–246.

Stowe, Noel Read

1970 Prehistoric Cultural Ecology in Northwest Alabama. Master's thesis, Department of Anthropology, University of Alabama, University.

Stiner, Mary C., Natalie D. Munro, and Todd A. Surovell

2000 The Tortoise and the Hare: Small-Game Use, the Broad-Spectrum Revolution, and Paleolithic Demography. *Current Anthropology* 41(1):39–73.

Streuver, Stuart

1968 Flotation Techniques for the Recovery of Small-Scale Archaeological Remains. *American Antiquity* 33(3):353–362.

Sullivan, Janet

1993 Morus rubra. In *Fire Effects Information System.* U.S. Department of Agriculture, Forest Service, Rocky Mountain Research Station, Fire Sciences Laboratory (Producer). Electronic document, http://www.fs.fed.us/database/feis/, accessed January 30, 2005.

Surovell, Todd A.

2000 Early Paleoindian Women, Children, Mobility, and Fertility. *American Antiquity* 65(3):493–509.

Talalay, Laurie, Donald R. Keller, and Patrick J. Munson

1984 Hickory Nuts, Walnuts, Butternuts, and Hazelnuts: Observations and Experiments Relevant to Their Aboriginal Exploitation in Eastern North America. In *Experiments and Observations on Aboriginal Wild Plant Food Utilization in Eastern North America,* edited by Patrick J. Munson, pp. 338–359. Indiana Historical Society, Prehistory Research Series 6(2), Indianapolis.

Taylor, K. C., P. A. Mayewski, R. B. Alley, E. J. Brook, A. J. Gow, P. M. Grootes, D. A. Meese, E. S. Saltzman, J. P. Severinghaus, M. S. Twickler, J. W. C. White, S. Whitlow, and G. A. Zielinski

1997 The Holocene–Younger Dryas Transition Recorded at Summit, Greenland. *Science* 278(5339):825–827.

Teller, James T., David W. Leverington, and Jason D. Mann

2002 Freshwater Outbursts to the Oceans from Glacial Lake Agassiz and Their Role in Climate Change during the Last Deglaciation. *Quaternary Science Reviews* 21:879–887.

Tennessee Valley Authority (TVA)

2005 TVA Reservoirs and Power Plants. Electronic document, http://www.tva.com/sites/sites_ie2.htm, accessed November 30, 2005.

Terrell, John Edward, John P. Hart, Sibel Barut, Nicoletta Cellinese, Antonio Curet, Tim Denham, Chapurukha M. Kusimba, Kyle Latinis, Rahul Oka, Joel

Palka, Mary E. D. Pohl, Kevin O. Pope, Patrick Ryan Williams, Helen Haines, and John E. Staller

2003 Domesticated Landscapes: The Subsistence Ecology of Plant and Animal Domestication. *Journal of Archaeological Method and Theory* 10(4):323–368.

Tucker, Bram T.

2001 The Behavioral Ecology and Economics of Variation, Risk, and Diversification among Mikea Forager-Farmers of Madagascar. Unpublished Ph.D. dissertation, Department of Anthropology, University of North Carolina, Chapel Hill.

Tucker, Bram T., and Alyson G. Young

2005 Growing Up Mikea: Children's Time Allocation and Tuber Foraging in Southwestern Madagascar. In *Hunter-Gatherer Childhoods,* edited by B. Hewlett and M. Lamb, pp. 147–171. Transaction Publishers, Somerset, New Jersey.

U.S. Department of Agriculture, Agricultural Research Service, Nutrient Data Laboratory (USDA NDL)

2004 USDA National Nutrient Database for Standard Reference, Release 17. Electronic document, http://www.nal.usda.gov/fnic/foodcomp, accessed January 30, 2005.

U.S. Department of Agriculture, Natural Resources Conservation Service

2004 *The PLANTS Database,* Version 3.5. Data compiled from various sources by Mark W. Skinner. National Plant Data Center, Baton Rouge. Electronic document, http://plants.usda.gov, accessed February 23, 2005.

U.S. Geological Survey, National Mapping Program

1997 Part I: General. Standards for Digital Elevation Models. National Mapping Program Technical Instructions. Electronic document, http://rockyweb.cr.usgs.gov/nmpstds/acrodocs/dem/1DEM0897.PDF, accessed March 10, 2005.

VanDerwarker, Amber M., C. Margaret Scarry, and Jane M. Eastman

2007 Menus for Families and Feasts: Household and Community Consumption of Plants at Upper Saratown, North Carolina. In *The Archaeology of Food and Identity,* edited by K. Twiss. Monograph 16, Center for Archaeological Investigations, Southern Illinois University, Carbondale.

Velleman, Paul F., and David C. Hoaglin

1981 *Applications, Basics, and Computing of Exploratory Data Analysis.* Duxbury Press, North Scituate, Massachusetts.

Wagner, Friederike, Sjoerd J. P. Bohncke, David L. Dilcher, Wolfram M. Kürschner, Bas van Geel, and Henk Visscher

1999 Century-Scale Shifts in Early Holocene Atmospheric CO_2 Concentration. *Science* 284(5422):1971–1973.

Wagner, Friederike, Lenny L. R. Kouwenberg, Thomas B. van Hoof, and Henk Visscher

2004 Reproducibility of Holocene Atmospheric CO_2 Records Based on Stomatal Frequency. *Quaternary Science Reviews* 23:1947–1954.

Walker, Renee B.

1998 The Late Paleoindian through Middle Archaic Faunal Evidence from Dust Cave, Alabama. Unpublished Ph.D. dissertation, Department of Anthropology, University of Tennessee, Knoxville.

2001 Refining Our Understanding of Subsistence Strategies at Dust Cave: An Analysis of a Recently Excavated Paleoindian Faunal Sample. Paper presented at the 60th Annual Meeting of the Southeastern Archaeological Conference, Chattanooga.

2003 Transitions in Animal Use at Dust Cave between 8500 and 5200 Years Ago. Paper presented at the 60th Annual Meeting of the Southeastern Archaeological Conference, Charlotte.

2007 Hunting in the Late Paleoindian Period: Faunal Remains from Dust Cave. In *Foragers of the Terminal Pleistocene in North America,* edited by Renee B. Walker and Boyce N. Driskell, pp. 99–115. University of Nebraska Press, Lincoln.

Walker, Renee B., Kandace R. Detwiler, Scott C. Meeks, and Boyce N. Driskell

2001 Berries, Bones, and Blades: Reconstructing Late Paleoindian Subsistence Economy at Dust Cave, Alabama. *Midcontinental Journal of Archaeology* 26(2):169–197.

Walker, Renee B., Lara K. Homsey, and Kandace D. Hollenbach

2007 Investigating Archaeological Correlates for Food Processing at Dust Cave, Alabama. Paper presented at the 64th Annual Meeting of the Southeastern Archaeological Conference, Knoxville.

Walker, Renee B., Darcy F. Morey, and John H. Relethford

2005 Early and Mid-Holocene Dogs in Southeastern North America: Examples from Dust Cave. *Southeastern Archaeology* 24(1):83–92.

Walker, Renee B., and Paul W. Parmalee

2004 A Noteworthy Cache of Goose Humeri from Late Paleoindian Levels at Dust Cave, Northwestern Alabama. *Journal of Alabama Archaeology* 50(1):18–35.

Walker, Renee B., and Nicholas Richardson

1999 A Consideration of the Taphonomic Factors Affecting the Faunal Assemblage from Dust Cave. Paper presented at the 56th Annual Meeting of the Southeastern Archaeological Conference, Pensacola.

Walker, Robert, Kim Hill, Hillard Kaplan, and Garnett McMillan

2002 Age-Dependency in Hunting Ability among the Aché of Eastern Paraguay. *Journal of Human Evolution* 42:639–657.

Walsh, Roberta A.

1993 Amaranthus retroflexus. In *Fire Effects Information System.* U.S. Department of Agriculture, Forest Service, Rocky Mountain Research Station, Fire Sciences Laboratory (Producer). Electronic document, http://www.fs.fed.us/database/feis/, accessed February 2, 2005.

Walthall, John A.

1980 *Prehistoric Indians of the Southeast: Archaeology of Alabama and the Middle South.* University of Alabama Press, Tuscaloosa.

1998a Rockshelters and Hunter-Gatherer Adaptation to the Pleistocene/Holocene Transition. *American Antiquity* 63(2):223–238.

1998b Overwinter Strategy and Early Holocene Hunter-Gatherer Mobility in Temperate Forests. *Midcontinental Journal of Archaeology* 23(1):1–22.

Wang, Yang, A. Hope Jahren, and Ronald Amundson

1997 Potential for ^{14}C Dating of Biogenic Carbonate in Hackberry (*Celtis*) Endocarps. *Quaternary Research* 47:337–343.

Waselkov, Gregory A., and Sid Hite

1987 Paleo-Indians in the Tennessee Valley: A Preliminary Report to the National Geographic Society (#3246-85). Department of Sociology and Anthropology, Auburn University, Auburn, Alabama.

Waselkov, Gregory A., and Robert T. Morgan

1983 *The Archaeology of Seven Mile Island: A Cultural Resources Survey of the National Register District.* Archaeological Monograph 7, Auburn University, Auburn, Alabama.

Watson, Patty Jo

1976 In Pursuit of Prehistoric Subsistence: A Comparative Account of Some Contemporary Flotation Techniques. *Midcontinental Journal of Archaeology* 1(1):77–100.

Watts, W. A.

1980 Late Quaternary Vegetation History of Southern Georgia and Central Florida. *Ecology* 52(4):676–690.

Watts, W. A., and M. Stuiver

1980 Late Wisconsin Climate of Northern Florida and Origin of Species-Rich Deciduous Forest. *Science* 210:325–327.

Webb, Thompson, III, Patrick J. Bartlein, Sandy P. Harrison, and Katherine H. Anderson

1993 Vegetation, Lake Levels, and Climate in Eastern North America for the Past 18,000 Years. In *Global Climates since the Last Glacial Maximum,* edited by H. E. Wright, Jr., J. E. Kutzbach, T. Webb, III, W. F. Ruddiman, F. A. Street-Perrott, and P. J. Bartlein, pp. 415–467. University of Minnesota Press, Minneapolis.

Webb, William S., and David L. DeJarnette

1942 *An Archaeological Survey of Pickwick Basin in the Adjacent Portions of the States of Alabama, Mississippi, and Tennessee.* Bulletin 129, Bureau of American Ethnology, Smithsonian Institution, Washington, D.C.

Welch, Paul D., and C. Margaret Scarry

1995 Status-Related Variation in Foodways in the Moundville Chiefdom. *American Antiquity* 60(3):397–419.

Wilkinson, Leland, MaryAnn Hill, Jeffrey P. Welna, and Gregory K. Birkenbeuel

1992 *SYSTAT for Windows: Statistics.* SYSTAT, Evanston, Illinois.

Winterhalder, Bruce

1981 Foraging Strategies in the Boreal Forest: An Analysis of Cree Hunting and Gathering. In *Hunter-Gatherer Foraging Strategies: Ethnographic and Archaeological Analyses,* edited by Bruce Winterhalder and Eric Alden Smith, pp. 66–98. University of Chicago Press, Chicago.

1990 Open Field, Common Pot: Harvest Variability and Risk Avoidance in Agricultural and Foraging Societies. In *Risk and Uncertainty in Tribal and Peasant Economies,* edited by Elizabeth Cashdan, pp. 67–87. Westview Press, Boulder.

2002 Models. In *Darwin and Archaeology: A Handbook of Key Concepts,* edited by John P. Hart and John Edward Terrell, pp. 201–223. Greenwood Publishing, New York.

Winterhalder, Bruce, William Baillargeon, Francesca Cappelletto, I. Randolph Daniel, Jr., and Chris Prescott

1988 The Population Ecology of Hunter-Gatherers and Their Prey. *Journal of Anthropological Archaeology* 7:289–328.

Winterhalder, Bruce, and Carol Goland

1993 On Population, Foraging Efficiency, and Plant Domestication. *Current Anthropology* 34(5):710–715.

1997 An Evolutionary Ecology Perspective on Diet Choice, Risk, and Plant

Domestication. In *People, Plants, and Landscapes: Studies in Paleoethnobotany,* edited by Kristen J. Gremillion, pp. 123–160. University of Alabama Press, Tuscaloosa.

Winterhalder, Bruce, and Eric Alden Smith
1992 Evolutionary Ecology and the Social Sciences. In *Evolutionary Ecology and Human Behavior,* edited by Eric Alden Smith and Bruce Winterhalder, pp. 3–24. Aldine de Gruyter, New York.

Wood, W. Raymond, and R. Bruce McMillan (editors)
1976 *Prehistoric Man and His Environments: A Case Study in the Ozark Highland.* Academic Press, New York.

Wymer, Dee Anne
1987 The Paleoethnobotanical Record of Central Ohio—100 B.C. to A.D. 800: Subsistence Continuity Amid Cultural Change. Unpublished Ph.D. dissertation, Department of Anthropology, Ohio State University, Columbus.

Yanovsky, Elias
1936 *Food Plants of the North American Indians.* U.S. Department of Agriculture Miscellaneous Publication No. 237, Washington, D.C.

Yarnell, Richard A.
1982 Problems of Interpretation of Archaeological Plant Remains of the Eastern Woodlands. *Southeastern Archaeology* 1(1):1–7.
1993 The Importance of Native Crops during the Late Archaic and Woodland Periods. In *Foraging and Farming in the Eastern Woodlands,* edited by C. Margaret Scarry, pp. 13–26. University Press of Florida, Gainesville.

Yarnell, Richard A., and M. Jean Black
1985 Temporal Trends Indicated by a Survey of Archaic and Woodland Plant Food Remains from Southeastern North America. *Southeastern Archaeology* 4(2):93–106.

Yu, Zicheng, and Ulrich Eicher
1998 Abrupt Climate Oscillations during the Last Deglaciation in Central North America. *Science* 282(5397):2235–2238.

Zeanah, David W.
2000 Transport Costs, Central Place Foraging, and Hunter-Gatherer Alpine Land Use Strategies. In *Intermountain Archaeology,* edited by D. B. Madsen and M. D. Metcalfe, pp. 1–14. University of Utah Anthropological Papers 122, University of Utah Press, Salt Lake City.

Index